JOSE STEVENS is a licensed psychotherapist, author, and educator in Berkeley, California. He is on the faculty of John F. Kennedy University Consciousness Studies Department and holds graduate degrees from the University of California at Berkeley and from the California Institute of Integral Studies. His workshops and classes include shamanism, transpersonal psychology, and developing intuition. He is the author of *Tao to Earth: Michael's Guide to Relationships and Growth*, co-author of *The Michael Handbook*, and the author of numerous articles on consciousness studies.

LENA SEDLETZKY STEVENS teaches classes and workshops in shamanism, developing intuition, and intuitive business approaches.

SECRETS OF SHAMANISM

TAPPING THE SPIRIT POWER WITHIN YOU

**JOSE STEVENS, PH.D.
& LENA SEDLETZKY STEVENS**

Produced by The Philip Lief Group

AVON BOOKS ◈ NEW YORK

SECRETS OF SHAMANISM: TAPPING THE SPIRIT POWER WITHIN YOU is an original publication of Avon Books. This work has never before appeared in book form.

AVON BOOKS
A division of
The Hearst Corporation
1350 Avenue of the Americas
New York, New York 10019

Copyright © 1988 by Jose and Lena Stevens & The Philip Lief Group, Inc.
Published by arrangement with The Philip Lief Group, Inc.
Library of Congress Catalog Card Number: 88-91497
ISBN: 0-380-75607-2

First Avon Books Printing: August 1988

AVON TRADEMARK REG. U.S. PAT. OFF. AND IN OTHER COUNTRIES, MARCA REGISTRADA, HECHO EN CANADA.

Printed in Canada.

UNV 10 9 8 7 6 5

For our wonderful children,
Anna and Carlos

We are deeply grateful to:

our family and friends, whose wonderful support and encouragement made this book possible;

our fellow students of the shamanic way for their experiences and insights into modern-day shamanism;

our power animals and guardians, whose advice and information gave this book direction;

Inetz Walker for her editing, typing, and all-around help in completing this manuscript on time;

Philip Lief for his support and effective efforts in getting this book into print;

Louise Quayle and Kevin Osborn of The Philip Lief Group, Inc., for their fine editorial assistance.

Contents

Preface 1
Chapter 1—Shamans: An Overview 6
    Shaman Specialties 9
    Shamans and Society 10
    The Making of a Shaman 10
    What Shamans Know 11
    Benefits of Shamanism 13

Chapter 2—Beginning the Journey:
        Soaring into the Unknown 15
    What Is Imagination? 16
    How You Limit Your Imagination 18
    Why Use Imagination? 19
    Detachment and Surrender 21
    The Nuts and Bolts of Visioning 24
    Beginning the Shamanic Journey 29
    Understanding Your Journey 35
    Benefits of Journeying 36

Chapter 3—The Secret World:
        What Shamans Know 38
    The Web of Power 38
    The Human Spirit Body 40
    Seeing Others' Spirit Bodies 51
    Defining Your Own Spirit Body 51
    Grounding 53
    Protection 55

Becoming Transparent   58
Shape Changing   61
Developing Neutrality   62

Chapter 4—Nature's Power: Spirit Helpers   64
The Power of Rocks   66
Locations of Power   68
The Power of Animals   75
The Power of Plants   80
The Power of the Elements   82

Chapter 5—Shaping Time: Learning to Be Present 87
Presence   100

Chapter 6—The Circle of Life:
  Creating and Destroying   103
Creating and Destroying   104
Appropriate Destruction: Possessions   106
Appropriate Destruction: Beliefs   108
Appropriate Destruction: Habits   111
Appropriate Destruction: Relationships   113
Creation   115
Creating with the Help of Guardian Spirits   118
Balance and Imbalance   120
The Infinite Potential of the Spirit World   124
Creating Balance: The Giveaway   125
Receiving   127

Chapter 7—Shamans and Opportunity:
  Goals, Problem Solving, and Success   130
Detachment   133
Keeping Up to Date   135
Problem Solving   138
Change   146

Chapter 8—Finding Your Place in the Shaman's
  World: Maps and Trails   153
Tunnels to the Spirit World   157

Guarding and Monitoring the Tunnels 169
Healing Others Using the Tunnels 173

**Chapter 9—The Sacred Marriage:
    Discovering Balance** 174
Head, Heart, and Gut People 174
Balancing the Body 183
Magnetic and Dynamic: Feminine and
Masculine Principles 185

**Chapter 10—Transformation Through Ritual and
    Ceremony: Practices** 193
Simple Opening Ritual 196
Opening Ritual for Journeying or Other
Shamanic Process 197
Power Songs 198
Shamanic Dancing 200
Using Quartz Crystals for Protection and
Empowerment 203
Creating a Clear, Safe, and Powerful Place 204
Creating Your Own Power Spot 205
Vision Quest 206
Harnessing Power Through Light 210

**Chapter 11—Playing the Shamanic Game of Life:
    The Big Picture** 211
How to Know That You Are Being
Successful at Shamanic Practice 215
How to Go Further 217

Appendix—Shaman's Resource Guide 221
Further Resources 223
Bibliography 224

Preface

This is a book about success, the success of the shaman over the ages and the success that you can achieve by following the shamanic way.

We wrote this book because we saw a need for the ancient art of shamanism to be reframed in the context of the twenty-first century. This has been particularly challenging because we have not wanted to change the meaning of any integral concepts but simply to make them more available to the everyday person. We did not want to be purists in this endeavor either, but rather pragmatists, weaving basic shamanic approaches together with age-old understandings about consciousness.

What follows is a short history describing the paths that led to our writing this book.

Jose

How did I, a Basque-Mexican-Irish-American, become involved in the world of shamanism? Answering this question brought numerous half-forgotten memories to the surface of my awareness. I discovered that many threads wove the rich pattern of my current interest in shamanic ways. As a small child growing up in East Hollywood, California, I spent much time with my Mexican grandmother, who filled me with stories of her childhood and the brujos of the Yaqui Indians in northern central Mexico, where she had lived. She was in awe of them and, being a fervent Catholic, she crossed herself many times as she told me strange tales of their methods and practices. She herself practiced some of their ways, and to my impressionable young mind, the magic and power of the shamanic perspective became a way of life.

1

I learned in childhood that I had "eyesight" in the palms of my hands; that I could read energy with them; that I could use my hands to ward off dangers or rid myself of unwanted negative influences.

Later I was introduced to the northern Native American perspective by Strongheart, a friend of my father who worked in the film industry. A part-time actor and film consultant, Strongheart would drop by my father's stage-lighting business, where I helped out. I was always impressed by his long hair, clawlike nose, and gentle demeanor. He did not teach me anything formal, just talked in his native style about the way he saw the world.

Perhaps these were some of the influences that led me to know that I wanted to become a psychologist and counselor from my earliest childhood. Perhaps this as well motivated my solo journey throughout India, Nepal, and Thailand, seeking alternative perspectives and ways of looking at reality. That journey would connect me with powerful teachers who only reinforced my already "eccentric" outlook on life. Those travels also solidified my relationship with Lena, my wife-to-be, who waited patiently for me while pursuing her own shamanic training.

Later I embarked on a series of psychic training courses that introduced me to powerful techniques that I recognized as shamanic in origin. This three-year period of formal training is what eventually led me to select the study of "Power Animals, Mental Imagery, and Self-Actualization" as the topic of my doctoral dissertation. My research led me to discover that people who actively used animal imagery in their dreams or reveries were actually more self-actualized and mentally healthier than people who did not. The statistics showed that they tended to be more present, more self-motivated, and more positive in their attitude toward life. This just confirmed what I already knew: that the shamanic approach leads people to greater success and effectiveness in the world.

During my doctoral studies at the California Institute of Integral Studies I had the wonderful opportunity to meet teachers who not only were knowledgeable about shamanism but practiced it in their daily life. Angie Arrien, expert in Basque shamanism and Ralph Metzner, master of transformative metaphors, each assisted me in my studies interfacing Western psychology with shamanism. I was fortunate enough to meet and study with anthropologist and shamanism expert Michael Harner, a truly excellent teacher and guide.

During this time I met many others who were studying shamanism and applying it in their daily lives with incredible results. A group of us formed a shamanic practicing group that met weekly for years to apply what we had learned and share discoveries with one another. Out of it evolved the Empowering Circle, a group devoted to working with others using shamanic techniques.

I had long since learned that the more I practiced shamanic techniques, the better I felt and the more effective I became in all areas of my life: as a parent, psychotherapist, channel, teacher, and business person. As I applied shamanism to my therapy practice and seminars, I discovered that not only were people open to it, but they were actually starving for these age-old methods of effective living. They became more insightful, more personally responsible, more capable of reaching their goals in a shorter time, and had more fun doing it. They also became healthier and suffered from fewer physical complaints.

I also discovered through my own children that shamanism is a natural approach to life, a perspective trained out of us through school and culture. What I discovered is that my children are naturally shamanic in their perspective and are exceptionally powerful when they use their inner skills to solve problems.

As I write, lecture, channel, and work with people, I consistently find that my most profound teachers are those guardians and allies whom I discover within. These are my tutors, my constant guides that provide me with valuable information and insight when I am confused or in need. They are the ones I have perhaps drawn the most from in writing this book. In truth, Lena and I wrote it together with them. We offer it to you as a helper. May your path take you to the light of self-discovery, the center of the universe.

Jose Stevens; Berkeley, California; January 1, 1988

Lena

My informal training in the shamanic perspective began at a very early age. Born of Russian-Polish-Swedish parents, I remember fairy tales in which animals were the helpers and guides, always assisting people out of trouble and helping them achieve great riches and happiness. I have had a great affinity for animals ever since. When I was seven my family moved from the city to Carmel, California, where I spent the rest of my childhood and adolescence. The magic and power of the Big Sur coast, an area where I spent much time backpacking in the woods, affected me deeply throughout my formative years. Many of these outings, in a land revered by Native Americans as sacred, revealed power spots and magical places that greatly strengthened my inner bonds with nature. One incident that brought the unseen power of nature home to me was a near-fatal fall off a steep embankment when I was thirteen years old. For all practical purposes, I should have been seriously injured if not killed. I distinctly remember the fall as if suspended in time: me falling, but somehow not touching the rocks and trees I was bouncing off of. It was as if some unseen cushion were guiding me down to place me gently in the creek two hundred feet below. I came out of the experience with only slight scratches and bruises, and with an altered feeling of great respect for the power of the spirit world. At that point, I also knew that I had allies who were helping me through life.

Perhaps knowing about this protection was what spurred me to take a year-long trip through Europe, trusting that I would meet the right people and always have enough to get by on. I was then twenty-one years old. My travels eventually took me to the far north of Sweden on a trek through the country of the Lapps. There I experienced intensely lucid dreams and feelings of déjà vu. Years later work with a psychic revealed a past life as a shaman in that northern region.

I devoted the rest of my twenties to intense studies in the realm of shamanism, psychic awareness, and channeling as well as business. Since my interests in art and music were not putting money into my bank account, I turned to real estate, to the surprise of my friends and family. The field for me has turned out to be an excellent vehicle for learning to negotiate in the business world using my now deep-rooted shamanic perspective and intuitive skills I developed in years past. My transition into management has been a natural way for me to teach what I know about the shamanic world to the sales agents, brokers, and clients I deal with on a daily basis. The shamanic perspective has become so much a part of me and the way of our family life that I cannot imagine living any other way. The fact that Jose and both our children share the same perspective has given us much joy. We are truly grateful to be able to share what we have learned with you in his book.

Lena Sedletzky Stevens; Berkeley, California; January 3, 1988

Although both of us have encountered near-death experiences, neither of us has undergone severe initiatory trials, nor have we received formal initiations as shamans. We do not believe that formal initiation is necessary to allow one to benefit from the shamanic perspective. Nor do we believe that severe suffering is necessary for a person to learn the value of the inner ways. Historically, extreme hardship and surviving severe trials has often been the only way that some people were willing to embrace the shamanic way of life. We believe there is another way, the way of slow, gentle learning about the powers of the inner world.

Two different approaches to learning are reflected in the way people come to learn the shamanic method. In the first, novices must undergo profound and often life-threatening experiences that propel them into shamanic work. After years of practicing the traditional techniques and forms, they gradually learn how and why the methods work. They can explain shamanism to themselves and perhaps to others. The second style of learning reflects more of the modern Western approach. Here novices learn about shamanism gradually and are gently guided into its ways, being able to explain it to themselves as they go. There are advocates of both ways and we believe that because people are vastly different, there are people who learn better under one style than another. Perhaps the best way to learn is a good mix of both hands-on experience under the tutelege of a teacher, a little self-reflection, and flying by the seat of your pants. There is no single right way to do it. Whatever way you learn will be the right way for you.

CHAPTER 1

Shamans: An Overview

It was an opportunity of a lifetime, an offer seemingly just out of reach. For years Shawna had wished for the anthropologist's dream: an assignment to Lima, Peru, jumping off place for the Andes. And now a group was being formed and she was asked if she wanted to go. But the obstacles seemed almost unsurmountable. Slaving over a maze of reports from her last assignment, Shawna was not even remotely ready to go. She was also flat broke. Shawna spent hours in the July heat of Los Angeles calculating the costs, pouring over the calendar, and figuring in any possible assets she could turn into cash. Neither the figures nor the dates on the calendar added up.

In frustration, Shawna threw her pencil across the room where it bounced and spun into her favorite cottonwood drum, a gift from her grandfather in New Mexico. He wasn't really her grandfather but she called him that. Old Bill was everybody's grandfather. Shawna had spent a few summers with the ancient Apache and now she suddenly recalled something he had taught her. "When your heart is sad and you have lost your path, go inside for help. When your heart speaks its truth, you cannot know failure." Suddenly Shawna relaxed. How could she be so foolish as to give up her dream because of a few calculations?

Swiftly crossing the room, she picked up the drum. Sitting quietly for a time, she began to sing a little song Old Bill had taught her, accompanied by a light drumbeat. "Falcon I am calling, Falcon I am calling, Come and be with me..." Closing her eyes, Shawna could see the ebony of the falcon's wing feathers as he flashed by her. "Falcon," she whispered, "I could use a little help. I want to go to Lima but as you can see I am stymied. Any suggestions?" The image of the falcon appeared to look her straight in the eye and say without opening his beak, "Melanie, call Melanie. You will go, you will go." Then he vanished across an imaginary horizon.

Shawna rubbed her eyes. Melanie? The only Melanie she knew was a former employer from pre-graduate school days; a prim, exacting woman whom Shawna had always found somewhat hard to please. Melanie also possessed power, money, and influence where it counts. It started to dawn on Shawna.

The following morning found Shawna on the phone with Melanie. "Ah, hello, I'm Shawna Michaelson, I used to work for you and—" Shawna was amazed. Not only did Melanie remember her but she also showed a genuine enthusiasm for Shawna's Peruvian plans. They agreed to meet the very next day.

"I can't believe you called me," Melanie exclaimed. "I've been hoping to start a foundation for scholars but had no focus as yet. Now I've got something to start with. How much will you be needing?"

Shawna's mouth fell open. "I, I, I don't know. Five thousand dollars will go a long way in Peru."

"Good," stated Melanie, "lets make it six for good measure. That's a good beginning for this year's endowment."

Excited beyond measure, Shawna decided she now must get down to that paperwork. Then she caught herself. "Falcon's working on it. I'm not going to fail. I'm going to Peru."

On her way home Shawna stopped at a gas station. "Hi, Shawna," a familiar voice called. It was her supervisor, Larry Jackson, from her last job, which was in Montana. He said, "I'm in town for some lectures at U.C.L.A. and was going to call you. I want Terry, that doctoral student, to finish those reports you're working on. It will be good practice for him and give you a break. What do you think?"

Larry wasn't expecting the big bear hug Shawna gave him. She mumbled thanks and hustled home to get her affairs in order. "Let's see: passport, shots, cold-weather clothes... *Thank you, Falcon!* My friend. This assignment is starting out right!"

Shamanic advising is an ancient and powerful form of information retrieval and inner consultation that can be adapted by anyone for use in the context of the modern world. Shamanism itself is a time-honored cross-cultural quest for knowledge and personal power that predates all known religions, psychologies, and philosophies. A set of techniques developed over ages, it allows individuals to learn consciously to bridge the apparent chasm between the physical world and the realms of imagination and vision. The great advantage of this form of guidance is that it requires no outside tools, no expenditures, and very little time investment. In fact, you might be tempted to overlook it because it does not fit into what we think of as a traditional path to success, whether personal or professional.

The shaman relies on inner powers to support his or her conclusions about a situation, rather than on material concerns as is often the case today. The only price you have to pay to use this form of consultation is that shamanism asks you to let go of your conventional belief systems about reality.

While shamans have no fixed dogma or religion, they all believe in the universal web of power that supports all life. According to shamanism, all elements of the environment are alive and all have their source of power in the spirit world. Rocks, plants, animals, clouds, and wind are charged with life and must be paid due respect for the maintenance of harmony and health. Shamans consider all life-forms to be interconnected, and a mutually supportive balance among them is essential for humankind's survival. Our job is to understand this balance and to live in harmony with it, always taking nature into consideration in every endeavor. The web of power in nature is the life giver and the source of all successful activity.

Shamans access vital survival information and knowledge through what is known as a spirit journey. As shamans put it, they travel within their imaginations to contact the spirit world or the world of the spirit self: they contact the universal source of all information by "flying" deeply within themselves. If they do this while focusing on a question or matter of concern, their ecstatic journey will provide an answer, allowing them to bypass the stumbling blocks of the material world and rely on a broader vision.

Yat squatted by the water's edge lifting handfuls of the cool drink to his lips. Although his thirst was quenched the water did nothing to ease the ache of hunger he and his scouts had felt these past five wintery days. If they did not find his brother's village soon they would surely starve. They made a hasty camp by the snowy riverbed and bundled in skins by the fire. Yat knew it was time to call for assistance. Drawing forth his drum he began a steady spirit song honoring his totem spirit, the kangaroo rat. With eyes closed he soon saw kangaroo rat flying in the air nearby. "Oh, rat, my friend, I have a special request. We cannot find my brother's village and we have run out of food. Can you help us find it?" Rat continued to hover for a moment and remained silent. Then with a flourish rat produced a large branch with a fork in it. He pointed to the left fork and in a flash was gone. Yat was puzzled. He pondered the vision and after a time began to laugh loudly. In the morning he led his companions up the stream. Shortly the river forked into two smaller streams. Immediately he followed the left-hand one and before long the village was in sight. Yat once again gave thanks to kangaroo rat.

SHAMAN SPECIALTIES

For shamans, imagination is more than cerebral activity, rather, imagination is an actual vehicle that carries them to unknown realms. Thoughts and feelings are forms of energy that go to specific locations in the web of power, not simply mental activity as most of us have been taught to believe.

Shamans fill a diverse and fascinating set of roles including sacred artist, poet, musician, mediator, ceremonialist, dancer, and singer. Four principal specialties of shamans are: healing; accessing new or lost knowledge; developing power; and prophesying or foretelling. Although most shamans have a knowledge of all these areas, they also tend to focus on one in order to master it. For example, curanderos or healers specialize in learning about the power of medicinal plants and herbs for the healing of infirmities. Other shamans develop the ability to forecast the weather, locate good opportunities, and warn of potential hazards. Still others become power brokers, masters of suspending the laws of gravity or space and time. Whatever their speciality, they are the medicine men and women of their communities and are found all over the world from North and South America, to Europe, Africa, and Asia. The shaman's power as visionary, seer, and healer has been traced to Siberia, India, and Tibet. Similar techniques have been utilized everywhere by shamans since Paleolithic times even though they were separated by vast oceans and continents.

In this book we will touch on all four principal areas of shamanic activity because they are integral to developing your power and becoming a successful human being in your own right. In addition we will provide you with exercises that draw from the shaman's artistic skills. Unless you can develop the artist within you, you will not be able to enjoy the shamanic approach.

SHAMANS AND SOCIETY

According to anthropologist Michael Harner, an expert on shamanism, shamans have always been pragmatists, doing whatever worked best to increase their reputations as powerful healers and visionaries. If the shamans' methods worked, they earned respect and a good reputation. If the shamans' methods did not work, they lost credibility. Through trial and error they found what actually proved effective and then applied their newly found knowledge with astonishingly successful results. In this way shamanism has survived through the ages despite a variety of persistent widespread attempts to wipe it out by: missionaries, who felt that it represented a threat to the vertical authority structure of their religions; the advance of science, which considered shamanism unscientific and subjective; the age of reason, which discarded shamanism because of its nonrational approach; the advent of technology, which superceded the nature-based shamanic perspective.

Despite earlier interpretations that shamans were simply tolerated psychotics, recent anthropological studies have revealed that shamans are actually the most productive, stable, and intelligent members of their communities. They often provide for many dependents through their efficient and shrewd handling of goods, livestock, and items of trade. Thus each community and tribe depends heavily on the local shamans for their knowledge and guidance because they have dedicated themselves to gaining knowledge and accessing power for the good of others.

Perhaps the most intriguing aspect of shamanism is the fact that it is truly a grass-roots phenomenon. There exists no dogma, no organization, no special texts (although we will be giving you examples and suggested exercises in this book), no leaders, no regulatory board. Anyone can practice its techniques and derive benefit from its methods. Historically any male or female who exhibited the talent or who had an intense desire for this personal spiritual quest could practice it. Shamanism has always been a people's spiritual practice. Each shaman has the right to access new information and new knowledge with no threat of expulsion or condemnation from any organized belief system.

THE MAKING OF A SHAMAN

How does one become a shaman? Typically individuals are initiated into shamanism in three ways: they are either self-selected; they are selected to be trained by older shamans, sometimes after having survived a life-threatening accident or disease; they inherit the role of shaman from their father or mother. Whatever the method of selection, shamans have traditionally undergone a long training period and often have had to pass a rigorous and sometimes brutal test before becoming a shaman in their own right. We are not proposing in this book that you become a shaman or that to be successful using shamanic techniques you need years of training or brutal initiation; many have found that the shamanic techniques translate successfully for use by the ordinary person and can definitely aid in the enrichment and success of life.

Actively using your shamanic abilities, however, is not a panacea for all problems. Shamanism will not eliminate the obstacles in your life. Shamanism can make solving those problems less of a chore—and it'll probably make you more successful at solving them, too—but you still have to take action to get the results you want. Tribal shamans, for example, may use their powers to help hunters locate the herd. But knowing where the herd is doesn't eliminate the challenge of the hunt or the job of skinning the animal and preparing the meal. You can use your own shamanic powers in much the same way, by being able to place yourself in the right place at the right time. Once there, you'll have to depend on your own abilities to succeed, but the edge you've given yourself will make your job that much easier.

What makes a shaman different from other members of his or her community? What are the ingredients that make up a powerful shaman? What do shamans know that makes them special or gives them that added talent for healing and coping with life? Let's take a moment to preview some of those qualities and beliefs. In subsequent chapters we will go into greater detail and give you pointers on how you can begin to develop these qualities in yourself.

WHAT SHAMANS KNOW

There is much that shamans know and many qualities that they possess. Below are listed a few of these characteristics:

- Shamans know about energy and how it works both in the environment and in the human body. They recognize the inherent power in all of nature and sense their own connection with it. They know about the spirit body and how to communicate with it for health and extra stamina.

- They have learned to relax their physical bodies and to reduce their level of stress so that they are more receptive and efficient. They are able to quiet the mental chatter so that they can better hear, see, or feel the internal message.

- Shamans use the powers of their inner vision and imagination to journey for knowledge and for vital information. They have learned to recognize that these clues and symbols are important and they believe that they are worth listening to. They learn how to suspend judgment and trust their inner guidance.

- They learn to work with natural images and symbols from within and know how to interpret these to overcome obstacles and problems. True artists, they often bring their symbolism forth into ritualistic song, dance, movement, and rhythms.

- Shamans learn how to understand people and how to work with them in a healing fashion. They have excellent insight into people's character structures. Shamans know how to laugh and have learned to be detached enough from the drama of life to find the human condition amusing.

- They learn to communicate both externally and internally at the same time. They truly have a foot in both worlds at once and lose track of neither. They alter their views about linear time and suspend beliefs in the limitations of the human mind.

- Shamans learn how to be successful and they certainly know how to take action when called for. Shamans are not armchair philosophers. They have practical skills for handling dilemmas. They have become quite comfortable with paradox.

- They know how to shift levels of consciousness at will. They are as comfortable with ecstatic states as with ordinary waking consciousness. This gives them a flexible nature, able to handle change easily.

- Shamans are fighters. They are disciplined and persistent in their attempts to gain power and apply it to the common good. They know how to protect themselves in formidable circumstances.

These then are the qualities and attributes shared by shamans throughout the ages from all continents of the world. These shamans are no more than human beings who developed themselves out of interest and dedication. Their talents are probably no greater than your own ability to experience a similar level of success. The secret to the power of the shamanic approach is interest and a willingness to believe that you can do it. As we mentioned earlier, this book is not about turning you into a traditional shaman. Rather it is about translating the often mysterious and magical world of the shaman into everyday terms that you can understand and apply in your own daily life. Shamanic techniques work in a modern urban environment just as they do in the jungle, the steppes, or under the harsh desert sun. Remember that shamanism is a strategy for gaining power and a set of techniques for exercising it created by and for people at the grass-roots level.

We have included vignettes and stories, both modern and ancient, to illustrate the shamanic techniques and their effectiveness in daily life. The contemporary stories are based on actual situations that we, our colleagues, and our clients have experienced. The ancient stories were given to us by our own guardian spirits to illustrate shamanic problem-solving in all corners of the world.

BENEFITS OF SHAMANISM

In the following chapters we will take you through a process that we have designed to bring you shamanic awareness and problem-solving abilities. Here are some of the benefits you can expect to receive:

• Your ideas about how events in your life occur and how they affect you and those around you will shift. Your conventional ideas about linear time will be altered, allowing you more freedom.

• Your understanding of who is in charge of your life will transform and you will no longer feel that you are the victim of circumstance.

• Your view of yourself as a separate human being will be called into question and you will begin to contemplate how you are related and connected to all of life. Your perspective will broaden.

• Your understanding about the nature of reality and how your goals manifest will undergo radical transformation. You will discover how to set appropriate goals for yourself in order to reach them effectively.

• Your understanding and experience of real power will be enhanced.

- Your awareness of personal relationships will change and your method of communicating will improve as well. You will gain a new insight into what compassion means because you will understand yourself and others better.

- You will feel inspired and challenged by obstacles that you are capable of handling and you will know how to avoid obstacles that you cannot overcome.

- You will understand how to access knowledge and information that you did not think you possessed.

- You will learn how to tap into an infinite supply of energy available to every human being who knows the process.

- You will learn how to feel more relaxed and less stressed in the face of obstacles.

To develop your shamanic abilities you'll first need to learn about energy and how it works, because the intensity of thoughts and emotions direct energy and initiate results both in the ordinary world and in the spirit world. You can then learn about the human spirit body, what it does for you, and how to understand and use it. You will learn how to manage the energy within your spirit body in a way that energizes you rather than depletes you. You will need to know how to ground yourself and protect yourself when you are involved in shamanic work. In addition, you will be introduced to the tunnels to the spirit world and you will discover how you can develop your personal gateways for greater power and mastery.

When you study shamanism you are studying a system of knowledge that predates all your familial, social, and cultural conditioning. You are cutting through the confusions and abstractions of centuries of theologies and dogmas and returning to a simple direct method of apprehending the world. Yet unlike primitive human beings, you have the benefit of the incredible discoveries of physics and biochemistry to validate your experience. You can see with the eyes of a child, yet act with the body of one who has centuries of experience and wisdom at your immediate disposal.

When you practice shamanism you become a co-creator in the collective will of nature. You become a change agent in the drama of evolution. More than that, you release yourself from the illusion of isolation and step into the reality of the interrelationship of all life. Finally the practice of shamanism leads you to eventually align yourself with the healing forces of nature. You find balance and integration. You know who you are and where you are going.

CHAPTER 2

Beginning the Journey: Soaring into the Unknown

Scraped and battered, the glider flipped upside down on the grass for the tenth time. "It just doesn't work, Dad," Tod said, his eight-year-old face screwed up in frustration. "The plane doesn't work." The big man squatted down beside him. "Well, I don't know, Tod, I showed you how to hold it. Maybe you're just not tall enough yet to make it fly. Come on, let's go in for some lunch." Tod just stood there looking angrily at his plane.

Grampa was watching them both from the porch. "Come here, Tod," he called in his gravelly voice. "Bring that glider over here and let me see it, my eyes don't work as well as they used to. Let's see if there's anything wrong with it." Tod loved Gramps and already his mood had changed. "Hmmm, don't look like anything's wrong with that plane to me. You're holding it just right. Let's see. Mind if I tell you a secret?" he said, his eyes twinkling. "It ain't the way you hold it, and it isn't the plane, and it isn't the way you throw it. Tell you what—it's about how you see it and how you feel about it that makes it fly."

"What do you mean, Gramps?" asked Tod.

"Well, see that hawk hoverin' over there? Close your eyes. Can you see the hawk still?"

"Sure, Gramps." Tod's eyes stayed closed tightly. "Hey! Now he's taking off." He opened his eyes and the hawk was gone.

Gramps laughed, "Did you notice how you could tell exactly when that hawk was leaving even with your eyes closed? You got a friend in that bird there and you got the power to fly that there plane. Close your eyes again and see that glider fly high and clear. Let it fly from your heart. Ask that hawk to carry it up for you. He knows all about flying."

15

Tod picked up the glider and closed his eyes. In his imagination he sent that little plane shooting into the sky and sailing round and round. That hawk was right there carrying it up higher and higher on his back. From his heart, Tod felt a rush of warmth and excitement. Opening his eyes he flung his arm back and let go. The little plane, catching the breeze, sailed up and away. "Lunchtime!" he heard his dad call from inside the cottage.

Grampa winked. "Remember now, Tod, it's our little secret." Tod raced for the door, happy and hungry.

WHAT IS IMAGINATION?

A child comes to you with a fantastic story about a purple polka-dotted monster that comes from the land of the magic mountains where the sun is pink and the flowers grow to be as big as houses! You laugh, thinking it's very cute, and say, "My, what an imagination we have today!" On the other hand, should adults other than perhaps writers of fairy tales, science fiction, or children's books, come to you with the same story, you might view them as being a little strange, off-beat, or perhaps highly eccentric. Certainly you would probably not consider them to be within society's norm. At best, you may consider them to be creative geniuses; at worst, raving lunatics.

As twentieth-century fact-oriented people, most of us don't quite know how to understand imagination. On the one hand, our power to imagine seems to be so illogical and so irrational, yet our imaginations allow us to realize our wildest dreams. Incredible feats of technology and architecture all began with creative images conceived in the realms of imagination. We tend to be skeptical of imagination because we believe that it creates false illusions, yet we admire its boundless creativity; uncomfortable with our fear of not being able to control it, we are fascinated with the visions it offers us. We doubt its usefulness in the face of logic, yet we delight in its fantastic images. We wish we had more of it, but regretfully feel that we have lost it forever to childhood. In all truth, each of us has imagination and can be highly creative; we're just a little rusty at it.

For shamans imagination encompasses more than just brain activity; a vital and principal vehicle, imagination connects us with the web of power and the spirit in all things. Imagination in shamanic terms links us with the spirit world or, as Michael Harner calls it, the world of nonordinary reality. The way or means we have of creating a line of communication with the spirit world is critical in shamanic work. Children, born with this skill, forget a great deal of it through enculturation and modern emphasis on strict logic to explain everything in the physical universe. The door that links children to the realm of spirit slowly begins to close in their attempt to master the physical, cultural ways of modern life. To a degree this is a normal process and a necessary one if they are to learn to distinguish between the nonordinary spirit world and the everyday physical world.

Joseph Chilton Pierce talks about this connection between the two worlds and the realm he calls "mind" in his book *The Magical Child*. As many others have done, he acknowledges the importance of preserving the childlike process of imagination and of reaching beyond the concrete and physical. The magical child, according to Pierce, translates to the child who has the ability to focus and yet does not get lost in content or memory.

Using shamanic skills requires the reopening of the door of imagination so that the link between the physical and the spirit world becomes reestablished. Exercising your imagination through visualization and shamanic visioning prepares you for the process of journeying, one of the basic techniques of shamanic work.

Drumming, Intzu closed his eyes and entered into the big dream. Instantly the golden bird spread its wings and, grasping Intzu in his talons, flew across the sky into the land of night. There was darkness all around them and all he could feel was the brisk wind that whistled through the feathers of the great bird. Suddenly the bird swooped low and lit on the branches of a mammoth silver-barked tree with eight magnificent branches stretching beyond the horizon. The top of the tree was lost in the heavens and the great roots penetrated to the very core of the Earth. Then the great golden bird sang to him in a soft voice: "Here find you at the center, go and come back, go and come back, the tree will always be your home. Sing with the spirit of the silver tree in your heart. Sing this song, sing this song and you shall be ever with your power." With a roar the bird was gone and Intzu awoke dazzled and filled with the spirit of life.

Intzu was overjoyed. Through his vision he had at last found his path of truth.

HOW YOU LIMIT YOUR IMAGINATION

You have probably heard it said many times that your beliefs limit you, and that you can only have as much as you can imagine yourself having. By this time in our historical development, human potential experts and metaphysical thinkers agree about the importance of being able to imagine yourself in the very situations that will bring you success. They suggest that the slogan of "I'll believe it when I see it" be replaced by "I'll see it when I believe it." Shamans are keenly aware of this perspective and create it for themselves. They emphasize the importance of being able to "see" the result before actualizing it physically. And yet they are also aware that people can only achieve as much as they can truly imagine for themselves. Thus a shaman will work at heightening a person's level or ability to have, do, and be. The ability to imagine raises our ability to have. Like a muscle that needs to be worked, strengthened, and stretched, imagination requires exercise. Shamanism is in part a strategy for expanding and empowering imagination.

Sandy sat cross-legged on the dirt floor of the shaman's simple shack. It had been quite an adventure tracking the old man down through the heat of the desert; even now in the shade, beads of sweat ran down her forehead and face; flies buzzed relentlessly around her eyes. I hope this is worth it, she thought to herself, recalling her friend Mike's stories about the shaman and thinking about the dwindling gas supply in her car. Reza was one of the few shamans around who spoke English and Sandy was looking forward to the full day she would spend in his company. She hoped to pick up a few tidbits about shamanic techniques, a subject that fascinated her. But that was tomorrow and now Reza seemed intent on telling stories involving many of the local people and the work he had done with them.

Months later Sandy was to recall a story that had stuck in her mind; the shaman had used his expertise in locating a herd of wild burros. Two villagers had come to him at different times on the same day to ask for guidance and information about the spot where these burros could be found. Both were told where they could find a herd of burros, but one was told the herd had six and the other was told it had eighteen. Thinking at this point in the story that perhaps Reza's memory wasn't the best, Sandy had asked if he had been describing the same herd. "Yes, same burros, same place" was the reply. "Not same is how many find," he offered in his broken English. What the shaman was alluding to was the fact that the first villager could not imagine owning more than six burros. When Sandy asked what would happen if this fellow went to the spot and found the eighteen, Reza answered, "Man will find only six; it is what he "see."

This is precisely the way your beliefs work to limit your level of success at any one time. Consider those people who suddenly gain an inheritence or win a lottery and come into a large sum of money. Studies show that too often they are unable to hold on to their good fortune and end up losing all or part through poor investments, squandering, or misman-agement. The same phenomena occurs with grossly over-weight people who suddenly lose a tremendous amount of weight. Only through consistent counseling and support systems are they able to ward off the tendency to gain it all back. They are ill-prepared for their newfound wealth or slim bodies because, although their situations have changed, their beliefs often have not.

The physical body has its comfort level, a state of homeo-stasis it settles into. The human body, like any animal, needs cajoling, massaging, and persuasion to come around to a new point of view. Even if the change is a positive one, inertia and habit must be overcome. To the physical body, any kind of change looks frightening because it represents the un-known. The "fear of success" syndrome is a very real one indeed and shamans have known about it and worked with it for centuries. They have been accused of lying or bending the truth as Reza may have appeared to Sandy, an accusation they mostly shrug off, knowing otherwise. In shamanic terms the physical self needs to be tricked, lied to, pampered, and bribed in order to get it to let go of the limiting beliefs that imprison it.

WHY USE IMAGINATION?

For a shaman who wants to retrieve information or a lost guardian spirit, "imagining what to look for" is the first step in achieving any result. "Imagining what you want" is as nec-essary for you when you desperately need a parking place (you've arrived minutes late for work) as when you wish to learn how to fly an airplane. Whether you realize it or not you use your imagination every time you are confronted with a new challenge and must decide what you want. You use your imagination to choose what question to ask or to decide what your focus will be. You create vivid sense-based images that help you see or feel what you are looking for. You then act on those images.

Visualization or visioning is a technique that uses imagination to create mental pictures of exactly what is wanted. For example, if you want a new car you create an image of that car and concentrate on it over and over until you get results. This method can be very effective and shamans sometimes use it to help them to manifest an outcome they wish to achieve. They manipulate thoughts and feelings to create a visual or sense-oriented picture of their goal. This helps them to formulate exactly what it is they want in the first place. Here is how to do it:

1. First create a mental picture of the exact item or experience that you wish to create in reality: perhaps a new house, a successful family gathering, or a vacation in the South Pacific.

2. Describe it in great detail to yourself.

3. Infuse it with all the excitement and enthusiasm you can muster. Include all your senses in creating a full image.

4. Let the image go. Repeat the exercise up to ten times.

The journey method is similar to visualization in that it is interactive with the environment, action-oriented, and power-based. In shamanic journeying you mobilize energy through your thoughts and emotions and send it out to intercede with the forces that exist in the world. If you have stored enough power you will be able to realize results with the hope of your allies. This emphasis on stored power is one feature that makes journeying different from simple visualization. A second difference between the two methods is the nature of the outcome. Unlike planned visualizations, in the shamanic journey process you don't always know what is going to happen in your visions. You don't control the events and situations that you experience but you can control how you respond to them.

Being able to visualize is an important prerequisite to developing the ability to journey. The more active your imagination and the more skill you have in using it, the more powerful you will be. The more powerful you are, the better you will be able to do the kind of maneuvering necessary in journeying, to meet challenges and obstacles in your path. You will need to open that door between the world of ordinary reality and the spirit world that was so available in childhood. Shamanic techniques rely on childhood skills. Specific visioning techniques are an integral part of the journey process. By exercising your imagination, you will be preparing yourself for using "shamanic vision" in the powerful journey method.

All of us have had experience with some form of visioning. For example, you may have daydreamed about an upcoming family vacation during a boring business meeting, or planned the scrumptious dinner you wished to serve for a romantic evening at home. In "daydreaming" two types of visioning can take place: passive and active. The passive form truly requires you to allow whatever thoughts and images you have to flow as in a dream. The active form, on the other hand, requires conscious thinking and manipulation of images.

Unlike many goal-setting and problem-solving techniques, visioning includes both active and passive forms of imaginative "daydreaming" or visualization. You must first actively focus on your question, problem or goal, be able to clearly "see," sense, and feel it, and then be receptive to the answer or guidance given.

DETACHMENT AND SURRENDER

Since shamanism is based on sensitivity and listening, the aspects of detachment and surrender play important roles in the success of any shamanic process. Coming up with a satisfactory solution to a problem while in the midst of an intense, emotional feeling about the problem itself is most difficult. Your intense emotional identification with a situation keeps you attached to it in such a way that the changes needed to bring about a result cannot be made. When you are heavily identified with your problem via these emotions, the result is a blockage of energy that stops progress toward your goal. Usually with time the emotional intensity fades and you can continue on your way. Thus the old saying "Sleep on it, things will look brighter in the morning" has a ring of truth to it, since your sleep state requires a surrender to the dream or spirit world.

This state of surrender is also important when it comes to goal setting and creating things or situations that you want. A great emotional attachment to these wishes can actually keep them from manifesting. You have heard that the "watched pot never boils." The same can be true for a desire you are too attached to. Often this is the case in dealing with relationships, since they are usually emotionally charged. For example, you would probably have more difficulty remaining detached in a shamanic process if you were asking about a quarrel you had with a member of your family. You would find it easier to ask about the weather or someone else's family affairs.

Shamanism takes this concept of detachment one step further. Not only are you required to surrender your attachment to achieve success, but you must also accept what comes in its place. Even if the information you receive during a journey does not seem useful to you, accept it graciously and do not resist or judge it. You may realize later the real value of what you experienced. For example, in response to your quest for clarity about a relationship problem you may see a bird circling round and round during your journey. You could dismiss this apparition as irrelevant or nonsensical or you could keep it in mind as a potential key to your dilemma. Later you may realize that the problem stems from your persistence in approaching that person the same way every time, just like a bird going round and round.

Shamans acknowledge that surrender and detachment are perhaps the most difficult concepts to master. Thus humor is used a great deal as an integral part of their advising process. Laughing helps in detachment by releasing stuck emotions and can be quite literally "the best medicine." It is difficult to remain identified with and intensely emotional about a situation when humor enters into the picture. Shamans know this and stress the importance of infusing their work with the humorous aspect. They invariably turn into clowns, acting out an exercise with wild gesturing, dancing, and singing. Western anthropologists used to think shamans were crazy because they seemed to laugh about everything. Crazy, perhaps; insane, hardly. Only truly sane people are able to laugh at the troubles humans get themselves into. The world of the spirit self is the true source of all amusement. Therefore, you will find that the advice you get from that inner world is often highly amusing, even teasing about your predicament.

The breakup of a relationship is never an easy experience, and for Andrea Clover it was downright debilitating. Andrea had been morose for weeks now: her writing career on hold; her letters unanswered; her social life dead in the water. Andrea felt so shocked about Jacque's sudden change of heart that she had been unable even to cry about her feelings of rejection.

Finally her closest friend Lynne persuaded her to come to the "empowering circle," a group of dedicated shamanic practitioners whom she met with weekly to dance, drum, and journey. Andrea had resisted going for months because the whole thing sounded so hokey and ridiculous: sitting, imagining silly animals, and hopping around like them. They must be a bunch of weirdos.

Andrea was rather surprised to find a mix of very ordinary-looking people from all walks of life. As the evening progressed she was introduced and the group let her know she was welcome to participate in all their activities. They began with some sharing and sage burning and then proceeded to perform a vigorous line dance accompanied by the drum that Andrea thought was silly. Why had she come? She thought about sneaking out but then began to see the humor of the situation. She started to laugh at the ridiculous picture of herself and the others hopping up and down in the semidarkness, loud drumbeats punching through the air. As she laughed, to her surprise Andrea inexplicably became tearful and for a few moments didn't know whether she was laughing or sobbing. When the dance ended Andrea felt confused but strangely energized. A group member then explained to her that they were going to "dance their animals" and that she could join them. He explained that since it was her first time, all she had to do was let an impression of an animal come through her.

As the drumbeat began again, Andrea was doubtful that she would get a sense of any animal but was again surprised at how quickly the image of a large deer came to her. Slowly, awkwardly at first, she mimicked the movements of a deer, feeling a warmth associated with the animal. She found herself assuming the stance of defense, head down, antlers protecting. As the drumbeat increased in intensity, the deer shifted to movements of attacking and sparring. Andrea suddenly felt an enormous relief and gave herself to the vigorous thrusts and parries.

Later that evening as Andrea drove home she had the strange sensation of a deer in the backseat of her car. She smiled to herself and sighed happily. Somehow Jacques didn't seem that important anymore. She had found a new friend and new power.

In order for Andrea to get up and dance the animal, she had to begin the process of surrender, which was greatly aided there by laughter and tears. Only then could she allow the helper, in this case an animal spirit, to come in.

THE NUTS AND BOLTS OF VISIONING

Shamanic visioning adds another dimension to visualization, the process of seeing or forming a mental image: that of incorporating nature and using all the senses. Because the spirit of all of nature is the source of true power, therein lies the key to successful visioning. And since nature and natural beings are three-dimensional, shamans re-create their images in a three-dimensional way by using sound, feel, smell, and taste, as well as sight. For example, if you were to re-create an image of an apple in your mind you would "see" it, feel it in your hands, smell it, take a bite and taste it, and hear the crunch as you chewed the bite.

The other aspect to remember about shamanic visioning is how important it is to re-create your images using natural phenomena as much as possible. If you are imagining yourself relaxing into a soft surface, have that surface be soft spring grass, a bed of cushiony leaves, or perhaps the fur of an animal you like rather than a nylon carpet or a piece of vinyl upholstered furniture. Likewise if you are re-creating the feel or hard piece of ground rather than concrete or plastic. Shamanically speaking, natural objects have more power than synthetic materials.

The same idea pertains to all the senses. Making a vision real for yourself should include sound, smell, and perhaps taste as well. Sound is more difficult because in most urban communities what we hear and can mentally reproduce are sounds of the city: cars, the hum of freeways, trains, cash registers, telephones, etc. But even in urban areas, if you really listen you can also hear natural sounds: the wind blowing through trees, birds chirping, water running (even if it's in your kitchen sink). And no doubt you can remember the sound of the surf at the seashore, or the rush of a rainstorm on a trip to the mountains. All of these powerful sounds from nature, if incorporated into your visioning process, help you create the three-dimensional image vital to successful shamanic advising.

The sense of smell is the most powerful sense of all. Memories of childhood smells, Grandma's baking, for example, trigger unprecedented emotional responses in people. Therefore adding the sense of smell makes a mental image very real indeed. Visions of flowers come to life when you add their fragrance, and fruit becomes mentally edible with added aroma. Likewise, visualizing the perfect place to live should include warm and comforting smells. A real estate agent we know always bakes chocolate chip cookies and lights a fire in the fireplace of a home she opens up for viewing. People walk in and immediately feel "at home." Needless to say she is very successful and has little trouble selling the homes she represents.

Infusing your visions with the sense of smell requires that you identify those smells that mean something to you. For example, one person may feel comforted by the smell of warm damp earth while for another it might be the smell of sea air. Whatever your favorite smells are, using them in your visioning adds a powerful dimension to the process of creating an image. Just remember to keep this sense oriented to nature as much as possible.

The sense of taste goes hand in hand with the sense of smell. Obviously it can only be used when you are working with edible objects and then the sense of smell is usually also included. But because taste enriches your image just that much more, you should use it whenever possible.

Here are a couple of simple sensing exercises to acquaint you with using the senses of feeling, hearing, smelling, and tasting. Because for most people the sense of sight is more developed, exercising the four other senses is important for developing balance and strength in shamanic work.

Sensing Exercise #1: A Synopsis

For this exercise you need to find a place to sit down for a moment without being disturbed, preferably outside. Close your eyes, relax, and explore your surroundings using your sense of touch; that is, if it is sunny or breezy notice how that feels on your face. If you are sitting on the ground or against a tree, feel with your hands the area around you. Notice its hardness, softness, temperature, etc.

Move to your sense of hearing. Listen to all the sounds around you. Focus on one sound at a time, really hearing it. If you are in an urban area, try to focus on just the natural sounds. Let the artificial ones fade into the distance.

Move to your sense of smell. Notice the different smells around you. Again, this may be more difficult for you if you are in a highly congested urban area. But in any park you may find smells of trees, grass, earth, etc. Focus on one smell at a time and try to follow the natural ones.

Now combine the senses. Notice all three at the same

time. If this is difficult for you, focus first on one, then add the others one at a time.

Exercise #1: The Steps

1. Close your eyes and relax.
2. Explore your surroundings using your sense of touch.
3. Listen to all the sounds around you.
4. Notice the different smells around you.
5. Notice all three senses at the same time.

Exercise #2: A Synopsis

For the sense of taste, it is not necessary to be outside. Your home, office, or anywhere else will do. This exercise works best with a piece of fruit. So choose a piece of fruit— for example, a pear. Then close your eyes and feel the fruit with your hands. Feel the texture and temperature. Smell the fruit and begin to eat it. Focus on the sense of taste while eating. Notice your sense of hearing as well.

Exercise #2: The Steps

1. Choose a fruit.
2. Close your eyes. Feel the fruit.
3. Smell and begin to eat the fruit.
4. Focus on the sense of taste.

These exercises are designed to be done in a short amount of time and just about anywhere. In doing them you increase your capabilities to enrich your visualizations and make them more powerful.

The sense of sight is the one most commonly used in creating mental images. When you are told to imagine an object, that object probably comes up as a visual mental picture. In shamanic visioning pictures make up the base that is then built up and filled out using the other senses. Therefore you must be able to "see" your image before you can begin to round it out.

For shamans not only is the shape or form of a visual image important but also the frequency at which the energy of that form vibrates. This is an abstract concept that perhaps only physicists, shamans, and mystics are aquainted with. Shamanically speaking each physical form, whether animate or inanimate, has a spirit or energy that vibrates according to a specific level or frequency. For example, gold would have a higher frequency than lead. This frequency can be most easily translated for the visioning process into color and density. Each color of the spectrum carries with it a certain frequency; thus, if you can create the color in your mind, you have also created the frequency.

A higher density or darkening of a color will lower the frequency, whereas the lightening or brightening of a color will raise the frequency or energy level. Darker, thicker colors such as brown or black carry with them the images of "black" moods, lethargy and depression; a fiery red invokes vitality, and a fluorescent turquoise may feel exciting and highly creative.

Colors and their frequencies are important as reminders of natural properties. The more you use these properties in your visions, the more powerful they become. Therefore we teach the use of color and density as it relates to natural beings. Shamans know that since all natural beings have spirit, duplicating their visual qualities in a mental process makes the image come alive and thus many times more powerful than using qualities from synthetic objects. The difference is subtle and you may well ask how one green is distinguished from another green. If someone asks you to close your eyes and think of green do you think of the green of your tablecloth or the green of your lawn? The shade may look the same to you, the difference being a purely energetic one.

Likewise if you imagine something yellow, you could recall the paint on your refrigerator. On the other hand you might use the warm yellow of the sun or perhaps the yellow of the skin of a ripe lemon. Using colors from natural objects replicates their spiritual properties. Thus, coloring your mental pictures with natural colors brings life to your visions and therefore more power.

Here is a type of guided shamanic vision. Although not truly a shamanic journey, this shamanic technique can produce powerful results.

Ahritmah sat by the fire huddled over his meager evening meal. For these past days he had been longing for the brighter days when his spirit soared and he felt full and virile. It was as if some darkness had descended on him, making his life miserable and cold. Only Saashima and a few of the women and children were left in the camp, the rest had moved on to camp on the other side of the great river. Saashima, young and beautiful, had been taught by an old wise one in the ways of the spirit. Ahritmah now called on her for help. She placed her palms on his eyes, closing out the firelight, and said, "Go inside, tell me what you see."

"Darkness," he answered. "Nothing but darkness and night in the desert."

"What do you wish for?" asked Saashima gently.

"For strength, for the new camp, for my life!" Ahritmah replied.

"Open your mind and find the sky," she told him. "Make it blue with the day. Look down and see the desert sand glowing gold like the sun. Find the camp across the great river and your tent warm as camel's milk and the color like the tip of the flame of your camp fire. Your mother is waiting with her heart warm and glowing as the embers. She hands you a bowl of liquid, red like fresh saffron; you drink it and feel your strength returning and the darkness washing away into the earth."

Saashima then removed her palms from Ahritmah's eyes, turned to the east, bowed low in thanks and was gone. Ahritmah lay for a long time near the dying fire, holding the lingering vision in his mind. Then he fell asleep. The next day he greeted the sun as it came up over the desert and, feeling himself again, left for the camp across the great river.

As reflected in the story above, the use of color and other sensual aids in visioning can not only bring about desired changes but help to motivate one to make those changes. A situation that appears grim or "dark" can be lightened just with the use of these techniques. For example if your present work situation is depressing, you might try changing the frequency of your office by lightening or brightening the color you give it in your vision by using natural colors.

The following exercise is a simple one and uses all of the principles discussed so far in this chapter. It will help you practice the basics of effective shamanic visioning. We recommend that you do this exercise several times in preparation for the shamanic journey we will introduce to you next.

Exercise #3: A Synopsis

Choose an object in your house. Relax and close eyes. Re-create the object in your mind as carefully as po ble, including every detail you remember. If you need open your eyes and look at the object again.

When you have re-created this object to the best of your ability, begin to focus on each part of it. Notice everything: color, texture, smell, sound, temperature. Take each quality that you have noticed and describe it to yourself in natural terms. For instance, if you are looking at a lamp with a rough brownish ceramic base and a silk white shade, you might see the base as having the same qualities and color as a rock, and the shade may resemble the white petal of a lily. Go through the entire object in this way using every sense you can.

Now let your imagination take over. Begin making some changes in your object, again using natural qualities and all the senses. You can make these changes humorous for added benefit. For example the lamp now can become furry like an animal, smell like cinnamon and dance around the room singing loudly. This step is an important once since it exercises your imagination as well as your ability to empower your images with the spirit of nature. Spend as much time here as you like. You may even try to allow the object to change on its own without your instruction. See what comes in; it may surprise you.

Exercise #3: The Steps

1. Choose an object.
2. Relax, close your eyes.
3. Re-create the object in your mind.
4. Focus on each part, notice everything, using all senses.
5. Describe each quality in natural terms.
6. Imagine changes using natural qualities.

BEGINNING THE SHAMANIC JOURNEY

Now that you know the basics of creating effective images in shamanic visioning, let us move on to the shamanic journey. By way of introduction, the shamanic journey is the most common method used in shamanic advising for the purpose of communicating with your spirit self and retrieving information. Your spirit self is in constant communication with all aspects of nature far and near. You have only to learn to journey within to communicate with your spirit self and thus become part of this hidden realm. As Michael Harner explains in *The Way of the Shaman*, the shaman is a "self-reliant explorer of the endless mansions of a magnificent hidden universe."

From ancient times shamans have used the process of journeying to travel to what they call the underworld. Whereas many schools of metaphysical thinking talk about reaching outward into the universe or the cosmos for information, shamans have always believed that the answers can be found within. Therefore the journey begins at an entrance to the earth usually in the form of a cave or hot springs, and the travel is generally through a tunnel. A friend of ours likens it to a mine shaft that goes deep into the earth.

Before beginning the journey you must first prepare yourself by focusing on a question or a subject that you wish to know about. Tuning into the process without focusing first is like turning on the TV to watch your favorite program without tuning the dial to the right channel: you are likely to get a lot of static and experience a chaotic mishmash. Be sure to focus and tune into exactly what you want to know about. Second, you need to clear your mind of everything, give up the need for control, and begin your journey without any expectations or preconceived notions of what you'll discover. We will provide you with a relaxation exercise that may help you for starters.

To focus their energy, shamans frequently use rapid rhythmic drumming that drives them on their inner journey. The drum is affectionately called the horse or canoe because of its use as a vehicle to travel to the spirit world. Although not absolutely necessary for a shamanic journey, the drumming sound helps you focus, decreasing the tendency to intellectualize, quieting what might be called "mental chatter," and allowing the images or visions of the journey to form in your mind. Creating a focus with the drum helps induce a sense of urgent movement that will help start you on your journey and, once you've arrived, will help you effectively retrieve information.

If you are concerned about being overheard, you can listen to a tape of a drum using a set of headphones. (You can make your own tape or order one [see resource directory]). You can even get away with tapping your fingers on the back of a tissue box. Remember that shamans are pragmatists:

they do whatever works. The good ones don't waste their time with empty ritual. If you are able to concentrate well, you, like the shamans, can certainly learn to journey without the aid of drumming.

In order for the journey to work for you, you need only to follow the steps and be willing to take what comes. If you put too much effort into it, bully yourself, make judgments about yourself or what you are about to do, or are impatient, you will only get in your own way. Hopefully your experience with the previous exercises will help you override these habits, the most common blocks for beginners. Imagine that you are going to talk to a very old wise man or woman; you'll want to be calm, patient, respectful, and receptive to everything he or she has to say. Shamanically speaking, your spirit self is that very old wise being. Remember to approach yourself the same way.

Retrieving information for ruthless personal gain or for winning an advantage over another is seldom fruitful. To want to deprive another of what they have or to defeat them is contradictory to the basic laws of harmony in the spirit world. You will therefore find yourself blocked because your process is based on inappropriate intention. If the subject you're focusing on does involve other people, take a win-win attitude—that is, you want everyone to benefit from your strategy. This attitude supports the notion of harmony and balance in all of nature and will strengthen your access to this universal information.

During your journey you may be given advice or information that you do not want to hear. If you are not willing for this to happen, don't consult shamanic advice. Unless you are open to wherever your journey may take you, you are only wasting your time. If you journey, be prepared for whatever insights you may receive, whether you like them or not. Usually, you will be pleasantly surprised by the images and messages you discover. If, however, you are in the habit of lying to yourself, you may find that you have some uncomfortable truths to face.

Occasionally you may be given a symbolic gift or present during your journey. Feathers, gemstones, lights, and books are all typical of these types of gifts. Always accept them and bring them back with you in an imaginative form. This is where your visioning skills will come in handy. Receiving a gift is always important. It makes the journey real and is a sign that you are on the right track.

You might notice judgments and mental commentary coming up as you journey. This part of your mind has to have something to do, so let it be. Simply acknowledge it, then ignore it and go on.

LEARNING TO RELAX

Helpful for successful journeying and many other shamanic techniques is the ability to relax your body completely and rapidly. This art, if cultivated, will result in a rich bounty of benefits. The deeper your body relaxes, the more powerful and effective will be your experience. There are many good methods to relax the body. We recommend the following because it has proved effective with so many people and at the same time it tunes you into the elements thus opening the senses. However, feel free to use any method of relaxation that works for you. With a little practice you can learn to reach a state of deep relaxation within a minute or so. Shamans can reach this state in seconds if they wish. You may want to make a cassette tape of the exercise and play it to yourself.

Exercise #4: Relaxation

1. Find a safe comfortable place where you will not be interrupted. It is best to turn the lights low and lie down on your back with your body stretched out.

2. Take three deep breaths and blow out all the tension you might feel.

3. Become aware of your body. Start with your feet and gradually move upward through each joint until you reach your head.

4. Begin to notice the effect that gravity has on your body. Notice that it pulls you downward, pressing various parts of your body more deeply into the carpet or floor. Notice how it holds down your clothes and your arms and legs. Feel its effect on your face. Realize that without gravity you would float up and drift around the room. Gravity gives your body weight.

5. Let go of any resistance you have to gravity. It is a natural and constant force. Give into it. Allow gravity to pull out all the tension left in your body. Let it drift downward deep into the earth where all energy is renewed.

6. Notice, however, that the thoughts and images in your mind are not subject to gravity. You are free to travel with them anywhere you wish to go.

LEARNING THE SHAMANIC JOURNEY

Like developing any skill, the shamanic journey takes practice to receive its maximum benefits. As the saying goes, "If at first you don't succeed, try, try again." You may find that when you first try to journey, nothing happens. All you get is darkness. Occasionally this happens even to those experienced at the journey process. Do not be discouraged by such obstacles, since they seldom persist. Eventually, after two or three attempts, you will achieve some results and then you will be on your way. If occasionally you find that you are not able to journey, don't try to force yourself. Simply try again at a different time. Timing has a lot to do with success in shamanic work.

The time required for the exercise below is three to twenty-five minutes, depending on the nature of your question, your level of proficiency, and how much time you have. Read through the exercise first to get acquainted with it. Then you can do it from memory with your eyes closed.

Exercise #5: Description of the Journey Process

Make yourself as comfortable as you can. Sitting is fine, but lying flat on your back on the couch or floor works better. Try turning the lights off, and make sure you won't be interrupted by the telephone or other people. If you are tired, however, avoid lying down as you may fall asleep.

Follow the relaxation exercise described above. Then focus on the issue that you want to know more about, shutting out any mental chatter and distractions around you. Form your issue into a question. For example, try stating your question in one of these ways:

- Will "x" make a good employee?

- How will the problems in my relationship be resolved?

- How can I spend more time with my family when I have so much work to do?

- How will my time be most effectively spent?

Ask your question or state in your own words what it is you would like to know about. Then, to enhance your receptivity say, "I will appreciate any help I can get on this matter. I will use the information I receive with integrity."

Resolve to see, hear, or feel with your visioning skills without censoring or making judgments. You don't have to follow the advice given, but you do need to be willing to hear the message for the journey to work.

Close your eyes and breathe deeply three or four times, once again allowing yourself to relax fully. Picture or remember with all of your senses the entrance to a cave or an opening in the earth that you have visited or seen. Clear your mind of everything but this image—you can also picture a pool of water or a hole in a tree trunk that you once saw. If you don't recall one, try to imagine as many details about an opening in the earth as you can, from its shape and color to the sounds and smells that surround it.

Approach the entrance or opening slowly and step inside. Imagine the cave walls or the texture of the earth. Remember to use as many of your senses as you can. Here you will be met by a presence that will act as your spirit guide: an animal, person, voice, light, ball of energy, or other form. If you are too uncomfortable with whatever appears, ask it to come in another form.

State your question to the guide and prepare to journey. It may tell you to ride on its back or accompany it in some fashion. Typically you will proceed at a rapid pace down a tunnel. This may be quite brief or take longer than you expected. Usually you will be surprised at the spontaneity of the ride and the destination. Sometimes you go up, sometimes down, sometimes you travel on one level. Rather than questioning this, simply notice it. Shamans of old had ways of naming these different pathways that led them to their different worlds. This concept will be described in greater detail in a later chapter. For now, just explore and learn through your experience.

There are many possibilities at this point. You may go to a landscape or a room and meet someone who tells you what you want to know. You might enter a library where a page in a book is open for you to read. You may be led to a place where a symbolic activity or drama takes place for you to understand.

Accept whatever happens with grace and when you are asked to leave, do so at once. Your guide will usually return with you but, if not, it is important to return via the same route that you took to arrive. If you do not, you might find that you are not able to remember what happened as well. You may even have a hard time becoming fully awake upon your return. Your return journey need not be lengthy. However, it is usually highly accelerated.

When you have returned to the entrance, thank your

guide, and emerge from the opening. Recall the room or place where you are, move your body and open your eyes. It is helpful to jot down in a notebook the main points of what occurred as soon as you can. These will be useful to you as you journey more and begin to piece together the meanings of the various messages you receive.

Exercise #5: The Steps

1. Lie down in a private place.
2. Relax.
3. Formulate the question you wish to ask.
4. Picture opening into the Earth.
5. Meet guide or ally.
6. State problem or question to guide.
7. Follow guide's lead and instructions implicitly.
8. Return via the same route.
9. Thank your guide.
10. Jot down your experience.

UNDERSTANDING YOUR JOURNEY

In most cases, the information that you receive on a shamanic journey is clear, direct, and to the point. It will say, "Proceed with your plan, good work, all systems go" or it will say "Stop, to proceed is disastrous."

Occasionally, however, your answer will come in symbolic form as in a dream. You may need to interpret its meaning for yourself. This usually means that there is more to the situation than meets the eye. Take your time if this is the case. Interpret the shamanic advice as you would any dream. Although only you can interpret your own experience accurately, you may find it helpful to talk it over with a trusted friend, experiment with possible associations related to each symbol or image, and sleep on it. Try not to analyze or figure it out too much. Its meaning will become clear in the appropriate amount of time.

Often practitioners of the shamanic advising technique report with amazement the profundity and depth of knowledge they receive. So, do not be surprised if you get a new slant on a situation that you may have overlooked before.

BENEFITS OF JOURNEYING

The more you practice the shamanic journey, the better you will get at it. Eventually you will be able to take a rapid inner journey as you walk down a busy street on your way to meet a friend with whom you've had an argument. You will look like any ordinary person to others, but like all shamans you will have a foot in two worlds: the ordinary physical world around you and the inner spirit world of all knowledge which you will learn about in detail over the next few chapters. This does not guarantee a happy reunion with your friend, but it does mean that you will approach your friend fully in focus, with an active intuitive sense, knowing what pitfalls your friendship faces.

One of the most positive results of developing your shamanic abilities is the discovery that the world of spirit is the true source of all amusement. As we mentioned before, shamans always include humor in their work; it allows for the often amusing advice you might get during your journey. The helpers you meet often tease you about your density or seriousness. When you return you feel lighter, clearer, and more objective about the issue you are dealing with.

Another benefit of the journey is that it helps you get a different perspective on your situation. In the stress of the corporate world, for example, a narrow focus on succeeding at all costs may shut down creativity and visionary ability. Obvious clues and signs indicating the probable boom or bust of a deal are simply screened out. This is the proverbial "forest for the trees" syndrome. The journey method always expands the focus to include all necessary information—it gives you a sense of the big picture. Journeying also encourages you to see the importance of other factors besides the immediate win.

Jon was so focused on cementing an upcoming contract that he was about to be debilitatingly anxious about a flight cancellation. The delay would cause him to be late for his appointment with a new client. As he bided his time in the airport he remembered that he could use the shamanic journey to explore the larger context of his delay. He found a comfortable seat in an out-of-the-way waiting area, closed his eyes, and began to journey. He was surprised by what was revealed to him.

After traveling through the tunnel, he came to a large meeting room. His client, Mr. Cormick, appeared to him as a lumbering friendly bear. He said, "Hi, Jon, you don't remember me, but I'm your friend. I'm going to help you out. Don't worry about being late. I needed that delay because I'm not quite ready for you. I needed to receive an important letter that makes it possible for us to proceed. In fact, I was ready to turn you down until I got this letter. Take your time."

Jon was able to relax during the delay and upon arriving, he discovered that something like his vision had happened. He and Mr. Cormick hit it off like old friends. And although Mr. Cormick had received no letter, he had gotten an important phone call that had made the deal possible. Seeing the big picture is the shamanic forte.

Finally, the truly hidden benefit of shamanic advisement is that the more you practice it, the more humane and compassionate you will become. You may think that these attributes have no place in your world, whatever it may be, yet the truth is that you will not truly succeed unless you develop compassion for yourself and others. This does not mean playing a sucker or martyr role but rather being cognizant of what you and other people need in order to feel safer and truly cared about. Only when you have achieved this state will you be truly successful.

CHAPTER 3

The Secret World:
What Shamans Know

THE WEB OF POWER

The summer storm came crashing through the mountains as Teema and her small son Yol scurried to find shelter in the barren high pass. The wind rose up to gale force, stinging their eyes with dust particles and flying sand. Teema knew that if they did not clear the ridge they could be blown off or, worse, struck by lightning. As Yol whimpered by her side, she grew calm inside and kneeled behind the sparse protection of a boulder. She felt her body go limp as she mentally focused on the spirit of the wind. Suddenly she felt her spirit body rise up to a great height, strangely impervious to the raging wind and intense flashes of lightning. A great hawk hovered near her and spoke to her calmly: "Go higher up the ridge and find the small cave that is just below the peak on the right. There you will be safe as the storm passes this way." Having spoken to the wind on several occasions before with good results, Teema did not hesitate. Up she scrambled with Yol to the peak above. The cave, though small and sparse, offered ample protection from the tempestuous winds. Now Teema had time to thank the spirit of the wind for her timely help. As the storm abated she felt strangely invigorated, as if she had received some of the power of the wind during the storm.

One of the basic concepts of shamanism is the notion that a "web of power" underlies all of life: the belief that all things of physical form also have "spirit." This spirit is the source of power for all life. For the ordinary person, the world appears to be just a physical environment that runs according to ordinary physical laws. It has some order but no meaning. In the shamans' world, the web of power creates coherency and gives meaning to the world. Without it, there would be chaos. For shamans this underlying source of power is not a theory or a metaphor but a definite reality that is as fundamental as the experience of gravity is to anyone who has dropped something. And for shamans, an understanding of this web of power is the key to success.

Shamans believe that without this knowledge a person is truly the victim of circumstance and can have no mastery over his decisions and actions. Shamans feel that understanding the physical world of form through modern-day science and technology is okay but certainly not adequate. These approaches fail to address the spirit realm that is so essential to their world view.

This world of spirit exists within all forms, but remains hidden unless you unveil it. In this chapter, we will begin to familiarize you with the spirit world and how you can open your senses to it. When you have unveiled it, realms of knowledge and therefore power become available to you. But like most treasures, they may elude you for a long time. You may walk over a diamond or a ruby many times before you discover that it lies beneath a layer of crust and dust.

So it is with all physical forms. To the uninitiated and inexperienced the wind is the wind, a rock is just a rock, and a tree is just a source of lumber or shade; water is for drinking and washing, animals are flesh-covered bones, and humans are flesh, blood, thoughts, and feelings. Take them apart and all you find are smaller pieces of them. Take them down to the atomic level and, surprise, they are all made of the same basic materials. Take them down to the subatomic level and, voilà, they are mostly space (or spirit). They are particles that are really waves or vice versa. At this level, chaos begins to reign for the physicist, but not for the shaman. Even this simple scientific breakdown just begins to crack open the door from the shamanic perspective. From the shamanic point of view, there is spirit within all wind, within all rocks and earth, within all plants and trees, water animals, humans, and every other form of life both animate and inanimate. Furthermore, this spirit, this source of energy is what you communicate with mentally in shamanic advising.

Mike slammed his fist down on the table. "That monkey's done it again!" The door to Max's empty cage stood open. Although Mike scoured his small animal hospital, there was no sign of the wayward rhesus monkey. By now, he could be halfway across town, dining on garbage in every trash bin in town. Mike realized that he would have to work fast if he was to get him safely back.

Mike knew if he were to be successful, he had to relax and go inward. First he spread out a map of the town in front of him and studied it. Using a shamanic technique he had learned recently, he sat down, closed his eyes and quieted himself. He reproduced an image of Max in his mind's eye and reached out to him with his feelings. Silently he called to the monkey, "Max, Max, this is Mike. I need you to come back. I've got some nice food for you and I'll keep you safe and warm." Mike continued in this fashion for a while until suddenly he felt a connection. He reached out and stroked the monkey's fur and soothed it. Then, using his shamanic vision, he reproduced the map of the town in his mind's eye. A little spark of light lit up on Elm Street just about where Carl's Pizza House was located. "Aha, gotcha. Stay right there," cried Mike as he grabbed his coat and keys. In a flash he was in his car on the way to Carl's. When he got there, Max didn't put up a fight but came to Mike amiably. He was stuffed with pizza.

Shamans have learned to communicate with the spirit within both inanimate and animate things, not just with the physical forms. It is this communication with the spirit that empowers shamans, for they know that the invisible web of power, that spirit within all forms, is in fact the real source of life. Through such communication they gain a deep understanding of and respect for the workings of the universe. The power they gain is one that comes with truly knowing something. As the shamans' power grows, they learn to manage and channel it appropriately.

Shamanic communication is almost always effective, even in modern-day situations like the wayward-monkey scenario. To give another example, one of our friends communicates regularly with the tree in her front yard and claims to receive information regarding the health of some of her house plants as well as coming weather conditions.

THE HUMAN SPIRIT BODY

Shamans believe that humans as well as rocks, animals, plants, and other natural phenomena have spirit bodies that can be communicated with. Unlike rocks, animals, and plants, however, each person's spirit body is unique and different. This spirit or energy body is associated with heat and to shamans it looks like flames or the kind of heat waves that can be seen shimmering in the desert on a hot day. The spirit body surrounds and interpenetrates the physical body and is made up of a blend of vibrant colors.

Historically, shamans have described these brilliant waves surrounding the head and body as a sign of the spirit of light that infuses each human being with life. Shamans of old believed the sun represented the fire of life and that the human spirit body was the internal sun. They believed that the brighter the flame of this in-dwelling solar fire, the more powerful the shaman. Much shamanic art depicts this internal sun as rayed aureoles emanating from the heads of spirits and influential shamans alike.

Shamans are famous for their ability to generate incredible heat from their bodies with an act of will. For example, Tibetan shamans are able to melt the snow all around them in the dead of winter with self-generated heat. This talent for generating heat is a shamanic sign of the incredible power available in the spirit body.

The spirit body has been seen and described for centuries not only by shamans but also by psychics, mystics, and intuitives. They have seen, sensed, felt, and worked with it via intuition, clairvoyance, and imagination. You may ask, how is it that so many powerful individuals have described this field of energy throughout history and cross-culturally the world over? Why is it that venerated saints and avatars are depicted with halos and flames surrounding their bodies? How is it that artists and visionaries are always the first to know what science later discovers? These questions point to the fact that over time and from all continents, sensitive people have noticed a similar phenomenon with regard to a certain kind of energy field within and about the body. In the discussion that follows we will assume that the energy body is a functional part of you and we will explain its fundamentals and how to use it. The description of the spirit body that follows is really a compilation of what both shamans and mystics have described over the ages.

Although the spirit body has its source in the spirit world, it actually exists in a kind of interface between the physical world of form and the spirit world. Kirlian photography and other sensitive instruments have been able to capture it, thus forcing science to admit that the physical body emits a form of energy that cannot be seen with the naked eye. This field is truly very subtle, but in fact can occasionally be seen by the naked eye although it is easier to "see" it using a shamanic visioning process.

The spirit body is a fluid energy field that typically extends from eighteen inches to three feet around a healthy body. It responds to thoughts, feelings, and your reactions to any situation by expanding, contracting, or changing color or density. Therefore it is an instant measure of how you are feeling and thinking at any given moment. This energetic field likewise responds to the thoughts, feelings and reactions of others.

As we mentioned in Chapter 1, shamans view thoughts and feelings as actual forms to be worked with in shamanic advising. They have an actual impact on the environment, both physically and spiritually, and this makes them very effective in shaping the spirit body. Thus shamans recognize both their positive and negative influence. Send a positive thought and a warm feeling and the spirit body glows healthily. Send a hostile feeling or a disparaging thought and the spirit body recoils and darkens a shade. That is why shamans would say that people who work around very negative surroundings, such as prisons, may at times suffer from the influence of negative spirits. If they do not know how to protect themselves or store power, they may need to have foreign spirits extracted from them, or in other words, the negativity removed from them from time to time. Shamans regard most forms of emotional imbalance as negative influence of a spirit nature.

A power-filled person who has learned to ward off such negative influences with his own positive feelings, can work in the most negative environments and remain untouched. Positive thoughts and feelings carry a high-positive charge that low-frequency negative thoughts and feelings cannot penetrate.

As we mentioned, the spirit body has been associated with heat waves, an association that can be attributed to its energetic field vibrating at a certain frequency. This frequency level, often read as color or density and prone to change along with mood fluctuations or changes in reactions to the environment, is actually related to the spirit itself rather than the physical body. Think of the qualities of air, which is basically colorless. Air heavy with moisture and humidity has a different quality from crisp, dry, mountain air. Smoke- or soot-filled air has a different density from air that is fresh and clean and full of sunlight. Even though the known properties of color are missing, there is a qualitative difference not unlike changes that can be perceived in a person's spirit self.

We frequently hear about people whose energy is so "negative" that no one wishes to be around them. Likewise, a person with "charisma" or "good energy" is someone we are drawn to. That is a reaction, an inherent sensitivity that we all have toward the spirit bodies or energy fields of others. As we mentioned, these frequencies and their fluctuations are also read as color. A person in a deep depression is slowed down and blocked. Thus the spirit body is of a thicker density and may read as dark brown or even black. People might say that the person is in a black mood. An angry person is riled up and that somewhat higher frequency reads as red. We say that the person sees red. We say a healthy person glows and that state reflects the much higher frequencies of bright blue, gold, or white. Shamans would say that the color of the spirit body reflects the power received and stored there. When people reflect a dense and dark color, it indicates the little power they have been able to access from the web of power. The more brilliant and light the color of the spirit body, the more power has been received and stored in the spirit body.

Marla worked at a hot springs resort in Northern California during her breaks and vacations from college. This gave her the opportunity to observe a great many people, and it was always interesting for her to watch their interactions as they relaxed in the crowded pools. She was particularly struck by a rather large woman who spoke with a thick Scandinavian accent. Although this woman spoke very little, each time she entered the hot pool, the people would clear out within a few minutes of her arrival, leaving her with the pool to herself. The other hot pools would absorb the defectors. When Marla closed her eyes and looked at her using her inner shamanic vision, she saw the reason why. This woman had an extremely dark and dense cloud around her chest and solar plexus. Although she was pleasant to look at physically, she had a most unattractive covering to her spirit body. Each time she left the pool she would look a bit lighter, only to return in a few days once again carrying the density.

Interestingly, a thin and balding older man produced almost entirely the opposite effect. Although he also was quiet and unobtrusive, whenever he came to the pool people would flock to it, apparently just to be near him. When Marla looked at his spirit body with her shamanic sight, she saw that he positively glowed with health and vibrant color.

In the everyday work world people tend to hide negative states because they want to appear successful and appealing. They wear clothes, makeup, and put on a happy face. The spirit body, however, always tells the truth about how people feel and think, no matter what the physical disguise. Incidentally, your own spirit body does the same for you. People that buy into appearances lose out in the long run, because they are not looking at the information that counts. People that read the spirit body are a step ahead because they know where to find real power and they have learned as well to see where power is missing.

Even those unacquainted with the realm of spirit are only somewhat fooled by outward appearances and words. Reacting also to a person's spirit body, they are not conscious of why they hired Mary over Sue, even though Sue was more experienced, qualified, and better dressed. They simply liked Mary better and felt she would do a great job.

Thus, one of the keys to success today is being aware of your spirit self: its change, and states. This is an awareness, a knowledge that to a certain degree can give you control over how others perceive you. Wouldn't it be useful if you could use a few simple shamanic techniques to make changes in your spirit body that would aid you in attaining a balanced and healthy state? If you learn to be sensitive to your energetic fluctuations and to those of others, you have gained power in the situation: remember that knowledge is power where shamanic advising is concerned.

Red Hawk had been dreading the meeting with his father that would decide whether or not he would be able to join in the Great Hunt. The party was leaving the following day and if Red Hawk was not with them, he would have to wait an entire year until the next summer solstice moon, the only time the tribe initiated a new hunter. He knew that his coming of age for the Great Hunt was theoretically not for three more moons, but Silver Fox had gone last year underaged and Red Hawk knew he had at least as much strength and stamina as Silver Fox had then. But there was the question of his father, whose permission he needed and who would be hard to convince.

The wise one had taught Red Hawk much in the ways of the spirit world, and he now sat down on his favorite rock and closed his eyes. Turning his thoughts inward, he noticed that his anticipation of confronting his father coupled with his fear of being left behind had weakened his spirit self in places. He drew from the spirit of rock, and the feeling of strength welled up in his chest. He asked for Rock to help him keep up with the others in the Great Hunt. Thanking Rock and aware that his spirit now showed the strength and stamina needed for the journey, he set out to meet his father. Red Hawk was initiated into the hunt.

When using the shamanic vision of intuition and imagination, the color density of the spirit body is easy to see. You see if a person is expansive or feeling contracted. You sense whether a person is open to you or not. As we have already pointed out, you also detect who has the real power in a situation and who does not.

Frank Skione, a physician familiar with the method of shamanic visioning, arrived at a hospital to consult about a patient who had complications following heart surgery. He met with the medical team responsible for the patient and quickly assessed the energy around them, using his shamanic visioning method. Frank realized immediately that the charge nurse, Carol, was the one who not only had the most affinity with the patient, but also could most effectively apply his recommendations. He saw that her spirit glowed around her chest when she spoke about the patient. He also noticed that her spirit body was large and more powerful than the fatigued and lifeless ones of the medical experts in the room. Frank could see that they did not really want to be there. They should have been home in bed, resting. He wasted no time theorizing with the specialists, but delivered all the necessary information to Carol and left. He knew she would provide the necessary assistance to the patient.

The best way to begin to understand how the spirit body works is by observing yourself. Observation is also the most fruitful because it will tell you instantly what is going on with you in ways that you wouldn't have detected otherwise. Your spirit self records instantly what your body may feel minutes, hours, or even days later.

When someone shouts at you, your instantaneous reaction might be to feel verbally attacked; an emotional feeling may follow that could remain with you for some time. Likewise if you were physically assaulted, your body would feel the immediate sensation, but you would have an emotional reaction that could remain for a long time. Most of us are unaware of how frequently our spirit selves are also affected, a change that often remains long after the emotion has died away. And the thoughts and feelings of others need not ever be physically expressed to affect your energy field. Often, the negative reactions in the spirit self will later manifest physically in some way.

For example, you meet with a polite but touchy client for an hour. You end the meeting and immediately go on to meet a friend for lunch. By the time you are back at work you have a terrific headache. You may attribute it to something you ate or mistakenly wonder if it had something to do with your lunch date. If you were attuned to your own energy field, you would have noticed changes in its frequency occurring during the meeting with your client. You would have seen that your spirit self was responding to your client's anger and her feeling that you were not listening to her. Your energy field was recording stress and tension that your conscious personality was not aware of while anticipating lunch.

By checking your spirit body after appointments and meetings you can make subtle adjustments. Remember that your spirit body responds directly to thoughts and feelings.

Here is a series of exercises designed to acquaint you with your own spirit self so that you can begin to be sensitive to it and make adjustments as needed. They are designed pragmatically, to be done anywhere, at any time, and without employing any tools other than your shamanic vision (imagination). Remember: to a shaman, imagination is a vehicle that sends thoughts and feelings to make real changes in the physical world.

As a reminder, since you cannot read and do the exercises at the same time, we suggest that you read each exercise through first. Then do it as best you can from memory. This should not be difficult because the exercises are all quite simple.

If you have a partner or are working with a group you can take turns leading one another through each exercise.

Exercise #1: Feeling Your Spirit Self

Relax and close your eyes. (With practice you can keep them open and use your shamanic vision at the same time.)

Discover the outside edges of your physical body; start with your toes and feet and move on up your body. This should be done somewhat quickly so that, within a few moments you can become aware of your whole body at the same time.

Slowly begin to expand that feeling, as if your skin were

elastic and you were being slowly filled with air. Continue the expansion equally over the whole body until you feel that you are approximately eighteen to twenty-four inches larger than the size of your original self all the way around.

Experiment with this feeling by imagining yourself fitting through a doorway or into your car. What does it feel like to brush up against a wall, a person, or tree with your outer expanded edge?

Now feel yourself shrinking back to your original size. Repeat this exercise as often as you wish, either in the same sitting or at a different time. You may find that eventually, as you gain a sense of your energy field, it will become more difficult to shrink all the way back down to just your physical edges.

Exercise #1: The Steps

1. Relax and close your eyes.
2. Discover the edges of your physical body.
3. Expand the edges to 18–24 inches.
4. Experiment with the expansion.
5. Shrink back to original physical size.

Exercise #2: Seeing Your Spirit Self

Now that you have a sense of your spirit body and the energetic dimensions, it is time to add the visual component. You begin this exercise by relaxing and closing your eyes. Now envision a field of energy penetrating through your body and extending eighteen to twenty-four inches around you. Remember to include the area behind your back and the space underneath your feet. If you have trouble seeing your body, you might try taking a couple of imaginary steps backward; then look forward, to see yourself from behind.

Once you have a clear image of your spirit body, notice what color or colors are there. Then notice the quality of the energy. Is it moving? If so, how? Is it dense like the earth? Is it light like the sun? Is it the same all over or different in places? Notice the differences.

If you wish to know something about what you are observing, or you do not understand the meaning of what you see, simply pose the question. Shamanic work is never done in isolation. You have unseen guidance at all times. Wait to receive an answer. The answer will come via words, thoughts, images, or sensations. The more you practice, the more information you will receive. You are building the channels of communication with your spirit self.

Do this exercise as frequently as you want. It is good to get into the practice of being able to do it quickly. This is the basis of the next exercise, "Checking In."

Exercise #2: The Steps

1. Relax and close your eyes.
2. Envision a field of energy through and around your body.
3. Notice the color/s and quality of the energy.
4. Pose a question or questions about your observation. (Optional.)

Exercise #3: Checking In

This exercise is particularly effective after business meetings, emotional confrontations, or any situation that leaves you with feelings of uncertainty or loss of power.

To begin, relax and close your eyes. Get a sense of your spirit self by using either the feeling or seeing method. You will probably notice yourself both seeing and feeling your spirit body. This is optimal since it includes both emotional and visual components.

Quickly scan over your spirit body from top to bottom. Take notice of what you see, sense, or feel. Especially notice any area where energy seems to be missing. These are potential problem areas that need attention. You can mentally direct your spirit energy to flow into these areas and fill them up. In the areas of concentrated energy, take note of the color. If dense but vibrant they are usually healthy; but if the color is murky, you may want to brighten it up by channeling a brighter shade into it.

Notice where the edges of your spirit body are. If any part is withdrawn and constricted, expand it a little. Likewise, you can shrink any part that feels too expanded and out of control. You are looking for balance in your spirit body and like an artist you can shape it harmoniously. You can use your hands to pat and shape it to your liking. Although someone else would see you patting what seems to be thin air, you are actually manipulating your spirit body. Remember! Shamanic processes are practical. Whatever makes them feel more real to you will ensure their success.

This exercise should be kept short. Its value lies in your ability to do it quickly, between appointments, prior to meetings, either business or social, and especially after confrontation. It is merely practice in being able to communicate with your spirit self and in using your spirit body as a gauge of what is going on with you at all times.

Exercise #3: The Steps

1. Relax and close your eyes.
2. Get a sense of your spirit body.
3. Scan and notice.
4. Direct energy to missing areas, brighten dense ones.
5. Expand or contract as necessary.

Exercise #4: Making Changes

This exercise is designed to help you gain control over your spirit body and direct its energy in ways that will serve you best. Here we reintroduce the use of visual aids from nature such as wind, sun, earth, rocks, animals, and so on. (In Chapter 3, you will learn more about the actual spirit in all natural things.) Be sure to enlist your other senses whenever possible to enliven the process, as we taught you in Chapter 1. You can use this particular exercise to help shift your moods and the way you feel. In addition you can use it to re-create the state you want to present in the world and how you wish to feel.

As with the previous exercises, begin with relaxing and closing your eyes. See, sense, or feel your spirit body. Remember, the more senses you can include in your vision the richer it will appear.

Acknowledge the state you are in before making changes, since often the reading your spirit self gives you is an attempt to communicate a neglected area, or something that needs attention. This acknowledgment lets your spirit body know you are not ignoring what is there, and that you will return to work on it as soon as you are able.

A client of ours was involved in a lawsuit that affected him emotionally. During that time, he had to perform a series of lectures that were important to his career. Although he found this exercise quite useful in preparing for his public appearances, he always acknowledged the obvious turmoil in his spirit body before he made changes in it. He then made sure to take time to work with that particular emotional state.

Postulate in your mind's eye the change you wish to make or the desired effect you wish to have. Perhaps you wish to be noticed more and want to appear grand, or maybe you would rather not be noticed as much. Reflect on the quality you need that will help you achieve the result you want. For example, if you are in turmoil about a situation, you may desire clarity and peace. If you are going for an interview, you may wish to get in touch with your competence and knowledge. If you have been feeling listless, you might want to shift into feeling fired up and enthusiastic.

Think of something in nature that has that quality that you want. For some, the warmth of the sun shining on a spring day may suggest clarity and peace; competence and knowledge might evoke a vision of an owl or hawk; fired-up enthusiasm might look like the spirit of fire itself. Begin to color your spirit body with the particular quality you want, using the image that came to you. You may wish to give it an actual color or simply fill yourself up with the feeling. Remember, the more senses you include, the richer the experience. Always thank the spirit of whatever it was whose quality you used for the exercise.

Exercise #4: The Steps

1. Relax and close your eyes.
2. See, sense, or feel your spirit body.
3. Acknowledge the state you are currently in.
4. Postulate the change or desired effect.
5. Identify the quality you need.
6. Find something in nature with that quality.
7. Color your spirit body with the quality of the natural image.
8. Thank the spirit of the natural image.

As with the others, this exercise should take only a few moments to do and you can practice it as often as you like. Occasionally you may wish to do a longer version, but the goal is to be able to do it in the grocery line or wherever you happen to be.

We understand that you may feel foolish or skeptical when you first try these exercises. However, as with all shamanic work, self-importance or self-consciousness is an obstacle to acquiring real power. Remember that shamans believe in being outrageous and are not afraid of looking foolish on occasion. They are also strong advocates of humor, laughter, and the bizarre.

SEEING OTHERS' SPIRIT BODIES

Once you are comfortable working with your own spirit self, you can move to using your shamanic sight to "see," sense, or feel other people's spirit bodies. You may use the simple method of closing your eyes, picturing the person in front of you, and seeing or sensing their field around them. Take notice of what you see, and if you need help in understanding what you see, just postulate the question and wait for the answer to pop into your head. If you are sufficiently relaxed, you are probably not making it up. With practice you will be amazed at the accuracy of your insights.

Never meddle with or make changes in other people's spirit bodies without first asking their permission. This is a misuse of power and shamans would say that there are unpleasant consequences to this kind of manipulation. For example, the person may not like your interference and reacts by sending you a bolt of energy that can give you an intense headache or a feeling that you are very ungrounded. On the other hand, the spirit world may cut itself off from you so that you no longer have access to its assistance. It is best to heed shamans' advice in these matters.

If another person has a headache or if they ask you to help them with another discomfort, go ahead and use the same methods that you have learned to use with yourself in Exercise 4. There will be more about working with others throughout this book. It is best to leave others alone though, until you have become proficient using these methods with yourself.

DEFINING YOUR OWN SPIRIT BODY

In the beginning of this chapter we mentioned that each human spirit body is a unique and creative expression of who they are. Animals, as you shall see shortly, have spirit bodies, too. But instead of each one having a separate and unique one, all the members of the same species belong to *one* overall spirit of the animal. Even though human spirit bodies are unique and separate from one another, they tend to blend together or match in frequency when in contact with one another, just like animals in a herd, flock, or school. A group of people working together on a project or gathered in a meeting tend to match their frequencies at the same level. The average color among them may manifest as perhaps blue or yellow, depending on what they are up to. They tend to match at the average or midpoint of the people making up the group. The presence of a powerful individual can, however, influence the entire group in a major way. When they separate and go their own way, they gradually resume their unique and original colors.

Researchers have discovered that people in close proximity to one another tend to match up on heart rates, blood pressure, and a host of measurable metabolic processes. The physical body responds more slowly than the spirit body, so this matching process can take place over the course of an hour. Spirit body matching is much more rapid and often takes place instantaneously. As you can probably foresee, matching everyone you are with is not necessarily the healthiest course of action. At the end of a long day, you may be left feeling irritable and cranky because, as the shamans would say, you came under the influence of alien spirits and you lost power. In other words, you matched too many unhappy, angry, or depressed people in the grocery line or in the department store or at the office.

When your spouse comes home in a lousy state, you might say he or she has brought the troubles of the office home with them. This is quite literally true. You may not be looking at the person you know anymore, but instead seeing all the frequencies of a variety of people he or she has met that day.

This, by the way, is one of several reasons that so many people are prone to drink alcohol at the end of the day. It tends to mask or knock out the discomfort of the foreign feeling.

Exercise #5: Clearing Your Spirit Body

A number of simple shamanic methods aid in clearing out the foreign frequencies and re-establishing your own comfortable equilibrium. Here is an internal method that again begins with relaxing and closing the eyes. Then using the methods you have learned, picture your spirit body around you. Define its edges and sense its shape. What color is it?

Imagine a warm, light waterfall of the purest spring water cascading into a shallow pool before you. Enter the pool with or without your clothes and allow the waters to purify, cleanse, and balance your spirit body. Take a drink and allow the cleansing water to penetrate throughout your entire physical body. Thank the waters and open your eyes.

If you wish, you can substitute an image of your choice for the waterfall. You may want to bathe in sage smoke or enter into a beautiful hot spring. Do what works for you.

Exercise #5: The Steps

1. Relax and close your eyes.
2. Picture your spirit body. Define the edges and color.
3. Imagine a waterfall and pool.
4. Bathe and drink to purify and cleanse.
5. Thank the water.

Now here are some physical methods that are helpful in reestablishing your equilibrium:

• Dousing with water has always been an excellent shamanic method to regain balance. So, take a shower when you feel off.

• Mud baths and salt baths (epsom salts) are equally effective, especially when you consciously release everything that is foreign into the bath. A dip in the ocean is also excellent. That is why so many people feel great during vacations by the ocean.

• Burning sage, incense, or epsom salts and letting the smoke drift over your body is an age-old shamanic cleanser and balancer.

• Vigorous exercise tends to knock out the foreign frequencies and sets up a fresh pattern.

GROUNDING

Another way to be aware of what is happening with your spirit body and to have greater control over your energy field is through what we call grounding. Being grounded means that you are aware of your body and you know how you feel while you are carrying out ordinary affairs of the day. It means feeling real, awake, and aware.

When you are zipping from one thing to the next during the day, planning for future activities or remembering past ones, it is easy to become "spaced out," or feel "unreal" or "ungrounded." You know the feeling of being ungrounded when you start to put your shoes in the refrigerator or you feed your cat Cheerios instead of catfood. You know you are ungrounded when you walk across a room to get something and no longer remember what it is you went there to get. Perhaps you have spent time searching high and low for your keys, only to find them in your pocket. Experiences like these usually mean that you are out of touch with the natural elements around you, that you no longer know how you are reacting to them. The connection between your physical body and your spirit body at these times is tenuous.

The secret to being grounded is to become aware of the web of power that manifests throughout your environment: through the sun, the moon, the stars, the air, the rain, the plants, and the more mobile living creatures around you. It is always easier to remain grounded outdoors than in an isolated indoor environment, where you are subjected to cramped conditions. Shamans therefore prefer to remain outdoors a good deal of the time. The connection between the spirit body and the physical body tends to be stronger out of doors.

How to Ground Yourself

Even if you work or live in a city environment where you are forced to be indoors much of the time, you can find ways to ground yourself by periodically taking a ten-minute break out of doors. The simple act of moving into a relationship with the natural elements makes you more real. It is hard to be ungrounded or spaced out when you are buffeted by a breeze, warmed by the sun, splashing in the rain, or crunching through the snow. You automatically become more aware and more real.

Exercise #6: Grounding

This shamanic method of grounding yourself to the earth takes about five minutes. First, relax and close your eyes. Take a couple of deep breaths. Become aware of your physical body from top to bottom, then shift your awareness to the earth directly below you. Even if you are in a tall building, you can still stretch your awareness downward into the layers of strata, rock, clay, and dirt until you become aware of the molten quality of inner earth. As you move down, say hello to each part of the earth. Remember that shamanically speaking, the earth is alive and responsive to your attention. The earth spirit delights in being acknowledged and is overjoyed to serve you as a result.

From the base of your spine establish a connection down to this molten center or core of the earth. With your feet feeling firmly planted on the ground, let your spirit body stretch all the way down as if you have a long tail that reaches and roots into the earth. Use this tail to first drain out all the excess tension (foreign spirits) that you are carrying. Then let energy from the earth rise up into your body, making you more solid and present.

If you have trouble making a connection, feel free to ask for assistance in this process. Often the same guardian that guides you in your journeys can be enlisted as a helper.

You can leave this connection with the earth in place, open your eyes, and go about your business. A simple check once in a while is all you'll need to keep yourself grounded at all times. Should you find yourself becoming ungrounded due to the scattered events of the day, repeat the exercise above. With practice you can bring back your grounding within thirty seconds.

Exercise #6: The Steps

1. Relax and close your eyes.
2. Become aware of your physical body.
3. Become aware of the earth.
4. Establish a connection with the center of the earth.
5. Drain out tension and foreign energy.
6. Bring up energy from the earth.
7. Open your eyes.

PROTECTION

When shamans are elsewhere, traveling through the various levels or worlds of the web of power with their spirit body, they leave their physical bodies behind. While they are traveling thusly, they deliberately let go of their awareness of ordinary physical reality for a period of time. In order to protect themselves while traveling, they have devised ways of keeping their physical bodies safe during their inward journeys.

When shamans journey, their physical body becomes more vulnerable and less powerful, just as it does during sleep. Therefore, shamans do not journey while driving a car or crossing the street if they can help it. Usually they journey from places where they know they will be relatively safe.

They often have someone present who can sit with them or drum for them if they are undertaking a particularly long journey. If they take a short journey, they make sure their physical body is in a safe spot where intrusions are unlikely. Even when they briefly check into the spirit world during a meeting, they do so momentarily, making sure nothing is required of them at the time.

During travel into the spirit world, shamans make sure that they carry protection with them at all times. They know that they are not invulnerable. Their existence is interdependent with all creatures on all levels of reality, and they must get along with these creatures and request their help often. Shamans know that by becoming too arrogant they will ultimately fail. Therefore, they humbly request the help or assistance of guardian spirits to help them and protect them on their journeys.

Therefore, we recommend that you always call up a guardian spirit before embarking on a shamanic journey. Your guide that meets you at the cave or entrance is a likely candidate. Not only is your guide there to help you on your way, but also capable as a guardian of protecting both your physical and spirit bodies as well. You can ask that guardian to take care of your body as you journey or you can ask it to handle any situations that appear dangerous or frightening to you on your journey. Guardian spirits are good at this; it's their expertise and they enjoy it. When in doubt, let them do the work.

Talismans and fetishes have been used by shamans for centuries to protect them on their journeys. However, it is not the physical object itself that protects or has the real power. The energy behind the object is what's important. Its physical form simply exists as a reminder that the power is there and available. Therefore, successful shamans do not confuse the object with the power. Some of their most powerful talismans are invisible to the naked eye but offer them enormous protection. A good shaman can perform powerful feats stark naked because the physical form of his tools is not necessary to get the job done.

It is a good idea to get into the habit of using some protective talismans in everyday life. However, these need not be physical. Some of the best talismans are those that you receive as gifts during your shamanic journeys. It does not matter that when you open your eyes they appear not to be there. Whenever you close your eyes, they are there and they can help you.

As nursing staff coordinator at a large hospital, Maria felt her power was constantly being challenged by several charge nurses who quarreled among themselves. At the weekly staff meetings, they made her life miserable by complaining and bickering about every scheduling plan she came up with. When Maria began to learn about shamanism, she discovered a powerful way of looking at the world that changed her perspective from victim to activator. She became exposed to a treasure chest of powerful methods that helped her feel more powerful and effective in her role as co-ordinator.

During a shamanic journey, Maria was given a bright lavender crystal by her Badger guide to carry with her whenever she felt she needed some help asserting her leadership skills. Although the lavender crystal was invisible to the naked eye, Maria was aware of it hanging around her neck on its invisible gold chain. That week, Maria looked forward to the troublesome staff meeting. For the first time she felt she had assistance in the face of so much opposition. As she entered the meeting room, Maria silently called upon the spirit of the crystal to boost her power and protect her from the bombardment of the difficult staff. As the meeting progressed, Maria found that she was able to communicate more effectively with the confrontative charge nurses. They became strangely cooperative after a time; by the end of the meeting she was amazed at the results achieved. They had managed for the first time to agree upon a new staffing schedule that would run for a full three months. Also, for the first time Maria felt energized and healthy after the meeting rather than her usual battered self. She did not fail to thank the badger for her special talisman. She found that she enjoyed speaking to the crystal and asking its advice on a variety of matters. All she had to do was listen for the answers.

Typically, a Western psychologist might interpret Maria's experience as a way of projecting her own unintegrated assertiveness skills onto an imaginary device that she could then rely on for safety. While this argument has its merit, shamans would say that this interpretation negates the relationship that human beings have with a very real spirit world. In fact, they would say that this is a very arrogant position to take, because it assumes that we get no help outside of our own psyches. For shamans, talismans and fetishes are constant reminders of their humbling relationship with the great power of the spirit world, the source of their lives.

BECOMING TRANSPARENT

A particularly effective shamanic technique for protecting yourself in difficult situations is the use of transparency or shape changing. Shamans often change their appearance or disguise themselves in order to go undetected or avoid unwanted attention. This may seem like a very mysterious feat but in fact it is quite a simple technique. There are many reasons why you might desire to avoid detection in everyday life. Perhaps you have a problematic ex-spouse who is always trying to find or see you. You may have annoying, gossipy neighbors who, whenever they see you, snare you and then eat up your time with drivel. You may want to appear undetectable while walking through a dangerous part of town at night. Perhaps you would rather not run into your clients while you are shopping for lingerie or food items. Maybe you simply want some privacy after a long hard day. This is especially a problem if you are a public personality like a television newscaster who is frequently recognized.

Shamanically speaking, people do not simply recognize you by seeing your flesh and blood or your clothes. You are recognizable because of the particular vibratory rate of your spirit body. If it weren't for your spirit body, you would simply be dead flesh and not very interesting to look at. So if you disguise your spirit body, your physical body suddenly becomes easy to miss or pass right by.

People can sense your spirit body in close proximity to themselves or they can sense it at a greater distance. They can spot you in your physical form at the market, in the hall, or walking down the street. On the other hand, they can sense your presence even if you are out of sight, perhaps next door or across town. Have you ever noticed that people start calling you even when you return from an out-of-town trip three days early? People know you are home because they see, sense, or feel that your spirit body has arrived. You are like a beacon of light to those who are interested in you.

Those coincidental or synchronistic meetings where you run into someone you know at an unlikely place are not accidental. They are inevitable when you realize how visible you really are.

Shamans know that all spirits are highly visible when looking at them with shamanic sight. That is how they locate whomever or whatever they are looking for. Recall the story of Max, the wayward monkey. He was discovered via his spirit self, not through his physical form.

Shamans have learned simple techniques to mask their spirit bodies or temporarily render them undetectable. Under extreme duress, many people instinctively use shamanic methods to avoid detection and are successful at it. For example, you can remain undetected in potentially life-threatening situations. We know of one Vietnam veteran who was caught in a village overrun by the Vietcong during the war. He was in a hut with no place to hide except for behind an old water jug that didn't adequately conceal him. Although the Vietcong searched the hut, he remained undetected. His desire to remain hidden was so great that he inadvertently activated his shamanic ability to be concealed.

A personal example happened to Jose on an excursion a few years ago:

"I was hiking in the isolated northern California coastal mountains one day and strayed off the trail to take a closer look at a magnificent stand of redwood trees.

"Suddenly, I came upon a clearing where a considerable number of harvestable marijuana plants were growing. It was obviously someone's private commercial garden. I realized the danger to me represented by the illegal status of the plants. If I were discovered by the grower, I could be shot and possibly killed; if I were discovered here by the law, I would be arrested. Almost immediately I heard voices coming closer through the woods. There was no place to hide or run, so I stood perfectly still and made myself transparent. Four large men emerged from the woods, talking among themselves about recent busts and the need to harvest the plants soon. They passed within ten feet of me, yet incredibly they did not see me even though I wore an orange parka and was standing in broad daylight. With a quiet but enormous sigh of relief, I crept away when the men had passed out of sight."

Exercise #7: Becoming Transparent

Here is one simple shamanic method for becoming undetectable or transparent. It works when you need it, because your strong intention is behind it.

Begin by relaxing and closing your eyes. Without effort, imagine yourself becoming transparent, like glass or mist. Notice that when others look in your direction, they see right through you. You are not available for them to notice you.

With an act of will you can make this a general transparency that includes everyone or you can make an exception and be visible to one particular person when you want contact. On the other hand, you can make yourself invisible to just one individual who is harassing you. Specify what you want.

If you feel this exercise is so simple that it is hard to do, ask your guardian spirit to do it for you.

Do not forget to reverse this exercise when you are ready to be noticed again. Using your shamanic vision, vividly see yourself becoming brighter and more physical. If you really want to attract attention, make yourself a shiny silver.

Exercise #7: The Steps

1. Relax and close your eyes.
2. Imagine becoming transparent.
3. Specify the scope of your transparency.
4. Reverse the exercise when ready.

Some children unconsciously become good at hiding themselves because it is a good way to avoid the attention of abusive or alcoholic parents who may attack them. Unfortunately, they get so good at it that by the time they become adults, they are often invisible to other people. They are passed up for promotions and people get in front of them in the bank line because they are not easy to spot. These people need to practice the transparency exercise in reverse. That is, they need to learn how to become more visible, to see themselves attracting attention and being noticed in a wide variety of situations.

MAKING POSSESSIONS TRANSPARENT

Just as you attract attention through your spirit body, your possessions often attract the attention of thieves and burglars because they are imbued with some of your spirit. They become highly visible. When you leave your car in a dark or unsafe area, it's a good idea to use the same shamanic technique that you used on yourself with your car. Make it transparent, unseeable, using the powers of both your shamanic vision and your guardian spirit. It will be passed by even by thieves, because they quite literally don't see it.

SHAPE CHANGING

Shape changing is very similar in technique to becoming invisible. The difference is that you may wish to appear dissimilar from the way people usually perceive you. For example, you may wish to appear somewhat larger and more dangerous than your actual size when you are forced to walk through a tough part of town late one night. Or you may want to make yourself smaller if you are traveling in a foreign country where you stick out like a sore thumb because of your height. Likewise, you can make yourself look a bit more like the indigenous people so you can blend in better. Whatever the occasion, you can subtly shift your entire shape or specific parts of yourself by following these simple steps.

Exercise #8: Shape Changing

Relax and close your eyes. Using your shamanic vision, step forward out of your physical body and turn around. See or sense your body in front of you. Decide on the changes that you want to make. Reach out with your spirit hands and stretch, compact, or mold your body like putty. Make whatever changes you wish to. Ask your guardian spirit to help you if you find this difficult.

Turn around again and step backward into your body. Feel the changes you have made. Remember to go through the exercise in reverse when you wish to return to normal. If you forget, you will gradually do so anyway, but it is better to get in the habit of being disciplined about the technique. That way you will become good at it quickly.

Exercise #8: The Steps

1. Relax and close your eyes.
2. Step out of your body and turn around.
3. See your body in front of you.
4. Decide on and make the changes.
5. Turn around and step backward into your body.
6. Feel the changes.
7. Return to normal when you wish to.

DEVELOPING NEUTRALITY

One of the best sources of protection is your ability to find a neutral position. When you are not neutral about an event or situation, you make yourself vulnerable because you put yourself under its power or influence. If people call you stupid and that upsets you, then you are immediately under their spell because at some level you believe them. If you resist them and defend yourself, you are probably worried about being stupid and you don't want anybody to know. If you realize you are not stupid, you may regard them with curiosity, wondering what truly troubles them so much that they would be so offensive. Neutrality, then, is the position of power.

This is not to say that you should never take a position on anything or that you should be an emotionless robot. Shamans have feelings, but they do protect themselves when there is a real threat. So should you. Most events, however, are not literally threatening and are best handled by neutrality. Truly great shamans are ones who can retain their neutrality even in the face of a crisis. That takes practice.

The shaman and Coyote were engaged in one of their favorite sports. They were taking turns insulting each other to see who could gain mastery over the other. Whoever lost would get hurled off the cliff. It would take them a month to climb back out. "Hey, Coyote!" the shaman sneered. "Your coat is so mangy that even your fleas get sick when they hear your name." Coyote laughed and countered, "Hey, Shaman, I hear all the people laugh at you when they see your drum, it's so full of holes you can't even hold dung in it." And so it went, back and forth, each one trying to get a rise out of the other until finally Coyote said, "Hey, Shaman, remember that old man that died during the full moon of deep snow. Even with all your shamanizing, you couldn't save him. He took all your power away when you irritated him with your poison smoke." Now, Coyote knew that the old man who had died was really the shaman's mentor. He was banking on the fact that the shaman was afraid he wouldn't be as powerful when the old man died. Sure enough, the shaman gasped and struggled to regain his composure. Coyote grabbed him and hurled him off the cliff. "Another shaman down." Coyote grinned as he trotted off into the forest.

Up till now we have focused on the spirit body itself and have given you some methods to get to know it and to begin working with it. There is, however, more to the spirit body than we have told you so far. The source of the human spirit body is a series of tunnels that lead to the spirit world. Each tunnel broadcasts a different frequency of the spirit world's energy and these emanations make up different layers of the spirit body. By looking at the different layers of the spirit body, shamans can determine the tunnel responsible for a particular difficulty they or others might be having. In this way shamans are able to work with the tunnels to access information and promote healing. You will learn more about these power tunnels and how to work with them using the shamanic journey in Chapter 7.

Thus far, you have learned to sense your spirit body and feel its size and shape. You have learned to read its textures and colors and you know something about what they mean. You know that your thoughts and feelings determine its health and condition and that those thoughts and feelings can be altered to improve that condition. You know now how to define your own spirit body as opposed to others' and you have learned to cleanse it of foreign influences, to protect and to keep it grounded. You may even have begun to read other people's spirit bodies and have altered your own behavior because of what you've seen.

The more you tune into the world of the spirit body, the greater will be your capacity to see, sense, and feel the true nature of the world you live in. This will give you a tremendous advantage because you will no longer be led astray by mere external appearances. You will have the ability to know exactly what you and others are feeling or thinking at any given moment. Not only will you feel supported by your spirit body but you will feel a sense of expansiveness and depth that comes with knowing you are more than what is physical. The more you open to the messages your spirit body gives you, the more sensitive you will become to your own genuine needs and wants. You will then know your limitations and your true potential in any situation.

CHAPTER 4

Nature's Power: Spirit Helpers

Latuk lay on his mat and looked out of the shelter onto the expanse of barren tundra. Discouraged and dispirited, he let his head drop back onto his arm. He just wasn't his old self these past few days and he did not know why. He had no energy to hunt or even to eat what food they had stored. Ever since returning to the hut from the last hunt, he had been apathetic. Worried, Misha his wife had called for Isk, the shaman from the village at the confluence. Latuk knew he would not be long in coming.

When Isk arrived, he spoke with Latuk in a gentle voice. He asked many questions of him, including where he had been during the days preceding. Then he made some passes with his hand over Latuk and, with his eyes closed, was silent for some time. "Ah, so you have been to the north at the place of green rocks. The spirit of green rock has chased away your strength and is weakening your blood. You cannot go to that place without the protection of the lavendar quartz." After drawing a rough piece of the quartz from his drawstring bag, he laid the rock on Latuk's chest. "Lie still on your back until moonrise. Your spirit will find new strength and your appetite will return." With that, the shaman was gone. When Latuk awoke at moonrise, the apathy was gone. Feeling invigorated and hungry, he had some fish. As he ate he marveled at the lavender quartz that had brought back his energy. What a power exists in the spirit of this rock, he thought.

Silently he offered a prayer of thanks.

The web of power applies to all elements of nature. By knowing how this power net works, you may begin to tap into its resources in ways that you may not have imagined possible. Discover how to use the power of rocks, plants, animals, and other natural beings on the planet by simply learning how to communicate with them. From a shamanic perspective, communicating with these creatures has one basic requirement: respect. Respect is the key to communication; any truly successful communicator knows that respect carries with it a lack of judgment and an openness to contact. The elements of nature are no different with regard to how they respond even if you are not able to see them with your eyes open. They respond to the respect that you show them.

You may feel skeptical at first because you have not been taught that gems, trees, clouds, and insects are reachable through your emotions and thoughts. Try to take their point of view for a moment. Suppose that you were suddenly confronted by your household pets. Suppose that you could hear them, yet they acted as if you were an inanimate object. Maybe you would hear them discussing among themselves whether or not you could feel anything. Wouldn't you be taken aback? Wouldn't you be outraged? Wouldn't you be fearful? Especially if you had given them some food to eat or provided them shelter for protection, you might feel that they were not only ungrateful, but showed the height of arrogance.

Therefore, do not expect the spirits of nature to warm up to you immediately when you first try to communicate with them. Give them a chance to trust you and your limitations. After all, they have been treated rather badly by people for a long time. You may ask, if we show this kind of respect to all of nature, is it not then a betrayal of this trust to kill an animal for food? to eat a plant? to cut a tree for shelter? Shamans know that the creatures of this planet do not mind serving people by providing food products, shelter, clothing, and the like if they are asked properly and thanked afterwards. The spirit world, their true source, cannot be destroyed; only the physical form can be altered for a time.

Shamans are aware of the importance of balance and the fact that the natural world thrives on the tensions that keep this balance. When the balance is tipped through exploitation and greed, the natural world rebels. For shamans, the crises that face the world today are no surprise. They are a result of imbalance caused by lack of respect, and this imbalance ultimately results in a loss of power.

As you read about how how to communicate with stones and animals, keep in mind that the secret of your success is respect. You will ultimately lose power should you divert toward exploitation rather than mutual service.

Remember that your goal is success and real power. For you to be truly successful, you need to cooperate with your environment. You do not exist in isolation or separate from your fellow beings, even if they are rocks, for example. If anything, you need them to walk on and to build with.

THE POWER OF ROCKS

The spirit within rocks sets up a certain vibration that emits a particular frequency. Rocks and mineral structures of different types have varied frequencies of light and sound. This is especially true for gemstones, concentrated mineral structures that humans place a high value on because of their beauty and practical applications.

A quartz crystal's crystalline structure emits a different vibration from the mineral content of a sapphire. The frequency or spirit of different rocks and minerals affects plants, animals, and humans in particular ways. To some individuals an amethyst is balancing and healing while to others a tourmaline or fluorite has a beneficial effect. On the other hand, some gemstones or metals may have a deleterious effect on the health of certain people at particular times. For example, for most people, wearing silver is not a good idea when they are feeling nervous or highly anxious, because it has the power to raise their metabolism level even higher. Gold would be a better choice, because it tends to mellow the body more. On the other hand, silver is the metal of choice if one wishes to feel zippier and more active.

Shamans know how to speak to rocks and minerals as well as feel their energy and discover what their influences are. By sensing their unique frequencies and speaking to the spirit of rocks, shamans can deliberately choose particular rocks that will have a positive influence and avoid ones that set up an inharmonious frequency.

You may find you have a particular affinity for a ring inlaid with turquoise, or an amethyst pendant, or even pearl earrings. If you are like most people, you may discover that you occasionally pick up a small rock on a walk and carry it around in your pocket for a while. Could it be that your latent shamanic abilities are expressing themselves by responding to the spirit of that rock? Shamans would answer affirmatively, saying that you are naturally drawn to rocks whose spirits are helping you. By being close to your body, they affect you and set up a harmonic that feels good.

Jewelry that is made up of metals, gems, and minerals has a subtle but definite impact on the body. Sometimes they are arranged in a combination that has a harmonious effect on you and other times not. Perhaps you wonder why you have always had an aversion to that legrandite and silver pendant given to you for your birthday by Aunt Mabel, even though it is pretty to others. The fact is, your body probably doesn't like it at all and thus you never wear it. On the other hand, you may just love an ornate silver ring with some turquoise inlay, a Navajo favorite. The spirit of turquoise tends to open the heart and allow creativity to flow. If you love it and it feels good, then it is right for you. Shamans pay attention to these allies and they notice how their bodies feel when around them.

Although wearing metals and stones next to the skin exercises a greater effect on you, larger quantities in the environment will emit their power and impact as well.

A hunk of jade, coral, or quartz in the room will influence you according to its makeup and size. You may love to enter a room with a large amethyst, but avoid a room decorated with onyx statues. You are naturally responding to the power and life in the mineral world.

Here we will not go into detail about the specific effects of different gemstones and rock structures. Although there are general influences and tendencies, people best discover for themselves by experience which rocks, gemstones, and metals are personally helpful and which are not. We will, however, give some exercises that will help you tune into the spirit of rocks and cooperate with them for more successful living. Not only will you become more knowledgeable about rocks, but you will gain some new friends as well.

Exercise #1: Rocks and Minerals

This exercise will acquaint you with the spirit of rocks and minerals. Becoming acquainted with their spirit will automatically open up the channels to communication and therefore to their power.

Choose a rock, mineral, or gemstone. Better yet, let one choose you. The right rock for you will automatically grab your attention, even if it is not pretty to look at. It could be any rock, even a simple small one found on the street. Let yourself be drawn to it. If you see it outside, always ask it for permission to remove it from its natural setting.

Sit down with the rock, mineral, or gemstone in your hands and study it carefully. Notice every detail; shape, color, temperature, and how it feels in your hand. Then close your eyes and ask it these questions:

1. What are your specific properties?

2. Is there anything you want to tell me?

3. May I have permission to use your properties? How can you be of help to me?

Wait for the answers: Take them at face value. If the information is confusing, ask for clarification. Ask, "What does that mean?"

If you happen to see the rock spirit with your shamanic vision or imagination, bear in mind that the spirit of the rock may look very different from its physical form. It may appear as a small or bright light of various colors.

Remember to thank the spirit of the rock when you have completed the exercise. You may repeat this exercise as often and with as many different rocks, minerals, and gemstones as you wish. The information you receive might be different with each one. Likewise, the information you receive from a specific rock might be different from the information someone else receives from that same rock. This is not a problem. Neither one of you has to be wrong. It is often the case that a rock affects each person in a different manner. What is appropriate for one is not for the other.

Exercise #1: The Steps

1. Choose a rock, mineral, or gemstone.
2. Study and notice every detail.
3. Close your eyes and ask about properties and information.
4. Ask permission to use properties. Ask for help.
5. Thank the spirit of the rock, mineral, or gemstone.

LOCATIONS OF POWER

The composition of rock in a particular landmass or area can have a similar effect on those who live or traverse upon it. For example, a mountain range may be made up of a type of strata that sets up an imbalancing frequency in most humans. Over the years, people learn to avoid the area, perhaps saying that dangerous spirits live there. For shamans, this is an accurate statement, but only they know why. They learn how to take countermeasures by carrying a neutralizing rock with them and are able to go there without harm. How do they know this? Simply by spending time with rocks, getting to know them and talking with rock spirits through their own hearts and minds.

There are certain areas where traditionally health is poor, crime is high, and everything seems to break down. There are other areas where a constant peaceful feeling is sustained, health is high, and people are happier. Typically, in urban areas, land values rise in places of high positive energy. This tends to result in a high concentration of commerce or wealth, crowding out people with lower incomes who are relegated to the less desirable areas. In time, the positive or negative attitudes of the multitudes that live and work in an area can influence the nature of the landmass there. Rocks record the intensity of human or animal emotion and begin to reflect that back. Thus positive areas can turn sour and negative areas can be uplifted.

Even with the same neighborhood you may notice that there are some perfectly reasonable locations where stores never succeed, for example. New businesses open and shut their doors within a few months of each other. Just a block away, however, business thrives and the feel is different. As you drive or walk through town, notice these shifts of energy and get a sense of the changing landmass underneath. At first you may not know what to look for, but if you simply focus your attention on noticing the differences, you will begin to get a feel for sensing the energy or frequency of a place.

For shamans who speak to rocks, there is no mystery. Nor are they likely to live in an area where the rock frequency is inharmonious to people, if they can help it. That is one of the reasons why shamans prefer to live under less crowded conditions where there is more choice in selecting a harmonious and balancing place to live.

SPECIFIC POWER SPOTS

Shamans are aware that particular locations emit tremendous amounts of energy or deliver a very high frequency of energy. These locations can be tapped into for harnassing power. Very large ones have been used by people for centuries: Stonehenge, Mount Shasta in Northern California, and the great pyramids in Egypt and in Central and South America. Numerous smaller power spots are either unconsciously used by local people as meeting places or are known to shamans only.

These locations are empowered by the frequencies and juxtaposition of the rocks beneath them. Some of the larger locations are formed by rocks that have a powerful effect on most human beings. That is why they have been noticed and built upon or used ceremonially for centuries. Other locations are supported by rock formations that have a beneficial effect on certain people only. These locations are attractive only to a particular group of people who gravitate there or choose to live there, as opposed to others who may avoid the spot, feeling strangely uncomfortable there.

Animals and plants naturally know the locations of major power spots and whether to seek them out or avoid them altogether. They too respond to the energy of these locations. We know of one major positive power spot in Southern Oregon near the small town of Gold Hill. Here, trees growing around the center of the power spot all lean away from its center, as if pushed over by the strong energy there. The sky above this power spot is known to pilots as a place where radar ceases to operate. This is a fairly typical phenomenon of the larger power spots.

Power spots tend to amplify the frequency of your own energy field and energize your existing thoughts and emotions. Spiritually oriented people have built temples and churches over large power spots, wishing to amplify inspired thoughts and emotions of a spiritual nature. The people who flock to these spots contribute to the collective feeling that is already there, making the spot more and more powerful and oriented with a particular flavor. Lourdes in France is a good example of such a location. Those who desire healing often find it by going there and staying awhile.

All power spots can amplify whatever thoughts or feelings you are having at the time. You need to be careful what state you are in before entering into the sphere of influence of such a spot. If you are feeling fearful or angry, it is likely that these feelings will be magnified for a time. If you have an intense desire, you will find this emotion amplified or strengthened. However, if you are fatigued, it is more likely that you will feel energized. That is why retreat centers and spas are often built in the vicinity of power spots.

We know of one power spot north of San Francisco, California, where people often go to meditate and rejuvenate. Mount Tamalpais has long been revered by Native Americans as an important site of natural healing. Nevertheless, rapes and even murders have taken place there much to the chagrin of the local people. The violent desires of people who came to Mount Tamalpais with such acts in mind were amplified there, motivating them to more readily carry out their primitive desires.

Shamans know that the power spots themselves are only

amplifiers. They simply magnify whatever the people bring inside of them. Therefore, it is a good idea to prepare yourself by centering and calming yourself before knowingly going to a power spot.

Within every vicinity are numerous very small power spots that may have a beneficial effect on one or a few individuals. Shamans try to be aware of these spots and gravitate toward them wherever they go. In general, people unconsciously use their instincts to move toward or away from these locations as they go about their daily affairs. For example, you may have a favorite spot in a park you like to frequent, or you may regularly avoid walking down some block for reasons unknown to you.

Children often identify a favorite or "secret" place where they go for fun, adventure, or comfort when troubled. Think back to your own childhood. Can you remember such a place? You might even recall meeting a sweetheart (or a series of them) at a special natural spot. The same emotional recognition occurs quite often when you buy a home: either the neighborhood feels just right or the home "feels" like the right one. And, just like any animal who circles around before sitting, you will carefully select your seat in a café or theater even though all seats offer adequate service or views.

Power spots influence the vicinity around them in direct relation to their strength. Huge power spots such as the ones located at Taos, New Mexico, and near Big Sur, California, influence a radius of one hundred miles. Of course, the closer you are to the center of the spot, the stronger the influence you feel. Very small power spots may influence only a few yards around them.

Selka watched nervously as Mendo headed into the forest, laden with nothing but his simple garb. This was to be a most powerful initiation for her brother. His task was to find his place of power, seek there a vision, and return before he had eaten or taken liquid. The forest was broad and no one knew what dangers lay in the lands beyond. Besides, a hunting band of a hostile tribe had been spotted recently near the base of the maze rocks.

Mendo approached the cleft in the rocks carefully. Although parched and hungry, he felt sensitive to the patterns of energy that shifted as he walked over the land. Now he knew he had come to a place that felt strong. Slowly he edged himself between the large boulders and felt the intensity of energy there. He felt elated. This was it. There was no question. He positioned himself carefully, feeling that he must face east here. Then he closed his eyes and received his vision.

When Selka next saw her brother, he emerged from the forest like a shining light. Despite the fact that he had gone without food or water for three long days, he appeared energized and powerful. Beaming, he proceeded into the village for the welcoming ceremony.

Exercise #2: How to Find Power Spots

How can you find and identify a power spot? These simple steps will help you do just that. Identifying the earth's power spots is not unlike identifying your own spirit body. What you will in essence be doing is envisioning the earth's spirit body and sensing where there are pockets of increased energy. You will be looking for the ones you feel drawn to and comfortable around.

Go to a place where you have plenty of room. We suggest a large park or somewhere in the country where you can be outside. If this is not possible, then work with whatever space you have. Find a place to sit down, close your eyes, and first get a sense of your own spirit body, then that of the earth around you.

Ask to be guided to the nearest power spot. You might have a visual sense of a brighter energy in a certain location, or you could just suddenly get the urge to walk in a particular direction. Whatever it is, trust it and act on it.

When you get to the spot, sit down and repeat the exercise. This is the self-validating part, for you will either get information about another location that is perhaps better for you (since not all power spots agree with everyone), or you will feel like staying where you are. Repeat this part of the exercise until you feel you have found a power spot that has a frequency in affinity with yours.

Now, with your eyes closed, notice what it is about this spot that feels different to you from the rest of the nearby area. Ask how you can benefit from being near this spot. Spend as much time there as you wish, but make sure you also remember to ask the Earth for the use of this spot, and to say thank you at the end of your exercise.

A variation of the above exercise requires a trusted friend who won't laugh at seeing you blindfolded and wandering about apparently aimlessly. Actually, you will not be wandering aimlessly. The key here is to allow yourself to move in the direction you sense without visual interference; let your

Exercise #2: The Steps

1. Sit down and close your eyes.
2. Get a sense of your spirit body.
3. Get a sense of the Earth's spirit body.
4. Ask to be guided to the nearest power spot.
5. Go to that spot.
6. Repeat steps 4 and 5 until you find your spot.
7. Notice qualities of the spot. Ask for its use.
8. Thank the spot.

feelings tell you where the spot is. Since feelings have a language of their own, we cannot tell you exactly what to anticipate. You might feel like reaching out, or you may recoil if the spot is not good for you.

As we mentioned, the larger power spots are usually more obvious because they have become important pilgrimage sites and in some cases centers of commerce such as the site of the Vatican in Rome. Near the center of these large power spots, you may feel slightly nauseous, dizzy, or emotionally volatile.

In small power spots you may notice a similar but milder sensation as you approach its center. You may also experiment by rubbing your hands together and then placing your palms outward or downward to feel the sensation of buzzing on your hands as you try to locate the spot. Some people feel this buzzing more easily on their faces and especially on their lips. You will have to experiment to see which one works best for you.

Experiment by doing a journey or any of the exercises described in Chapter 2 in different locations. For example, sit down in a corner of your living room and check in with your spirit body. At another time try the same exercise in your bedroom or in the kitchen. Notice the differences in the locations and how they feel. It may be consistently easier for you to focus on your exercises in the living room or perhaps in the bedroom, as opposed to other locations. In this way, you can find the small power spots in your house and begin to use them effectively.

BENEFITS OF USING POWER SPOTS

Knowing about locations of power can be of tremendous value to you if you set about using them with the proper intention.

Personal power spots energize you and reduce your need for rest and recuperation. They naturally balance and heal you so that you can increase your productivity and enjoyment of life.

They intensify your feelings, allowing you to release them for emotional clearing and tension reduction.

Power locations are capable of inspiring you, energizing and propelling your latent creativity to express new ideas and feelings.

Power spots raise your frequency level, making you less vulnerable to illness, discouragement, and depression. You are supported in feeling encouraged and ready to tackle whatever is next for you.

Being aware of and searching for power spots keeps you alert and sensitive to your environment. When you know what is happening around you, you are in a position to be more successful because you have the information you need. Even though you cannot change the Earth's spirit body as much as you can your own, you can still control to some degree the potential influences the Earth's energy can have on you. You can be sensitive to the power spots you should seek out and those you should avoid.

Knowing about power spots helps you avoid places of potential negativity so you can place yourself instead in ones that positively influence you. There are "energy sinks" that can drain you of energy, making you feel apathetic or listless. It is best to avoid these areas.

Jack Pierson smiled as he headed up the highway in his late-model sedan. As he approached the convention center, he felt a twinge of anticipatory excitement. Here, on the first day of the convention, was his chance to validate his shamanic skills. He had already wrangled his way onto the committee that was to decide where the convention would be held this year. After checking out numerous sites, he persuaded the committee to choose the Bayview Convention Center even though it was not in the "right" part of town. It was by far the most peaceful and inspirational site of them all. And yet, it was nothing really to look at.

Jack had been surprised when, five years ago, he had

attended a series of software training seminars there and
had not felt the usual exhaustion from information over-
load. When, the following year, the series was moved to a
much plusher, more modern facility uptown, he felt the
typical wipeout after each class. Since that time, Jack
had discovered that places of power exist even within the
city environment, and he had begun to learn how to find
them. He just "knew" that the Bayview Center was such a
place.

   Although no one else knew quite why, the fifteenth an-
nual computer software convention was a huge success.

As a final note, you need not always be physically present
at a power spot to benefit from its special properties. Once
you know where a power spot is, you can journey there shamanically or re-create it in your mind's eye. Try developing
this habit with a favorite power spot so you can recall it
whenever you wish. You can even shamanically create or
build your own clubhouse or workshop, where you carry out
tasks and hang out whenever you want to replenish yourself.
This can be your own secret place, guarded by your power
animal, an ally that is described next.

THE POWER OF ANIMALS

The shamans' power is directly related to their totems, or
in other words, their animal allies. The greater the totems,
the stronger their power animals, the more influential they
are. To a shaman, a human being is not better or more aware
than an animal, even though humans largely depend on animals for their source of food. Animals, like rocks, have powerful spirits, each with its own talents, and are uniquely
qualified to assist people in specific areas. The shaman's relationship with animals is a mutually beneficial one. The shaman offers the spirit animal respect and devotion, while the
animal offers guidance and assistance with a great many
tasks beyond the shaman's personal abilities. One of the
chief gifts that power animals offer is protection and guardianship to the shaman during arduous tasks. Animal allies
may also be used to help find lost objects, mediate problematic relationships, and in general assist in the achievement of
a challenging goal.

   Each power animal has a specialty, so the shaman may
need to consult with several if a problem has a variety of
aspects to it. The hawk is good at seeing things from afar
while the fox is known for its intelligence and cunning. Gen-

erally speaking, power animals are wild animals, not domestic ones. Shamans feel that domesticated animals have lost their power in large part; They serve people in more physical ways than spiritually.

For the shaman, physical animals are just the outward form of the great spirit of that animal species. So the shaman's totem or animal ally is the bear, not this or that bear. Even so, the outward form of the bear spirit may be revered and honored. If you do not have the relationship with a power animal, or you have lost yours through neglect, the shaman would say you are in a very vulnerable and weak position. You have lost touch with your own animal nature. Is that not the case with modern urban dwellers today?

Yet even in a highly technological and in many ways alienated culture, the power of the animal expresses itself in ways that we often ignore. Automobiles, political parties, athletic teams, and clubs often have animal names, or totems if you will. The language is fraught with animal metaphors such as "sly as a fox," "quiet as a mouse," or "strong as a bull." Children are raised with stuffed animal toys and stories with animal characters. Wild animals are used frequently as emblems and symbols in every form of advertising. To the shaman, this is only natural. We cannot ignore the power of the animal spirits.

How do shamans find power animals in order to gain mastery? First of all they do not select an animal and then go about establishing a relationship with it. The contact is made in the reverse. The spirit of the animal selects the shaman. Historically, if a shaman survived the attack of a wild animal, it was felt that that animal was actually the shaman's totem spirit, testing him or her for strength and endurance. The animal demanded a sacrifice; through the wounding, the shaman proved his or her dedication and capacity to handle the power of the guardian animal.

Not all power animals come to the shaman in this dramatic fashion, however. Typically shamans discover their power animals by allowing them to emerge through a spontaneous dance or by seeing the animal in a vision. Other power animals show themselves in dreams. Children, usually naturals at shamanism, will often have recurring dreams involving an animal who will sometimes appear frightening and sometimes masterful and protective. They may also be inexplicably drawn to that particular animal at the zoo.

Pat threw her bags into the taxi as Louie directed the driver to the airport. Both of them were sunburned but satisfied with their sojourn at Playa Escondido, the beach paradise over the mountains from Oxaca, Mexico. We'll be home in two days, Pat thought with some regret as they eased into the airport parking area.

The airport was dark. Something was very wrong. "Sorry, airport closed. No planes until Monday," offered the lounging guard. A quick look through the airline tickets revealed the awful truth. Unbelieving, Pat read the date. The Mexican travel agent had written *April 21*, not today, *March 21*. Their tickets were for next month.

Back at the hotel Pat and Louie reviewed their situation. This couldn't be happening. Suddenly she hated paradise.

That night, as she walked on the beach, Pat suddenly thought of the pelicans she had seen throughout their stay there. The Pelican had been appearing in her dreams since childhood (helping her out of trouble of this sort and that) and, growing up in a coastal town, it was a familiar sight to her. Knowing something about shamanic techniques, she squatted down on the sand like a fat pelican and began waving her arms in flapping motions, croaking from her throat. She closed her eyes and asked the spirit of Pelican for advice. In her vision Pat saw a pelican shoot up directly into the air and zoom away. When Pat opened her eyes, she was suddenly positive there was a solution. Early the next morning, she insisted they go to the airport. Louie resisted, but finally, reluctantly agreed. "It's Saturday and there's nothing flying out of here until Monday."

Pat remained silent. When they got to the airport, it was deserted except for a clerk and a couple of pilots of private planes. Suddenly the silence was torn by a dull *thup thup thup* coming in over the building. A modern French helicopter settled down for a landing not fifty yards away. The Mexican pilot got out and stretched before dumping out a satchel of mail and parcels. Pat yelled out to him, *"Oxaca?"* *"Si"* was the reply.

Pat watched the shadow of the helicopter race along the trees as they glided over the mountains. Mexico never looked more beautiful she thought as she sprawled over the mail sacks and Louie. "Thank you, Pelican," she said silently.

Exercise #3: Meeting the Power Animals

You have probably wondered how one goes about getting a power animal. Here is a simple journey method, commonly used to draw in a power animal or guardian spirit. This exercise will also familiarize you with the spirit of animals.

Relax and close your eyes. (Drumming or a drumming tape is especially helpful here.) Imagine your cave or other entrance to the earth. Meet your guide and begin the journey. Allow a landscape to open up before you. It can be a forest, a meadow, a beach, or a cave. Then allow an image of an animal to enter that landscape, or perhaps simply think the name of an animal. Remember that the spirit of the animal may not always look like the physical form. If you get nothing, that is fine. Try the exercise again later. By the way, it is best to avoid animals that are overly hostile with bared fangs. They do not represent helping spirits but rather obstacles to be dealt with another time when you have assistance.

Should an animal appear, ask the animal to tell you about its particular qualities. Listen to the answers. Shamanic success lies in the ability to listen. Don't worry if it seems to you that you are making up the answers. It often feels this way at first. With practice you will be able to discern the difference.

Allow that image to fade and another to come in. Repeat the exercise with as many different animals as you wish. The animal that repeatedly appears to you or often acts as your guide during a journey is the important one. Always remember to thank the animal for its information and communication.

Exercise #3: The Steps

1. Relax and close your eyes.
2. Begin the journey.
3. Go to a landscape.
4. Have an animal enter the landscape.
5. Ask the animal about its qualities. Listen.
6. Let the image fade and another come in.
7. Notice the animal that shows up most often.
8. Thank the animal.

Exercise #4: Honoring the Power Animals Through Movement

Later we will explain how you can make contact with your spirit animal through dancing. Here we will simply suggest that you try the animal on for size, much as children do naturally. For this you will need to find a private space and get comfortable (wear loose clothes). Relax and close your eyes.

Mentally greet the spirit animal and allow the feeling of that animal to flow through you. Let yourself become that animal by repositioning your body in a posture that that animal would take: a turtle would creep, a lion would crouch, a bird would hop or fly. Make sounds that the animal would make.

Become the animal to the best of your ability, just as if you were a five-year-old. Enjoy the feeling of vigor, grace, or power that the animal has. See with that animal's eyes.

When you feel the power ebbing, thank the animal and return to your usual posture. Open your eyes. Later, as a child would, you might try to draw the animal as it appeared to you or sculpt it in clay.

Exercise #4: The Steps

1. Relax and close your eyes.
2. Greet the spirit animal.
3. Assume the posture of the spirit animal.
4. Become the spirit animal. Assume its qualities.
5. Thank the animal, return to your posture, open your eyes.

HOW POWER ANIMALS HELP YOU

When you establish a regular relationship with one or several power animals, you can call upon them at will to advise and assist you. The usual mode of communication is through shamanic imaging or internal listening. They talk to you in words or they use symbols that you decode.

You can call upon their assistance for:

• Extra vigor for an interview, a meeting, or an athletic event. Creative ideas for a writing project, artwork, or brainstorming about anything.

• Directions to find a lost object such as keys or a wallet, a missing person, or someone you have lost contact with.

• Prevention from contracting disease in a risky area. Help with recovery from an illness or cold.

• Protection from thugs or muggers; guardianship over your car when you have to leave it in a bad part of town; guardianship over your home when you leave on a trip; protection in travel—automobile—airplane—boat.

- Assistance with a test, growing plants, repairing your car or keeping it running.

- Getting along with relatives, bosses, or improving communication with an antagonist.

Power animals can assist with all these things and a myriad other tasks that you might need help with. They love to serve you because they learn by helping you with your challenges. Spirit animals are not static things, but beings that are interested in evolution and growth. Just as you like to help someone in need, so do they. Yet just like you, they like to be acknowledged and treated with respect. If you don't treat them well, they will simply go to someone who will treat them better.

THE POWER OF PLANTS

According to shamans, plants too have their spirit essences, potential allies to be communicated with and cooperated with for mutual benefit. Plants, like rocks and animals, have unique spirit frequencies that can help or in some cases interfere with your health. In every culture, shamans have gotten to know plant spirits and their properties in order to harness their power for healing, treating the sick, and assisting in other tasks. They have discovered which ones can be consumed in the proper quantity to aid digestion, strengthen blood cells, or soothe the nerves.

Shamans have learned which ones can be boiled and made into teas and which ones must be burned to release their beneficial odors. For example, sage is a powerful medicinal plant that can both be made into a healing tea and also burned for its cleansing and balancing properties.

As with power animals, the greater the number of plant spirits shamans have as their allies, the more powerful they are regarded to be. Harnessing plant spirits is a specialty, however; only shamans who are interested in the world of plants pursue contact with them over and above the usual shamanic sensitivity to them. You can decide for yourself whether you have talent that lies in this direction.

GETTING TO KNOW PLANT SPIRITS

To become acquainted with plant spirits you need to exercise a great deal of patience. Plants are stationary beings used to experiencing life at a very slow pace. It takes a great deal of time and patience to tune into their frequency. That is why people who like to putter in their gardens and spend time talking to their plants get such good results.

In order to get to know plant spirits, shamans sit for hours with a particular plant, sensing it, talking with it, listening to it, and just being with it. The plant eventually may tell you what its properties are good for.

All members of a single species share the same spirit essence. For example, each sunflower plant represents the physical form of the Sunflower spirit. Therefore if you get to know a sunflower in New York and a sunflower of the same species in Colorado, you are still speaking to the same spirit.

Exercise #5: Getting to Know Plants

Here is one simple method the shaman uses to contact plant spirits and establish a relationship with them. Begin by choosing a plant in your house, yard, or any other place outside. Again, think in terms of the plant selecting you by grabbing your attention. It could be a small flowering plant, a bush, or even a tree.

Study the plant, carefully noticing every detail: color, shape, smell, etc. Be sure to spend plenty of time here. Then close your eyes and try to get a sense of the plant in your mind. Accept whatever comes in. Remember, as with rocks, plant spirits do not always look like the physical form of the plant. If you have any trouble, go back and repeat step 1.

Once you feel that some spirit connection has been made, ask for a message from the plant. Then listen. If you get nothing here, ask again, then listen. If you are still unsuccessful, go back and try the entire exercise over again with the same plant.

Exercise #5: The Steps

1. Choose a plant.
2. Study it, noticing every detail.
3. Close your eyes and sense the plant in your mind's eye.
4. Ask for a message. Listen.
5. Thank the plant and open your eyes.
6. Repeat the exercise if necessary.

You can repeat this exercise as many times as you wish, either with the same plant or with different plants. Experiment and get to know them! Ask them for information, but always thank them afterwards. We have a close friend who makes an effort to do this exercise every day using different plants in her house and garden. She has been able to establish relationships with each of them and has learned about their distinctive properties. For example, she claims that one of her trees is great at giving business advice and her camelia bush helps her with health issues. Considering how expensive medical advice is these days, it may be wise to listen.

THE POWER OF THE ELEMENTS

For shamans, all elements have their source in the spirit world and therefore are infused with spirits that can be contacted for any number of purposes. The spirit of air, for example, takes many forms. Each form may be called upon for its unique contribution of knowledge. Light breezes, whirlwinds, tornados, cyclones, dust devils, jet streams, hot winds, and cold winds, all have at their source the spirit of air or wind, yet each has a particular job to do. Each form has a special store of wisdom that may be garnered by forming a relationship with it. By acknowledging the wind and talking to it, shamans gain in wisdom, power, and mastery because they know what the wind knows. They can be ready to take whatever precautions they need to in preparation for storms and the like. Shamans who speak with the wind do not need to listen to the local weather reports because they know firsthand what the wind will do.

Old Ted pulled his tractor into the barn and then ambled to the farmhouse door in the clear morning light. The air was already beginning to warm for a perfect spring day.

Just then his neighbor Frank pulled up by the fence in his pickup truck. "Perfect planting day," he called out.

Old Ted wandered over to the fence. "Think I'll wait for two weeks before setting those crops in. I just have a feeling we haven't seen the end of winter yet."

Frank looked incredulous. "You must be out of your mind, Ted," he said. "Why it's always over by this time of year. Besides, all the reports are for a warming trend. We're clear of it now. You'll never get a second crop in if you wait. I'm planting. So's everyone around. What gives you that crazy idea anyhow?"

"Oh, you might say a little bird told me." Ted grinned in his mischievous way, a twinkle in his eye.

Frank shook his head. "Well, it's your skin," he said

aloud as he pulled away. Crazy old coot, he thought to himself, but I wonder. That old guy always seems to know something. Maybe it's that Indian in him. Naw, he's just getting old and nutty.

Two weeks later Old Ted sat by his toasty wood stove and glanced at the snow drifts outside the window of his farmhouse. "Well, it wasn't exactly a little bird that told me," he reflected. "Brother Breeze told me direct."

For shamans, the spirit of fire has a special significance because fire and heat are associated with ecstatic journeys. Shamans the world over use intense heat to purify themselves prior to ceremonies and rituals. These heat purifications were in fact the early origins of the modern Swedish sauna and the Turkish steambath. The Native American practice of the sweatlodge is a good example of heat purification and healing that continues to this day.

When used ceremonially, smoke and heat from the fire carry the shaman up to the sky realms and to the land of spirit. This is the basic significance behind the Native American use of the pipe. When the pipe is lit and shared, all present are united through the world of spirit.

Shamans are considered to be masters of fire, and this is sometimes displayed by their immunity to its ability to burn them. Firewalking has its origins in this shamanic display of mastery over the physical properties of fire. In order to do this, shamans must first have a relationship with fire. They must know it so thoroughly that they actually merge with it or become its spirit. When there is no difference between themselves and the spirit of fire, it cannot burn them. Lightning, hot springs, smoke, and fire in all its forms are spirit powers that shamans seek to know and learn about so that they can become more powerful.

This does not mean that you should go out and attempt to walk on fire or play with it in a way that can cause you danger or harm. These are strictly advanced practices that require guidance by a master, and they are not necessary for you to become a more successful person.

Water, like wind, has a spirit self that takes many forms. Rain, snow, hail, ponds, streams, rivers, lakes, oceans, falls, torrents, and so on are each wise in ways that people can benefit from. Each form of water can be contacted and spoken with to discover what it knows that can be helpful to people.

The sun, the moon, the planets, and the stars are all important sources of spirit information. The shaman knows that each is vital to basic survival, and a personal relationship with them is critical to living a successful life. Furthermore, the most competent shamans know that these powers are all representatives of the greater spirit that unifies the cosmos and is the true source of life itself. By communicating to the sun or the moon and thanking them for their warmth or light, the shaman, through humility, grows powerful because he speaks directly with the source of life itself.

You too can learn to tap into the tremendous power inherent in all the elements of nature. As we mentioned earlier, all you need to start with is respect for these forces, a belief that you can make contact with them, and a desire to do so. If you have all of these ingredients, with practice you cannot fail to be successful.

What can you gain from developing your shamanic ability to talk directly to the elements? First of all, by learning to communicate with the wind, the water, fire, the moon, the sun and the stars, and all the elements, you can, at the most basic level, develop an uncanny ability to sense the larger weather patterns months in advance. Shamans know in summer whether the winter will be mild or heavy, wet or dry, long or short. When it is yet winter, they know if the spring will bring rain or late snow, heat or raw cold wind. You can learn to know this too. You can regulate your travels, plan building projects, avoid disasters, simply by learning to tune into the elements before hand. These elements always know what they are up to and will be glad to tell you if they feel you are a friend. Shamans know that the world of nature need not be the enemy.

Not only is it possible to read and understand the larger weather patterns but with practice and focus one can harness the elements as allies in a cooperative relationship. Master shamans call in rain and clear weather, or avert tornados and flooding with their ability to communicate directly with the elements. Through their contacts with these allies, shamans learn to let go of their resistance and merge directly with fire, wind, water, and earth for productive results.

Communication with the elements teaches you to become more fully integrated with the powers that surround you. You are then part of nature, not an antagonist or victim of it.

Second, you can greatly enhance your ability to successfully handle a career that works with natural forces. Chemistry, agriculture, physics, geology, electronics, water and power, petroleum, pharmacology, astronomy, to name a few, are all fields that stand to gain tremendously by simple and direct communication with the spirits of the elements they focus on. By adding spirit communication to your store of (sometimes questionable) scientific knowledge, you can produce results that can be of great service to humanity. Unlike deciduous scientific knowledge that can be completely invalidated overnight by a new discovery, direct shamanic knowledge tends to be perennial. When wind tells you that, to stay healthy, you must avoid the hot winds of early fall and seek out the fresh breezes of late spring, you can count on it.

Einstein is a good example of a man with latent shamanic powers. His greatest discoveries occurred not in the laboratory but in flashes of direct intuition. A shaman would say that he knew how to contact the spirit world for hidden knowledge. He must have had powerful natural allies. So it has been with many of the truly great discoverers, inventors, and pioneers.

We will give you an exercise designed to open up your communication channels with the spirit of the elements. It is a simple feeling exercise that you can do anywhere and at any time. The exercise is most effective when you are actually in the presence of the element you are working with. For instance, if it is windy outside, work with wind; if you are near a creek or you are swimming, work with water. Notice how much the exercise resembles child's play. This is not accidental.

Exercise #6: Knowing the Elements

Choose an element that you can physically hear, see, smell, taste, or feel at the time. Now focus intently on how that element looks, feels, or sounds to you. Close your eyes and, without losing touch with the sense of the element, ask yourself what qualities you would have if you were that element. For example, water would be fluid, wet, powerful in a flood, and perhaps warm or cold. Wind could feel light, free, cold, hot, formless, caressing, threatening, and so on.

Try on each of the qualities you come up with. Take a

Exercise #6: The Steps

1. Choose an element currently present.
2. Sense the qualities of the element.
3. Close your eyes. Ask how those qualities translate to you.
4. Try them on for size.
5. Thank the element. Open your eyes.

moment and feel like you are the wind, water, or sun. Move like they would move.

Repeat this exercise as often as you wish. You will find yourself gaining respect for the elements as well as developing an open line of communication with their spirits.

You are now familiar with the basics of the web of power and the great allies available in the natural world. These allies long for cooperative contact with human beings because they do not regard people as something outside themselves, as we do them. The element, animal, plant, and mineral worlds know that we humans are a part of them and they are a part of us and it grieves them when we treat them as enemies. After all, human bodies are completely made up of minerals and plant and animal material. We are largely made up of water; we breathe air; and we produce heat. All of the essential elements are represented inside of us. Yet we imagine that we are somehow separate and different from what appears to be outside of us.

The spirits of nature are incredibly patient with people and even after all the abuse and neglect we have heaped on them they continue to offer their help and assistance when asked. Learning to acknowledge them as family is a key to shamanic power. Shamans know that only people who have acknowledged their support system in nature can develop harmony and balance in their environment. They are ones who have become more simple in their relationship to nature. They say, "Good morning, Grandfather Sun," "Hello, Brother Rock," "Welcome, Grandmother Rain," and they sound like children speaking. Indeed, they are extraordinarily powerful children of nature and stewards of it as well.

CHAPTER 5

Shaping Time:
Learning to Be Present

Sally Gordon wasted no time preparing for her physiology exam. Medical school was hard enough without falling behind. Then disaster struck. A fire in the apartment upstairs caused water damage all through her own apartment. She would have to move everything out immediately for the repair crew to clean up the mess. By the time she moved, stored all her belongings, and found a place to stay, the physiology exam would be one day away. Only a miracle could bail her out.

Her roommate Cathy had an idea. "Let's try some time-stretching and see if we can borrow some more time for you to study."

Sally looked at her incredulously. "That's impossible!"

"Let's just try it," Cathy said seriously. "My uncle is a shaman in British Columbia. I used to spend summers with him and he taught me some valuable lessons about time. You'd be surprised what you can do."

"First, let me check with a friend of mine." Cathy closed her eyes and was silent for a time. "Great, my friend Wolf will help you. He says to use the drum my uncle gave me." Cathy instructed Sally to lie down and then helped her relax by tuning in to the pull of gravity. Then she told her to visualize a cave entrance or opening in the earth. "Wait there and if the wolf shows up, do exactly as he says," Cathy instructed as she began to drum.

Some time later, Sally opened her eyes and looked around her. "I felt like I was gone for hours," she murmured. "But something did happen. Your wolf did show up and he took me down this long narrow tunnel. Then we shot out of a geyser hole into this land filled with activity. Then the wolf flew up to the sun and froze it in the sky. Everything stopped except for the wolf and me. The wolf handed me a stick and said, 'Now you have your time.'

87

Then he grabbed me and we flew back up the tunnel and came back to where we started."

"Great," exclaimed Cathy. "That's the best way to do it. You always want to end up back where you started. Well, time's a-wasting, so to speak. Better hit the books."

Sally was amazed at her energy level. She seemed to go from one chapter to the next without getting tired. When she glanced at the clock, she was surprised to see that it had hardly moved. What's going on here, she thought to herself. I've never covered so much material in so little time! And on she went.

One week later, Sally got the results of her final. Max'd it, she thought proudly. I thought Cathy was a nut with her wolves and weird uncle. Now I'm not so sure.

For shamans, Sally's experience is not an unusual event, but rather an everyday possibility. Shamans view time differently from the way most of us are taught. Time, if held rigid, creates containment, restriction and limitation. For shamans, time is a flexible, malleable vehicle that can be manipulated with simple know-how. When time is made to stretch or constrict, it becomes a tool of power necessary for success. How can this be?

Picture the world this way. Ordinary reality is the world of form or, as some shamans call it, the "tonal." It is the reality where differences exist and where everything seems to be separate. It is the world of tables and chairs and trees and rocks. For shamans, the source of this world of form is the nagual or spirit world, where everything that cannot be named exists. Thus the physical world and its source create a reality where the tonal and the nagual exist in a dynamic tension to one another continually.

Within the nagual or spirit world, time does not exist as we know it in the tonal or physical world. Since the nagual is the source of the tonal, in order to manipulate time, you simply need to dip into the spirit world and call forth its resources. Putting it another way, if you want something done, you go to the top. In this case, you go to the source.

By going to the source, shamans gain access to all time frames. As a result they are free to retrieve information from the store of all knowledge both past and future. Imagine for a moment that all present experiences are being eternally recorded on a giant blue record. Imagine however that this record is alive with life energy and animated continuously. Envision that the record has an infinite number of green records stacked on top of it and below it representing the past and future. You can go even further and imagine that on all sides around the blue and green records are stacked an infinite number of yellow records representing alternative or probable pasts, presents, and futures. Now visualize shamans traveling into the spirit world where they emerge in the hole at the center of the blue record. Here, from a central point, they have immediate access to a great range of possibilities. The important consideration for them is to know what they are looking for. Allies and power animals act as guides to this living library, leading them to find out exactly what they want to know.

Not only do shamans gain entrance to this living record to retrieve knowledge, but to learn to shift the course of events so that the outcome emerges differently. This does not mean that the original result did not occur. It means that the original result is relegated to a side stack or probable occurrence and a more desirable one is shifted into the central stack.

Shamans are able to manipulate time in a number of ways. First of all, they know how to stretch time or make it slow down, as was the case with Sally and her exam deadline, or, in some radical cases, to avoid an accident. There are many reports from people who, in the midst of an automobile accident, experienced time slowing down, allowing them to make decisions and take protective action that saved their lives. Shamans would say they used their shamanic ability unconsciously to perform the act. Shamans carry out these time warps consciously.

Although Ron had been playing football for three years, he had never felt the pressure of a game like this one. It was first down, fourth quarter, with one minute to go in the big game. The noise in the stadium was deafening. The only problem was the score. After winning almost every game this season, they were now tied seven to seven and the other team had the ball. As he approached the line of scrimmage, Ron felt a strange feeling in his stomach. He felt odd, almost as if he weighed half of his 210 pounds. The ball snapped and there was the usual flash of jerseys, mud flying, and grunts as the teams slammed together. Just as he thought, this was a pass play, and he fell back to prevent the long throw. But he was much too far away from the ball as it rapidly arched through the air toward the receiver. Suddenly the whole world slowed down and became like a slow-motion instant replay. The ball seemed to be moving incredibly slowly as the players gradually moved their arms and legs in a slow-motion ballet. Oddly, Ron was not moving slowly, however. He suddenly had plenty of time to run toward the ball. Unbelievably, taking a flying leap, he intercepted it with his gritty, outstretched hands. Still the players moved like molasses as he began to run through the openings between them. As he crossed the goal line, Ron already knew the game was won. Ron did not tell anybody what he had experienced out there. He already had a reputation for reading those metaphysical books. They would just think he was crazy. But he was glad it happened.

A second way that shamans manipulate time is by speeding it up so that a long time goes by very quickly. Shamans can sit still for long periods of time and experience that time as if it had gone by in a twinkling. Yogic shamans of India put themselves into suspended animation for long periods, sometimes asking others to bury them in the ground for the duration to demonstrate their powers. When their followers dig them up after days or weeks they emerge smiling and very much alive. There are countless shamanic stories related to this theme of time suspension. Here is one with a surprise ending.

Masapa cinched up his satchel containing his few ritual items, hoisted it over his shoulder, and waved to the villagers. He was headed up the mountain to commune with his guardian spirits. The villagers were used to his comings and goings. As their shaman, he seemed to need the time alone to gather his power and seek the knowledge that made him such a good healer and seer. When Masapa had climbed high enough to look back at the tops of the clouds hiding the now distant village, he sat down to rest. Suddenly, he was confronted by a large grey coyote. The coyote grinned at him and said, "Say, Masapa, you are out of breath. Why don't you have a drink?" Masapa replied, "I do not have any water with me. I cannot take a drink." Coyote said, "Well, you are not very well prepared to spend the time you will need up here to learn everything you want to know." Masapa countered, "But I came up here only to spend the day." With that the coyote laughed at him long and hard. "I think you'd better come with me," he said, wiping away his tears. Masapa followed him into the bushes. Suddenly they were in a beautiful land where many animals danced and played on the plain below. He went down among them and danced with them all day long. When he had grown tired, he looked for coyote. "Coyote, Coyote," he called. "I want to go back to my village, but I have lost my way. Can you show me the way back?" Coyote showed up and looked at him with a grin. "OK, follow me," he said, and led him up the mountain and into the bushes. Suddenly Masapa recognized where he was and returned down to his village. The villagers looked at him in amazement. His clothes were in tatters and he had grown very thin. "Where have you been these last three years?" they cried. "Learning a lesson about time," he said sheepishly.

Exercise #1: Stretching Time

To stretch time you need to accelerate your travel speed in the spirit world first. When you have learned to accelerate in this fashion you can then learn to accelerate the speed of your operations in ordinary reality. This takes practice and intense concentration. The idea here is not to learn to rush around but to experience a relaxed effortless pace in high acceleration.

For this exercise you will need a drum, rattle, or percussion instrument and a timer.

Sit with your drum in front of you or lie down using one hand to shake your rattle. Better yet, have a friend drum or rattle for you. Set the alarm on your watch or set the timer for four minutes. Close your eyes.

Visualize your cave entrance and begin to drum or rattle using a methodical beat (approximately one beat per second). As soon as your guide or power animal shows up, ask them to help you make time slow down. Increase the tempo of the drumbeat threefold so that there is a sense of urgency to it.

Exercise #1: The Steps

1. Relax and close your eyes.
2. Set your alarm and begin to drum.
3. Envision your cave or opening and ask your guide for help with slowing time.
4. Increase tempo of drumbeat threefold.
5. Follow the instructions of your guide implicitly.
6. Return.
7. Write or tell your experience.

When you hear the beep of your alarm or timer it is time to return. Increase the tempo of your drumbeat or rattle slightly and rush back the same way you went. About one minute.

How much did you experience in five minutes? Chances are you experienced enough to spend longer than an hour writing it down and understanding it.

Exercise #2: Contracting Time

To contract time you need to slide entirely outside the present time frame in ordinary reality. Essentially you place your body comfortably in park and then travel with your spirit body to other locations where you busily take care of a variety of interests. This is exactly what you do when you fall asleep for several hours. Time passes and you are barely aware of its passing. The secret is to be so absorbed and involved in your travels that you lose track of the passing minutes in ordinary reality.

There is no formal exercise that we can think of to lead you into this phenomenon although you have probably experienced it many times. Storytelling is probably the best time squeezer that we know of. Shamans are usually quite good at telling stories. As you listen to a story from a good storyteller, your imagination travels extensively to the location and time frame of the tale being told. A simple way to experience this is to play professional tapes of an exciting novel or story while you are driving on a long trip in the car.

You, however, are your own best storyteller. The more exciting the story of your life, the faster it will seem to unfold.

A third way shamans play with time is to fly into the future, take a look at it, and bring back the news of what is going to happen. This is the art of foreseeing or prophesying for which shamans are well known. They travel into the spirit world via one of the many tunnels available for this purpose and, in the world without time, they can reemerge through an opening in so-called future time.

This, of course, has many practical advantages. When you know the probable outcome of a situation, you can plan for it well in advance and set yourself up to be in the right place at the right time. You may recall the tale of the farmer who waited to plant until after the late snow. By knowing about the late snow in advance, he saved himself a ruined crop.

On the other hand, shamans know that the future is never firmly fixed, but rather is based on probabilities. They can foresee that a course of action may lead to a catastrophe. But by altering what they do now, they can avert the catastrophe. One method of forestalling an undesirable outcome is to give the disaster a token opportunity to play itself out. For example, if shamans foresee a flood inundating their villages, they may avert the disaster by building tiny little mock-ups of the villages and then inundating them with buckets of water. By giving the event a token reality, shamans control the situation, possibly averting a large-scale disaster that might happen to a big village. The fact is, what they foresee does happen, but to a tiny village instead.

An entertainer had a recurring dream that she would be up on stage before an audience and suddenly lose control and laugh hysterically in front of everyone. Needless to say, this caused her considerable anxiety. She tried to put the thought out of her mind, but the more she avoided the dream, the more she would think of it. It began to interfere with her work to the extent that she was turning down jobs out of fear. Finally, she consulted a counselor that had some training in shamanic practices. The counselor heard her story and then suggested that they stage the scene. This, of course, took some powers of persuasion on the part of the counselor and several meetings to work up to it. She set up the office like a small stage at one end and lined up chairs as the audience at the other end. They rehearsed the scene as it had occurred in the entertainer's dream. She would be performing in front of the audience and suddenly would loudly pretend to laugh hysterically at all the people (represented by dolls, teddy bears, and pillows). Soon they both were laughing, and the entertainer felt more relaxed and unafraid. Her dream stopped recurring, with no substitute symptoms.

Some behavior-modification techniques similar to this one are actually based on age-old shamanic techniques. The reasons given why the techniques work are different, however. For the psychologist, the practice run relieves the client of anxiety, permitting her to master the problem. For shamans, the dream or fear is based on an actual probable event in the future. By giving the tragedy a harmless day in the sun, shamans control the future event and render the obstacles harmless.

Exercise #3: Looking into the Future

Use your drum or rattle. Tempo: three beats per second.

Lie down, close your eyes, and relax. Think of a future event that causes you anxiety or worry. It may be a public speaking engagement, an exam, an interview, the birth of a child, or your own death.

Imagine the entrance to your cave or opening into the Earth. Meet your guide and ask them to help you see into the probable future of the event that you selected. Tell them the event or time frame you are interested in. Follow their instructions to see into that event. They may take you to a specific location first to observe it. You may see something that appears strange to you. Do not be concerned, because events frequently look different in the spirit world from how they do in ordinary reality.

Notice the details of that event. Ask yourself what is not okay with you about what you are seeing or sensing. Stay in touch with the emotion that arises as you contemplate the outcome. If it is okay with you, there is nothing for you to do when you return.

Return when you are satisfied that you have seen the probable future event. Don't forget to thank your guide. If what you saw was not all right with you, then try to set up a three-dimensional model of the event the way it happened initially. Using clay, matchsticks, toys, or pillows, run through it as a child "making believe" might do. Then, if you wish, run it through again the way you would prefer it to happen.

Exercise #3: The Steps

1. Lie down, relax.
2. Choose worrisome future event. Commence drumming.
3. Enter cave entrance and meet guide. Ask for help.
4. Journey to examine the future.
5. Examine the event for details and emotions. What is not OK?
6. Return.
7. Reconstruct the event three dimensionally.

The fourth way that shamans manipulate time is through journeying into the past to retrieve lost information, bring forth ancestral knowledge into the present, and control present events from the past. This is a technique from ancient times, when no written language existed nor were there libraries and databanks to record the wisdom and knowledge that people gained through their experiences. Had shamans not developed a method to retrieve this knowledge and bring it forward, each generation would be doomed to rediscover the same information and no progress would be made. Shamans made it possible for people to know vital survival information in all parts of the globe at any time.

Queta watched the sleet as it slanted down onto the thatched roofs of the village, ice collecting between the fronds and bindings of each dwelling. Never had he remembered the weather to be so cold in this usually tropical climate. Not even the most aged elder could remember when the people needed to wear more than a simple shawl in the balmy time they called the Season of the Late Sun. The people were cold and fearful that the normally plentiful game would become scarce.

Queta knew it was time for Big Flying: the time to talk to the ancestors and find out whether they could help with their ancient knowledge. He had spent the usual seven days preparing for the journey through fasting and chanting. Now he called for his apprentice Anka to bring the drum and the great clear crystal. He raised the crystal to his forehead with the point raised. With Anka drumming, he began to enter the dream. "Oh, Great Crystal," he chanted, "take me to the land of our ancestors. Assist us now that we are so cold. Please help us." For some time, Queta sat pleading for help, until quite suddenly he felt so heavy that he could no longer hold himself up. He collapsed onto the matting and lay very still. His spirit body was flying, riding the crystal across brilliant landscapes of every hue. With a jolt he found himself in a bark shelter. A fire was burning and the room felt safe and cozy. An old woman sat before him. Looking at him steadily, she began to speak. "So, you are cold. Here, warm yourself." She handed him a mug of something sweet and hot. "Long before your land became sunny and balmy, long before the jungles grew up tall, this land was cold and bitter. We, your ancestors lived here in contentment because we knew the ways of the cold winds and Grandfather Snow. Come, I will show you how we live." Queta remained with the old woman for six months, learning her people's ways. He learned to make warm clothing from the furs of the animals and how to build sturdy shelters from the bark of trees. He learned the art of making strong shoes for protection from the sharp ice and cold.

One day the old woman said to him, "You have learned enough to help your people. You must now return to them for they need you." So after thanking her profusely, Queta drew forth his crystal and returned to his own village of the future. When he awoke, he was lying on the ground. Anka had fallen asleep, the silent drum lying on the ground next to him. When Queta sternly shook him, Anka awoke apologetically. "I'm sorry, Queta. You were gone for so long, I fell asleep. You have been lying there for two whole days." Queta taught his people the ways he had learned to cope with the cold. The people would live now and be warm.

Exercise #4: Retrieving Lost Knowledge

This exercise involves a very simple journey format. Use a drum (or tape). Tempo: approximately three beats per second.

Follow the usual relaxation procedure. Think of a skill or talent that you wish you had. It could be that you wish you were better at making friends or you were a better skier.

Imagine your entrance to the Earth. Meet your guide or power animal and ask them for help retrieving lost knowledge in your area of interest. Allow them to take you to a location or place where you can find that knowledge.

During your journey you may read what you want to know in an ancient book or talk to someone expert in that field as Queta did. On the other hand you may see someone who resembles you, performing the activity that you wish to know more about. Notice the details about that person. Introduce yourself to them. They may give you a gift or a symbol.

Upon returning and thanking your guide, recall the details about what you saw. If you saw a version of yourself performing the activity, remember what they wore and how they acted. For example if you noticed that they wore a silver ring on one finger, go out and get yourself a silver ring like it and wear it. Try acting like they acted for an hour or so.

Reproducing a detail from the dream as a kind of symbolic reminder is a most important aspect of this technique. The symbol acts as a channel for wisdom to penetrate through the time barrier into present reality. You don't have to understand this for it to work. We suggest you try it out for your own experience.

Exercise #4: The Steps

1. Relax and close your eyes.
2. Choose a wished-for talent or desired condition.
3. Commence drumming.
4. Imagine cave entrance and meet your guardian spirit. Make your request.
5. Journey to recover lost knowledge.
6. Return and thank your guide.
7. Recall details and reproduce one in your everyday reality.

Journeying to the past is not only a method of retrieving lost knowledge, but a way of actually working with history so that the present turns out differently. In Queta's case, the villagers were saved because he was able to bring ancient knowledge to bear on the current crisis. However, as you shall see in the next story, shamans can also enter into the past to alter the events there in such a fashion as to shift their current reactions. They need not feel trapped by a problem because they can literally intercede into the past to change the present reality ever so slightly. They call this changing or erasing personal history.

John Lager was an excellent sales representative. For three years running, he had been the top water-filter salesperson in his company. Then his company decided to send him to a rural area that showed great promise. His sales plummeted. The problem was dogs. No one but John himself knew that he had a desperate fear of dogs. In the city he could screen the homes with dogs, but out here in the suburbs every house and yard had a dog. Even with a sure sale, he couldn't bring himself to pass by that dog at the gate.

John knew he had to get some help with his problem so he asked for a referral to a local counselor who had a reputation for handling such fears.

Unbeknownst to John, Fred Crane used shamanic techniques in his work with phobias. When John asked him what he could do for him, Fred explained that he used some unconventional techniques that were very effective with problems of this sort. Fred outfitted John with earphones and a tape recording of shamanic drumming. He explained that John was to relax, close his eyes, and allow the image of a cave to form in his mind's eye. At the cave entrance, he was to meet an animal who would be his guide. He was to ask that animal for help with his problem.

Within five minutes, John was relaxed and entering the entrance to his cave. He was met there by a large golden lion who greeted him in English. Since the lion was a cat and not a dog, John had no problem with it. He explained his fear and the lion told him to climb on his back and hang on. With a tremendous leap, the lion flew into the ribbed tunnel at the back of the cave. The narrow tunnel wound this way and that, until they emerged into the middle world in a place that looked familiar to John. It was like the countryside where John had grown up. He looked across the field and saw a very little boy, running from two large dogs who were jumping up on him. As John watched with mounting anxiety, the boy ran into a barbed wire fence in his efforts to escape and began to flail, tearing his clothes. In a single bound, the lion sprang to the boy, warding off the dogs. John sprang off the lion's back to untangle the boy from the barbed wire. With a shock John saw that the boy was he himself, many years before. The boy was senseless with fear, and it took John some time to calm him down. He smoothed his hair and wrapped a gash with his handkerchief. Then he called the dogs over and lectured them. "I know you guys were just roughhousing, but you are big and scary to this little boy and he could have been badly hurt. When you approach children, you have to be more gentle." The dogs were chagrined, but soon they wagged their tails and came over to lick the boy's scrapes. The boy, with the invisible lion standing guard and John holding him, began to stroke the dogs' backs. Soon he was laughing and playing with them. "Come on, John," the Lion called, "time to go." John leaned down and snuggled the boy that was himself. "Just think, if we hadn't come along you might have gotten stuck on that fence for hours. I know how scary that can be. That actually happened to me long ago. Anytime you need some help, just call me and I'll be glad to help. I've got some powerful friends." With that, he hopped on the lion's back for the speedy trip home.

John awoke with a jolt in Fred's office. "Boy, you must have had a real powerful trip," Fred said, grinning. "You were out for almost half an hour." John remained silent for some time, integrating his experience. Somehow he just knew dogs would not be such a problem anymore.

John did not completely overcome his fear of dogs overnight. His body had built up a habitual fear response to dogs ever since that early childhood event, so he needed some time to learn to relax around them again. Nevertheless, the shamanic journey had torn the heart from his fear. Not only was John on the road to relief from his fear of dogs, but he had gained a powerful ally in the Lion. Now he could call upon the Lion anytime he wanted to, whenever he made house calls. Somehow with a big lion at his side, even large dogs paled in comparison.

Exercise #5: Altering the Present from the Past

Follow the simple journey method again and, of course, drumming is helpful.

Relax and close your eyes. Choose an obstacle or difficulty present in your life. Get in touch with your feelings about it by noticing where your body reacts when you focus on it. Spend some time with this.

Imagine your cave entrance and meet your guide there. Ask their help in recalling the origins of your present difficulty in the past. Let them take you to a locale where you can witness or reexperience the earlier event.

Deliberately interact with the characters within the situation as in the story of John and the dogs. You may wish to offer guidance and advice to the "you" who is having difficulty there. You may wish to consult your guide or power animal about possible choices. Act as if you are directing a play. You can rerun the scene with alterations as many times as you wish. The dialogue between the people can be important to reconsider. Remember to keep in touch with the

---

Exercise #5: The Steps

1. Relax and close your eyes.
2. Choose an obstacle or difficulty.
3. Imagine your cave entrance and meet your guardian spirit.
4. Journey to the past.
5. Reconstruct the past event.
6. Return and thank your guide.

emotions of the event until you feel a release or sense of relief.

Return from that locale when the situation seems resolved to you. Thank your guide and open your eyes.

PRESENCE

With all this time travel and time manipulation, you might think that it would be easy for shamans to forget where they are. Forgetting can be a real problem for shamans, so they have disciplined themselves in a way that helps them always to know where they are. Simultaneously, shamans have a foot in both the physical world, where their body is, and in the spirit world, where they are traveling. If they don't know what they are doing or where they are, they easily resemble schizophrenics who have lost touch with the reality of the physical world. But shamans are not psychotics by a long shot. They are masters of their trade and they have become so through much practice and discipline.

If you find yourself having trouble knowing who you are as you do the exercises we describe, we suggest you discontinue them right away. Perhaps shamanic techniques are not for you until some other time. Perhaps you first need to learn the basics of being present in physical reality. This is a perfectly reasonable approach to take. When you have mastered this presence, then you can return to developing your shamanic abilities.

The secret to maintaining your stability lies in your ability to stay present, balanced, and grounded. To be present means to have mastery in the present world of form. It means to be able to make a living, obtain food and shelter, handle challenges, and care for others. Shamans are therefore not only balanced in the present but masters of time in more than one world.

Although shamans are experts at time travel and maneuvering between realities, they know that only by being present can they exercise their greatest power. For a shaman, wishing and hoping about the future or worrying about the past are totally ineffective methods of producing desirable results. Wishing or worrying tend to remove you from the power of the present. Deliberate or conscious time manipulation originating from the present moment is the shaman's key to creating desirable reality.

Exercise #6: Developing Presence

Set up a wastebasket across the room from you or about ten feet away. Crumple up a sheet of paper into a ball and toss the ball into the wastebasket. Set up the distance so that it is possible to reach it, but not too easy. Shoot some baskets.

Now, purposely think of doing something else. Imagine that you are driving your car or shopping or anything you can vividly imagine. Throw some more baskets without taking your mind off your imaginative pictures. How well did you score?

If you are like most folks, your score for direct hits dropped dramatically when your thoughts were elsewhere. You were not present. You are not present whenever your mind is occupied by endless worry, rehearsing for future showdowns with the boss, or mulling over recent conversations. Presence has to do with being here with whatever you are doing now. It has to do with your spirit body being in the same time frame as your physical body. Whenever there is a disparity between the two, you lose some of your presence and therefore some of your power to handle the situation at hand.

When you are tossing the paper ball into the wastebasket, your physical body is present. Your body is always present in this time frame. But where your thoughts and emotions go, so goes your spirit body. So your spirit body has gone shopping, or driving, or wherever you imagined yourself to be. That means that your spirit body grows dim around your physical body, making you look and feel less real.

When you are in a meeting or talking with someone and your mind wanders, you become less present, less real, less impactful, less powerful. We say that powerful people have presence. That is true. They are present with their thoughts and emotions. Their spirit body is strong within and around their physical body. They are all there and they are the ones who get results. Shamans know how to be powerfully present in physical reality.

They also know how to be consciously present in the spirit world when they are journeying for knowledge or guidance. As you have seen, shamans make sure their physical bodies are protected during their forays into the spirit world. If they are going to deliberately shift their attention away from the present physical reality, they take the necessary precautions to ensure their own safety.

You have learned something about the shamanic perspec-

tive concerning the fluidity and flexibility of time. Although
for most people time is an enormous barrier to getting things
done, for shamans, time is not only plastic but a vehicle for
accomplishing a great many tasks. In shamanic terms, all
time and all knowledge are accessible through the technique
of journeying into the spirit world.

In this chapter you have discovered some ways to play
with time and learned some rudimentary methods of manipulating it for your advantage:

- You can both stretch time to your advantage or contract
  time when you find it a burden on your hands.

- You can peek at the future probabilities and discourage
  ones that you would prefer not to create major obstacles
  for you. By looking into the future you can encourage probabilities that open up more choices for you.

- You can retrieve knowledge and information from the past
  and even manipulate past events to alter your condition in
  the present.

- You have also learned about the importance of presence in
  shamanic work and how that relates to developing power.
  When you know something about your presence in the
  world and how to strengthen it, you can then create the
  conditions that will make you more successful at getting
  what you want.

CHAPTER 6

The Circle of Life: Creating and Destroying

The dressed gourds hanging from every tree rattled in the strong prestorm breeze. Mannaca shivered, not with cold, but with the realization that if the gourds were not properly decorated and ritually prepared, the tribe would be vulnerable to attack from the angry spirits of the dead. Each season of the rains the gourds had to be painstakingly prepared to ward off the spirits of ancients who might be offended by Mannaca's tribe, who had come from the distant mountains to live here in the forest.

Mannaca, tribal shaman, followed the ways of shamans before him. He did not know how the ritual of protective gourds began, but he did know exactly how to prepare them and when they needed to be hung. Each year he worked hard on the gourds because he wanted his people to live in harmony and peace.

That evening a terrific storm broke over the forest. Mannaca and his tribe huddled in their huts, afraid that perhaps the storm had been sent by angry spirits who were not happy with the gourds this season. As the storm raged, Mannaca fell into a deep trance and had a strange vision. He saw a huge gourd come down and smash all the little decorated gourds that he had so laboriously prepared. Then, from inside the great gourd came ancient ones who began to approach him. He cried out in terror, certain that this was surely his end when a strange thing happened. The oldest of the ancient ones stretched out his hand and comforted Mannaca. "Don't be afraid," he said. "We will offer you and your tribe no harm. We wish you to be happy in this place that we once knew. We have sent the storm to scatter your gourds because you need them no more. Make a great fire and burn all the rest of your gourds. We wish a dance instead, in our honor." With that the ancient one gave him detailed instructions about the movements of the dance. When Mannaca woke the storm had passed and outside lay the debris left in its wake. The gourds were broken and crushed beneath fallen branches and seed pods from the trees. Mannaca called his tribe together and revealed to them his vision. They collected the remains of the gourds, built a great fire, and burned them. The people were happy because a great fear had been lifted from them. They celebrated the new dance with vigor.

CREATING AND DESTROYING

Every shaman knows that in order to create something new, something first must be destroyed. The old form is taken apart and from its energetic source, something new arises. Shamanically speaking, all creating is based on some form of destruction. Shamans are comfortable with destruction and have learned not to fear it because without it they know there can be no life.

Nature offers the best examples of this constant destruction in the form of the seasonal changes. As each season gives way to the next, something is destroyed in the process. The fall sweeps away the summer sunlight, kills off the green leaves, and lays bare the landscape. Winter snow kills off the grasses, the insects, and the weakest animals. It covers over the gold of fall in a frozen white blanket. Spring destroys the snowpack and floods tear out trees and embankments along the riverside. The longer day pushes back the dark nights and destroys the cold of winter. The summer sun bakes the land and gradually dries up the water and grasses. Summer kills off spring as surely as summer dies before fall. And so it goes.

Everywhere in nature are examples of terrific destruction that reform the land and seas and create a new canvas for change. Tornados, earthquakes, floods, slides, tsunamis, hurricanes, erupting volcanoes, and withering droughts destroy the landscape as it was, leaving devastation in their wake. And from this terrible destruction comes new life, new forms, new possibilities.

Shamans acknowledge the terrific power of transformation that comes with destruction and seek to harness that power for their own use.

One powerful universal shamanic motif is the destruction of the apprentice during the initiation as a shaman. In many cultures, shamans experience initiation through a near-death experience that literally threatens their lives. This may occur via an accident or illness from which they recover totally transformed. Other shamans go through this experience symbolically during a trance state or ecstatic journey. Typically, during this symbolic death experience, they see their limbs ripped off and their bodies chopped into tiny pieces. Sometimes their flesh is stripped from their bones and the bones are dismantled and thrown in a heap.

In Tibetan Buddhism, similar meditations are used by apprentice lamas to reduce the hold of the ego on the personality. Interestingly, Tibetan Buddhism is based on the much earlier shamanic spiritual practices of the religion Bon. To this day, many Tibetan Buddhist lamas practice shamanism in their ministrations to the local people and use it to strengthen their own spiritual practices.

Why, you may ask, do shamans focus on such morbid internal images and experiences? Shamans understand that becoming a shaman requires the death or destruction of one's ordinary way of looking at the world. This is dramatically symbolized by the near-death experience or by the images of bodily destruction that shamans have historically endured.

It is not necessary to fall deathly ill or have an accident to begin to adopt the shamanic perspective. But it is necessary to become comfortable with the destruction of your old beliefs and ways of looking at the world.

Here is an advanced exercise, using the journey method, in which you can experience this type of initiation symbolically. There are countless versions of this exercise and if you wish, you will discover your own version that works for you. If the exercise is too disturbing to you, you should not attempt it. Wait until you can do it with a little more neutrality. Drumming is helpful with this practice as it keeps you focused and moving through this challenging journey.

Exercise #1: Symbolic Initiation

Relax, close your eyes and approach your cave entrance or opening into the Earth. At the opening, meet your power animal or other guardian spirit and tell them that you wish to go to the underworld, to the place of symbolic initiation. Follow your guardian's instructions explicitly. They may refuse to take you, saying you are not to go there today, or indicate that you are not ready. If this happens, stop, go no farther and try it again another time. If you get the go-ahead, proceed.

Allow your power animal or guardian to take you to the underworld place of initiation. It could look like almost anything, so avoid having preconceived ideas about it. Find your place there and begin the initiation.

Begin to shred your skin off (this may be done for you by your power animal or other guardians of the place) and pile it in a heap on the ground. Begin to pluck off all the flesh on your bones all over your body. Systematically pile on the ground all your organs and flesh until you are just a skeleton. Take apart your skeleton until there is nothing of your body left intact.

Heap wood on the pile and burn it until there is nothing but ash left. Mix some water with the ashes and use the clay to remold your bones and body parts with it. Systematically build your body back up again until you are whole.

Return with your power animal or guardian to the entrance or opening into the earth. Notice how you feel.

Exercise #1: The Steps

1. Relax and close your eyes.
2. Approach your cave or other opening.
3. Meet your power animal or guardian; state your purpose; follow instructions.
4. Travel to the underworld; find your place to begin.
5. Take your body apart from the skin to the bones; pile it.
6. Burn the pile down to ash.
7. Mix water to make clay; remold yourself.
8. Return with and thank your guardian; notice how you feel.

APPROPRIATE DESTRUCTION: POSSESSIONS

Destruction and death are an integral part of the web of power that supports all creativity and new life forms. Therefore learning how to use destruction appropriately and how to get rid of anything that does not contribute to your stated goals in life is important. Shamans know that all possessions have some of your life force invested in them to the extent of your attachment to them. Remember again that to a shaman, thoughts and feelings are forms that go out and become attached anywhere they are sent. Anything you hang on to makes you less rather than more powerful. To become more powerful and therefore more successful, do as the shamans would. Eliminate and let go of as much as possible of the unnecessary things in your life.

Here are some different categories of things that you can

destroy. Keep in mind that in this context, *destroy* means give away or throw out. It means "you" won't have it anymore.

Appropriate destruction includes getting rid of old possessions that no longer work for you or serve you in productive ways. These include clothes, household items, furniture, electronic devices, tools, vehicles, to name a few.

Exercise #2: Appropriate Destruction: Possessions

Head for your clothes closet and dresser and go through all your shirts, blouses, slacks, jackets, dresses, underwear, shoes, and weed them out. Ruthlessly toss out any item that you have not worn for one year or more. Toss out anything that you "do not enjoy" wearing! Keeping clothes because they might come back in fashion someday or because Aunt Mabel gave them to you is usually just a way of fooling yourself. If they still have life in them, let someone else benefit from wearing them.

As you cart them to your favorite charity or to the trash bin, thank them for their service and then mentally let them go; completely give them away.

If you still do not see enough space in your closet, go through it again. You can be sure that no matter what your circumstances, your closet will somehow fill up again in a few months and you will have to do this again.

Of course, if you want to hang on to all that old stuff, then your closet will have no room left for new things to flow into it. Your closet symbolizes your mind. When it is cluttered, there is room for nothing new. Go back over it once more. Be ruthless.

Go through your house, office, yard, garage, car, and everything else you own. Apply the same ruthless tactics that you used with your closet. You will not regret it.

Exercise #2: The Steps

1. Go through closet and dresser; toss out clothes you don't wear or enjoy wearing.
2. Thank them for their service; mentally let them go.
3. Go through your closet and dresser again.
4. Go through everything else you own in the same fashion.

APPROPRIATE DESTRUCTION: BELIEFS

Now that you have divested yourself of burdensome unwanted possessions, you have paved the way toward eliminating outdated and worn-out beliefs that once served you but no longer do. This includes old limiting beliefs and ideas about what you can and can't do. As with possessions, beliefs are imbued with your life spirit and require a constant supply of it to keep them in your current memory bank (mental closet). When your mind is filled with a mishmash of competing and sometimes opposing beliefs, you tend to become paralyzed and unable to make decisions or initiate action.

It is easy for us to identify so closely with our beliefs that we get mixed up and think that our beliefs are actually parts of ourselves. Unfortunately, this is the stuff of wars and feuds. How many battles have been fought over the belief that one side has dishonored the other simply because they had a different set of beliefs? How many religious and ideological wars have been fought over nothing more than conflicting belief systems?

Here is an opportunity for you to go through your beliefs systematically and discover how closely identified with them you are. Remember that it takes some courage to disidentify from some of your cherished beliefs and stand apart from them.

You can probably recall a belief that you once firmly held that you no longer hold. Perhaps it was a childhood belief in Santa Claus or a conviction that you would be struck by lightning if you told a lie. Although these beliefs were once "held" by you they were not "you." You went on to change your belief, and you *continue* to change your mind about things without losing your overall integrity as a person. Keep this in mind as you do the following exercise.

Exercise #3: Appropriate Destruction: Beliefs

Sit down and make a list of beliefs and ideas that you hold about different categories of experience. For example, make a list of everything you believe to be true about "men" or "women" or "money" or "work" or "who you are" and so on. Particularly list those beliefs that you wish you did not have, but have to admit are there. You will find this exercise, like the possessions exercise, to be both relieving and somewhat anxiety provoking. Stick with it. It's worth knowing what you've been dragging around.

Now go back and next to each belief, write out the exact opposite belief. You may find yourself feeling uncomfortable with the polarity, but stick with it. This takes some courage, but it will bring you face-to-face with your attachment to certain limiting beliefs. Shamanically speaking, to the extent you hold on to those old beliefs, you are totally run by them. They determine exactly what you will experience in life unless you shift your beliefs.

For example, one of your beliefs might be "I'm just no good at seeing anything when I close my eyes." The opposite belief would be "I have excellent visioning powers and I am able to have vivid and effective journeys when I close my eyes." Go ahead and lie about it for a while. Soon your lies will become the truth. Remember that shamans have a reputation for being liars; they know that the physical body needs to be tricked and cajoled into letting go of any pattern it is used to.

Tear up your lists or burn them for symbolic destruction.

Examples of beliefs worthy of destruction:

Outmoded Beliefs	Opposing Beliefs That Become True
• Only cheats get ahead in life.	• Honesty helps me to get ahead in life.
• There's never enough time to get everything done.	• I have all the time I need to get everything done.
• There's never enough money.	• There is always enough money for all my needs.
• I should be able to do it all myself.	• I can ask for help when I need it.
• This shamanism stuff is unreal.	• This shamanism stuff is very real.
• People don't like to see my emotions.	• People are supportive of my emotions.
• It is difficult for a woman to be successful no matter how intelligent she is.	• A woman can be both smart and successful.
• Men have all the breaks in life.	• Women as well as men get all the breaks in life.
• Women make no sense.	• All people make sense, including women.

Outmoded Beliefs	*Opposing Beliefs That Become True*
• Men are all callous creeps.	• Men are generous and loving.
• It's safer not to confront anyone because then you can't get hurt.	• It is exhilarating to confront others.
• I should take care of everyone else.	• I can take care of myself best.
• Everyone's out to get me.	• Everyone's out to help me.
• I never have any luck.	• I always have a lot of luck.
• I always get taken advantage of.	• I create my own reality.
• I can never get ahead.	• I am getting ahead.
• You've got to work very hard to get ahead.	• I get ahead easily.
• Life isn't fair.	• Life is always fair.
• I need someone special to make me happy.	• I am happy with myself.
• I am the only one who can get the job done.	• I am one of many who can do this job.
• I'll never change.	• I am changing every day.
• I'm better than everybody else.	• Everyone else is as good as I am.
• Nothing is worth doing.	• Everything is worth doing.
• Nobody loves me; nobody takes care of me.	• Everybody loves me; everyone takes care of me.
• I'll never be healthy.	• I am always perfectly healthy.

Exercise #3: The Steps

1. Make a list of your beliefs and ideas.
2. Next to each belief write out the opposite belief.
3. Tear up or burn your lists.

APPROPRIATE DESTRUCTION: HABITS

Now that you have started thoroughly cleaning up your beliefs, you are ready for the more difficult challenge of eliminating habits that do not serve you. These include all those behavior patterns that you perform mechanically and unconsciously and that keep you deadened to the greater web of power around you.

Heyokas are Native American shamans whose job it is to keep the people from becoming too entrenched in their set ways. They do everything backward and upside down just to show that nothing has to be done a set way. They dry themselves with water and wash themselves with dirt. They walk backward, sit when others would normally stand, stand when others would sit, cry when they are happy and laugh when they are sad. This destroys the habits and patterns that keep them and others asleep. Secondarily, they make people laugh, a process that in itself breaks up old patterns and set ways.

Exercise #4: The Heyoka's Way with Habits

Try being a Heyoka to yourself for just a couple of hours and you will learn a lot about your patterns. This is best done when you have some private uninterrupted time. You will need to go slowly to get used to the unfamiliar approach of doing everything backwards. You will find that with a little thought, you'll see new possibilities of reversals that surprise you. For example, take your shoes off to walk around and try eating your meal in the reverse order. Walk backwards through the house or yard. Practice saying out loud what you don't mean. This is great fun with a friend or housemate that agrees to do it with you. The possibilities are endless and the process can be enormously funny. On the other hand, you may find some of your actions or sayings sobering when you discover that your reversal is more true than what you usually say or do.

Realize that set patterns and habits are convenient structures set up to make life easier and more comfortable. For example, if you have formed the habit of avoiding grapefruit because it upsets your stomach, you have probably saved yourself a lot of stomachaches. On the other hand, you have made your world a little smaller with that belief. It may be that grapefruit once made your stomach upset but now, due to a change in your metabolism, it no longer does. From a shamanic perspective, it is a good idea to adopt a questioning attitude about any pattern or set way that is done just because it has always been done that way. If you find true value in the pattern, you can continue with it more consciously. If not, try substituting a creative approach and see what you experience.

If you look closely at your habits, you will find that many of them are no different from primitive superstitions that you probably laugh at. Superstitions tend to close off life experience to you and prevent the risk of novelty.

The first step toward eliminating any habit is simply being able to tell the truth about it to yourself. Just admitting that it is a habit can be confronting. In this simple exercise, you can take a first step toward recognizing your habit patterns.

Exercise #5: Recognizing Habit Patterns

Make a list of habitual actions that tend to keep you more asleep than awake. Become aware of these habitual patterns and watch yourself each time you do one of them. Do not judge yourself for your habit; rather, find the humor in it. If you are unable to laugh, you will find the habit harder to break. As we mentioned before, laughing tends to break up patterns and shifts your perspective, enabling you to dissolve habitual behavior.

Next, examine the pattern or habit in detail. Pay attention to exactly how you do it or when you do it. If you smoke, notice when you feel the urge to smoke. When do you actually pull a cigarette out and light it? How do you smoke it? What does each puff taste like, smell like, etc.? Become conscious of the entire process. Apply this dissection to any behavior pattern that has become a habit, whether it is the way you eat your meals or the way you avoid asking directions when you are lost.

Without trying too hard, see what alternative actions are available to you. Try them out. For example, if you are in the habit of walking the same way to work each day, try a different route even if the difference is slight.

Here is a sample list of habitual behaviors you may want to change:

- Traveling the same route to work, school, shopping, etc.
- Eating the same foods for breakfast day after day.
- Getting up or going to bed at the same time each night.
- Wearing the same clothes day after day.
- Using the same figures of speech or phrases.

- Clearing your throat or nose.
- Drinking every night.
- Smoking.
- Going to the same eating places or stores regularly.
- Going out with the same people all the time.
- Reading the paper every day.
- Seeing the world from the same perspective, skeptically, cynically, idealistically.
- Watching television. Watching the same programs.
- Avoiding being alone.
- Avoiding people in general.
- Avoiding old people, children, disabled people.

Exercise #5: The Steps

1. Make a list of your habitual actions.
2. Watch and notice each time you perform one of them.
3. Find the humor rather than judge yourself.
4. Examine the pattern in detail.
5. Identify alternative actions. Try them out.

APPROPRIATE DESTRUCTION: RELATIONSHIPS

Your relationships can be the most difficult aspect of your life to sort through. Shamanically speaking, they also have the capacity to deaden you the most because they support and reinforce old patterns that keep you stuck. Unlike beliefs or habits that you can erase or transform, you cannot necessarily change other people. Socially speaking, what they think and feel about you matters a great deal. Therefore the people you surround yourself with are vitally important for your well-being, growth, and personal satisfaction.

Just like your closet full of old clothes or you bag full of old beliefs, you can carry a number of relationships around with you that no longer serve you and perhaps never did. These are relationships maintained out of habit and in some cases a false sense of duty.

From the shamanic point of view, your relationships are

highly influential in determining your store of power. Relationships have a way of either enhancing and contributing to your power by supporting who you are or draining your power by subtly undermining and attacking you. Remember again, that for a shaman thoughts are actual forms and the way people hold you in their esteem directly affects your well-being. Jealousy, envy, and ill will can be a real attack on your power base. Recall the effect of your own thoughts and feelings on the spirit body and you will get a sense of the effect relationships can have on you.

Shamans do not cultivate relationships that undercut their personal power. This does not mean they avoid constructive criticism or the natural emotions that come up during a disagreement or quarrel. It means they do not continue relationships that regularly drain their resources and attack their goals in life. Following their example could be beneficial, although it may mean looking pretty hard at some relationships that you have put up with out of convenience or guilt. If you have trouble with this, just ask yourself, "Do I want to be a powerful and effective person in my life, or do I just want to avoid guilt?"

Exercise #6: Relationships

By now, you have a pretty good idea of what to do. Follow the pattern of the exercises above.

Your challenge is to make a list of your relationships and judge which ones are worth keeping because they truly offer you something and which ones deserve to be dissolved. The ones worth keeping shine like a bright light. The ones that you have to think about and argue with yourself about are the ones that perhaps should be let go. How many relationships do you keep alive simply because you are afraid of what that person would say or would think if you no longer showed interest?

To start with, you can list the positives and the negatives of each relationship. Inspect the balance sheet. Do the negatives far outweigh the positives? If so, you will have to decide whether the relationship is worth keeping. If you decide that you would rather keep it, list what you must do to revise the balance sheet. You may find that you must talk with that person about certain imbalances in your relationship. If you decide that no amount of talking or shifting will help, then perhaps it is time to let that relationship go. The exception here could be a very difficult relationship that you have elected to take on as a good deed or as a challenge for your own growth. For example, you may wish to continue caring for an invalid, an elderly person, or difficult child because, although they give you little in return but difficulty, you have consciously chosen to help them as a challenge. It is important to know your limits, however.

Exercise #6: The Steps

1. Make a list of your relationships.
2. Check the ones that raise doubt in your mind.
3. List positive and negative features.
4. Inspect balance sheet.
5. Choose your course of action.

CREATION

You have seen from the shamanic perspective how important destruction is to the ongoing flow of life and how essential it is to your becoming more powerful and successful as a human being. We are now going to shift to its apparently opposite pole, creation. When you clear and open the space through destruction, you prepare the canvas for the shaman's forte, creativity.

If you clean up a room or a closet, there is the natural tendency for it gradually to become messy and cluttered again with items very similar to those that cluttered it the first time. Try to keep a closet neat, sparse, and up-to-date for any length of time, and you will find out what a difficult task it is. The creative principle in the universe is so strong that vacuums are instantly filled with more somethings. These somethings are usually just the same as what was there before. In nature, when a lake dries up in the heat of summer, it tends to fill up with more water when the rains come. Year after year, the lake fills up with more water unless something different is introduced.

Similarly, you will notice that the spirit world fills your life up with the same old things that you get rid of time after time—unless you introduce something new. If you passively expect your life to fill up from the outside, then you can expect more of the same. However, if you want something new, you will have to give the spirit world new instructions or directions. You have to get the spirit world to notice that you are now ready for something new and different.

Shamans know that if they are to manifest power, they must be co-creators with the web of power. They must exercise their own creativity and help create the order that makes life meaningful. So they have learned to give the spirit world suggestions concerning what they would like to have happen. You might say they help the spirit world along.

Shamanically speaking, you need to give the spirit world very specific instructions about what you are looking for, because you will receive exactly what you ask for. Let's take a simple example. Let's say you drive a car that often breaks down and has difficulty starting. If you get tired of this and say, "I want a different car," chances are that every car you get will end up having the same starting problem and will tend to break down. You have given no specific instructions for what you want or can have. You simply indicated that you wanted a change, not what kind of a change. So you get a different car with the same problems. Until you specify exactly the type of car you want to drive, the specific features and price range, you will be unlikely to get what you want.

Sometimes, if you are not specific and realistic, you will get what you thought you wanted, only to realize that it is not truly what you wished for in your heart.

What you get, of course, has to do with what you believe you are capable of having or what you believe is possible. You may recall the story about the shaman and the two men looking for mules in Chapter 1. Because one man could envision more mules than the other man, he was directed by the shaman to find more than the other.

Jerry had women problems. It was not that there was any shortage of women in his life; it was the kind of women he attracted. Every woman Jerry got involved with seemed to be addicted to something: pills, alcohol, cocaine, chocolate, you name it. The result always turned out the same. He became the rescuer and they turned more and more to their addiction. Eventually he gave up and tried another relationship.

Jerry even tried visualization techniques in which he imagined having many women in his life to choose from. Sure enough, he seemed to meet women everywhere but the end results were similar. He worked hard in psychotherapy trying to get to the bottom of this pattern. Although he understood intellectually why the pattern existed, he could not seem to break it.

Then one night Jerry had a dream. He dreamt about a witch who was groping for him and tearing at his clothes. He screamed and tried to get away. Then the witch turned into his mother. Horrified, he gave a tremendous shove and broke away in a panic. In the dream, he ran out into a field and there saw a row of withered sunflowers. Each was in a different stage of withering. When he touched them, they crumbled and turned to dust. Unexpectedly, a small brilliant green bird appeared, beckoning him. He turned to follow the bird and saw for the first time a row of rosebushes each with roses in a different stage of bloom. He went up to the one with roses in full bloom, reached out, and the dream ended.

When Jerry awoke, the solution to his dilemma was clear. He had somehow known all along that each addicted woman was just another version of his alcoholic mother. He didn't want that kind of relationship anymore. Up till now, Jerry had not understood or believed that there were any other choices for him but wilted sunflowers. He had never bothered to define exactly what kind of relationship he was looking for. Knowing now that alternatives truly existed, he set about defining what he was looking for in a woman. Within four months, the pattern ended. Jerry found a healthy woman who liked him and they were becoming close.

Exercise #7: Creating

Creating is the most wonderful, magical, mysterious ability known to human beings. And yet, it is phenomenally easy to do. Creating happens first in your imagination. The clearer and more specific your picture, the more likely you will actualize your creation. This exercise is meant to illustrate the simplicity of the creation process.

Close your eyes and relax. Imagine that three feet in front of you is a large screen onto which you can project anything you want. Project onto that screen a beautiful flower. Color it any way you wish. Give it a stem with leaves and dew-

---

Exercise #7: The Steps

1. Close your eyes and relax.
2. Create projection screen.
3. Create flower on screen.
4. Transform the flower's size and color a number of times.
5. See the flower bud, bloom, and wilt.
6. Re-create flower in bloom and give it to a loved one.

drops. Give it a smell and a texture. Now change its size. Make it very large. Make it very small. Change its color several times. See it in its bud stage. Watch it grow and bloom and then see it wilt and fall apart. Re-create it again in full bloom. Imagine giving it to a loved one. See the smile on their face as you give it to them. You have just executed a series of powerful creations. Shamanically speaking, you have just given an actual gift to your loved one. They will respond to your creation. All creation is that simple.

CREATING WITH THE HELP OF GUARDIAN SPIRITS

One of the keys, in the world of shamanism, to getting what you need is communicating as clearly as possible to your power animal or guardian spirit exactly what you want. They are, of course, the power brokers who pull strings in the spirit world to get results. However, keep in mind that when you deal with them as agents, you lose a bit of your control. You cannot make demands on or bully them and expect results. In communicating with them, take a humble position and make a request for their assistance. Also, it is best if you state that you will accept whatever is most beneficial for you at this time. The truth is that you can't see the big picture as well as your guardian spirits can. They may know that the new convertible sports car you want will kill you prematurely before your life's work is done. So they will arrange for the next best thing. You get what you need, not necessarily everything you want.

When you ask your guardian spirits to help you get things, you need to give up your control of the time frame as well. Perhaps you want that new position that is opening up in your company and you want it within two weeks. When you ask your guardian spirits to help you, they may be able to see that next month a much better position is opening up and it would benefit you more to skip this one and go for the next one. The reason you asked for their help in the first place is because of this access to the big picture of the spirit world. You can rely on it.

You may wish to ask your guardian spirit to show you the big picture scheme so that you can understand better why you are not getting what you want when you want it. This can be fruitful. Yet don't be surprised if this information is withheld from you either. Your guardian spirits know how tricky you are. They may see that showing you the big picture is interfering with your free choice and creativity. Here you must let go and trust that your guardian spirits know best how to handle the situation. They never work against your higher interests.

Your guardian spirits are capable of offering you much assistance, but they cannot override your basic belief systems. They cannot help you get or provide more than you are capable of having at any one time. What you can have is entirely based on how much power you have stored and how much power you are capable of handling in a variety of spheres. For example, you may be powerful in the realm of relationships but not so in the realm of financial matters. So your guardian spirits have more freedom in helping you with relationships than with finances, since you are capable of having more in that arena. They can help you only up to your capacity. Therefore, remember that your guardian spirits don't do the basic work for you. They help you most after you have already shown some growth or promise in a life area.

Exercise #8: How Much Can You Have?

The following is a process for helping you get in touch with your level or ability to have.

Begin by relaxing and closing your eyes. Imagine that before you is a landscape that reflects how much happiness and satisfaction you can have in your life at this time. Let happiness and satisfaction be represented by a clear blue sky (or any other image that works for you) while anything less than that is represented by dust clouds and soot in the air. You may wish to add a gauge at one side that gives you the actual percentage of clear sky that you can have. What percentage of clear blue sky can you see? Fifty percent or less? More?

Let the gauge drop all the way down and let the sky become black with soot. How does this feel?

Determine to increase the clear blue sky with an act of concentration. If you can get the sky to become clearer and the gauge to rise, notice the feeling in your body. It is not uncommon for people to feel uncomfortable and anxious as they expand their ability to have more. Now let the sky and the gauge return to the norm.

You can repeat this exercise, focusing on any aspect of your life that you want to check on. You may be happy with your relationships with people but unhappy about your state of health. Or you may be happy with your health but unhappy about your relationship with money or your bodily appearance.

Exercise #8: The Steps

1. Close your eyes and relax.
2. Invision an open sky. Create a gauge for clearness.
3. Dirty up that sky. Cloud it over with smoke.
4. Let the sky clear. How clear can you let it be?
5. Check gauge.
6. Check into your feelings of comfort or discomfort.
7. Let sky and gauge return to norm (where you are comfortable).

When you wish to increase your power in any sphere of life, it is best to proceed slowly and in small increments or you will cause yourself anxiety, confusion, and discomfort.

BALANCE AND IMBALANCE

Most people feel they are lacking or burdened in at least one of these seven main categories:

- Money
- Possessions
- Health
- Bodily appearance and attractiveness
- Relationships
- Sex
- Time

Few people feel they have complete satisfaction in every one of these areas. Most people's lives are filled up with what they don't want in each category, rather than what they do want. For many, problems come with having either too little or too much of each category.

For example:

1. There is too little money, causing feelings of hunger or deprivation. Or there is too much money, and managing it becomes an exhausting full-time operation that destroys the pleasure in life.

2. Life is cluttered with too many possessions and the spirit is spread thin keeping track of them all. Or there are too few, causing a feeling of scarcity.

3. Health conditions are unwanted—such as colds, flus, diseases, and allergic symptoms. Although you can't have too much health, you can feel that being in good health is just too good to have on a regular basis.

4. One or several main bodily parts detract from appearance: nose too big, teeth crooked or stained; body too tall, too short, too fat, too thin; skin too dark or light, hair too straight or kinky, feet too big, hands chubby, hips too large, stomach paunchy, ears stick out, no neck, eyes too small, and so on.

5. Relationships are too sparse and there is loneliness and depression. Or there are too many relationships that cause unhappiness.

6. Sex life is either unsatisfactorily out of control, or on hold with droughtlike conditions.

7. There is an abundance of time, causing restlessness or boredom. There is a scarcity of time, causing impatience and anxiety.

Shamanically speaking, too much or too little in any category is a state of imbalance; it signals being in a state of disharmony with the web of power and the natural order of things. However, keep in mind that having too much or too little in any category is a state of mind, not something based on any objective criteria. For example, one person can have ten relationships and feel perfectly happy with this amount. Another person may feel that ten is much too many and wish to reduce that amount to five. Still a third person may feel deprived with only ten relationships.

The way you feel about what you have or don't have is the criteria for balance or imbalance.

Exercise #9: Finding Balance

Under each category described above, make three lists. On one list, write all the ways that you feel deprived under that category. On the next list, write all the ways that you feel troubled by too much in that category. On the third list, write the ways that you feel in complete balance under that category.

Look over your lists and determine where you feel most balanced in your life and where you feel least balanced. The categories that have longer lists of "too much" and "too little" are the areas of your life where shamans would say you have lost power. You will recognize where you need to focus in order to gain back power and control over your own destiny. These are the areas that keep you from being successful and satisfied.

The lists of "too much" in any category can be handled by the exercises that we gave you earlier for divesting yourself of excess. This would fall under the destruction or discrimination theme. The lists of "too little" under any category can be handled by using the creation exercise that we will discuss shortly.

Whether you have trouble with too much or too little in any arena, by all means ask your guardian spirits and power animals to help you. You are already familiar with the journey method, one of the most powerful shamanic techniques to help you achieve your state of balance.

Follow the usual method of beginning the shamanic journey. When you have met our power animal or guardian spirit, tell them that you are having trouble with having too much or too little of x. Tell them you want some information that will help you resolve the problem. Follow their lead for the rest of the journey.

Exercise #9: The Steps

1. Make three lists: a. deprivation; b. excess; c. balance.
2. Inspect lists for length.
3. Plot course of action.
4. Ask guardian spirits for help.
5. Journey.

Bob Anderson seemed to have a continual problem with money. No matter how much he brought in every month, to him there never seemed to be enough. And yet realistically speaking there was enough. He had ample savings and good investments but he just couldn't kick the feeling that he didn't have enough for his family. Bob, his wife Mary, and their boys worked hard at their construction business, but even though their business was up by 30 percent this year, Bob insisted that they work overtime just to make sure. Despite all the hard work, Bob would not stop worrying. He even thought of taking a second job to get ahead. Mary Anderson was a long-time student of shamanism but somehow she had not felt bold enough to teach her husband how to get help with his money worries. One evening as they were discussing their situation Mary worked up the courage to tell him about shamanism. She was rather amazed at his willingness to hear more about it.

Apparently her timing was perfect. She explained how he could rely on an ally to help him with any problem. She said it might help if he took a shamanic journey, using his fears of economic poverty as a focus. After explaining the method, Mary had Bob relax and get comfortable in a darkened room. She gave him her drumming tape to assist him with focus and intensity.

As he approached the entrance to the cave Bob was immediately greeted by a silver-coated timber wolf. He told the wolf his problem and his wolf guide said to him, "Come and I'll show you." With that, Bob grabbed his tail and hung on as they flew down a passageway and then through a series of side branches until they emerged on a hillside above a small valley. It was late evening and almost dark. Below in a clearing a large fire danced, and in its light Bob saw dancers leaping about. They looked free and unfettered and he longed to go down and dance with them, but somehow he could not move. Looking down, he realized that he was burdened by heavy chains that hung all about his shoulders and around his waist down to the ground. He could not join the dancers because of the weight of the chains. Bob knew that the chains that held him were the same as the financial worries that burdened him back in ordinary reality. He asked the wolf how to unfetter himself and was shocked when the wolf showed up in Bermuda shorts, and carrying an air mattress, which he proceeded to lie down on, and then read a book.

He could see that the title of the book was *Vacations by the Sea.* At first Bob was confused, but then a light began to dawn. He had wanted a coast vacation for years, but had never allowed himself to go. He always disappointed his family by saying that they had too much work to do and couldn't afford it anyway.

The wolf sprang up and said, "Very good, you're beginning to get it." He then turned into the spitting image of Bob's deceased father, complete with his overalls and toolbox. His father spoke: "Sorry, Bob, I can't let you go to camp, you know. We're not like those rich folks who can just send their kids off to camp every year. Besides, I need you here to help me this summer." Bob felt a great turmoil growing in his heart. In a few short moments he felt rage well up inside of him and then intense sadness. He began to sob and in his sadness he felt sorry both for himself and then for his father, who was never able to get out of his own financial bind. Then the wolf was back, smoking a large cigar, wearing a tall silk hat, and an expensive-looking old-fashioned watch and chain. "Well, my boy, sounds like you have a bit of catching up to do. Are you going to live with what is, or are you going to keep thinking that it's forty years ago, huh?" Bob smiled through his still tearstained face. Then he looked down and noticed the chains had disappeared. He felt a great sense of relief and ran down to join the dancers around the fire.

After he returned to the cave entrance, the wolf handed him a gift. "Here is a gold ring with pyramorphite inlay. Whenever you start thinking scarcity, remember the ring on your finger and it will remind you of your journey. Then you will have a choice, rather than acting out of habit. Now, get your family to the coast. They deserve it after putting up with you all this time." Bob laughed and thanked the wolf. When he opened his eyes he felt for the gold ring on his finger. Even though he couldn't see anything there to touch, he knew it was there. Again he began to laugh.

THE INFINITE POTENTIAL OF THE SPIRIT WORLD

The idea of letting go of material goods, beliefs, habits, and relationships can raise the fear that if you let go of what you have, you will be left with nothing. This is a nonshamanic belief in scarcity within nature. For shamans, nothing could be more laughable. Nothing is further from the truth. The one thing that you can be assured of is the continual abundance of everything in nature. Shamans believe that the invisible web of power is infinite in its potential. From the world of spirit all physical forms are supported and infused with life energy. From this infinite source of power there is no limitation. Nature reflects the abundance of the spirit world in its own bountiful expression. Trees and plants distribute seedlings by the billions and take every opportunity to spread and grow wherever they can. Millions of species have developed over eons and have distributed themselves over every part of the earth. When undisturbed by people, animals proliferate and thrive in every kind of environment. There are ample water, air, and raw materials to live in harmony and peace for as long as humans need them.

To the shaman's way of thinking, only two things cause scarcity and imbalance. The first is the limitations within a person's own imagination. If you believe there is limitation, there is. The second cause of scarcity is a person's own greed and selfishness generated by fear (the lack of power). When people act from these imbalanced perspectives, they perpetrate acts of violence toward their own environment and support systems. This upsets the natural balance maintained by the dynamic tension between the ordinary world (tonal) and the spirit world (nagual). The result is incredible pain and suffering in the ordinary world and general alienation from the spirit world. People especially suffer because they have cut off the flow of power that comes from the spirit world into the ordinary world. Without power, they suffer from disease, depression, anxiety, and helplessness.

From the shamanic perspective power flows mainly one way, from the spirit world into the ordinary world. Therefore, when people interfere with the flow of that power, only the ordinary world suffers. The spirit world cannot be harmed, only frustrated in its attempts to provide for and support the ordinary world.

CREATING BALANCE: THE GIVEAWAY

For shamans, the spirit world is a great benefactor providing them with everything they need. As you have seen, the spirits of all the elements, plants, animals, and ancestors can be requested to provide assistance, information, healing, and advice. During shamanic journeys, shamans are often given talismans for protection and other gifts that offer a wide variety of benefits. The spirit world provides all of these benefits and gifts without charge to those who have earned them through discipline and dedication. If the gifts are misused through greed or violence toward others, however, they may be withdrawn.

Native American shamans have spoken of this generosity as the "giveaway" and have tried to emulate the spirit world by initiating their own giveaway rituals. Occasionally, a family would give away every shred of their possessions to the other families in the tribe. In the morning after the giveaway, they would find piled up before them heaps of new skins, moccasins, robes, and everything needed for living. By giving away what they had, they reaped even greater rewards.

From the shamanic perspective, giving away always begets increase in the form of power. Native Americans take their example from the spirit world. When the spirit world gives, it benefits by becoming even more powerful. So the rule here is that the more you are able to give, the more powerful you will become. It does not matter that you are able to give only a little bit to start with. Each offering increases your power little by little until you have a large enough store to make significant changes in the world.

In general, shamans do not charge for their services but are pleased to get a donation as a kind of exchange from those who can afford to do so. Now, the truth of the matter is that shamans are often rather well-off members of their communities who never go hungry for lack of means. They are usually repaid handsomely for their many services in the form of livestock, grain, clothing, and utensils. Historically they have lived in societies whose economy supports this form of exchange.

The challenge for people today is learning how to apply this principle of giveaway in a modern nonshamanic culture that does not operate from these rules. This means understanding and operating according to the spirit of giveaway and not necessarily according to the typical ways shamans have practiced it.

First of all, giveaway does not just apply to material things, but to many other qualities of life. When you give away your love, you increase love returned to you. When you give away your time, people make time for you. When you give away your attention, you gain the attention of others. When you delegate authority, you become a greater leader.

When it comes to money or possessions, in our culture it is not a good practice to give away more than your means, because the economy will not support you if you do. Therefore a good rule of thumb is to give "some" money or goods away that you can afford to give away on a regular basis. This should feel good to you and not cause you great discomfort or fear. It is good, however, to stretch a bit in order to increase your capacity for giving things away. If you do, following the example of the spirit world, you will always increase your supply of money or possessions.

RECEIVING

Just because you develop the capacity to give does not mean that you are good at the balancing end, receiving. Shamanically speaking, in order to keep the balance in nature, you need to be as good a receiver as you are the initiator of giving. Nothing in nature gives endlessly on one end without receiving on the other end. A lake has an inlet whether it be springfed or filled by a stream, and an outlet through a stream or evaporation. Cut off the source and the lake dries up. Fruit trees bear in relation to the amount of sunlight, water, and soil nourishment they receive. When the tree is not capable of receiving these anymore, whether by age or disease, its ability to bear ceases.

Human beings are peculiar in the animal kingdom because they are the only ones who think they can exist autonomously or in isolation from the rest of the community. They think they can cut off their supplies of nourishment either from the natural environment by contaminating their drinking water and air or by shutting out the love and support that comes from their fellow humans. They even believe that they can shut out the resources of the spirit world and expect to make a go of it.

Similarly, humans are the only ones who cut off the outside resources via self-imposed punishment. Because they feel they are not worthy of love, relationships, health, money, or material goods, they refuse to admit these resources into their lives even when they are given freely by others. From a shamanic point of view, nothing could be more insulting or desecrating than to refuse a gift offered unconditionally by the spirit world or by any of the creatures in ordinary reality. To turn down the gift of love or anything else creates a condition of severe imbalance that leads to more suffering and unnecessary wounding.

A wealthy American, traveling in Portugal, hired a taxi driver to take him to an isolated monastery. During the long drive they swapped stories and got to know one another. The taxi driver said that it would be a great honor for him and his family if the man would consent to go to dinner at his house. The traveler agreed and several days later, upon returning from the monastery, he arrived at the taxi driver's very humble abode and saw that his family was very poor. He knew that the feast would be expensive for the family, perhaps even a month's wages or more. He insisted upon taking the taxi driver's family out to dinner. The driver's feelings were crushed and the dinner out was an awkward uncomfortable affair. They did not part on the best of terms.

Only much later, in retrospect, did the wealthy American realize his egregious error. He had refused a gift of the heart and mistakenly placed the emphasis on a misguided consideration about means. He robbed the taxi driver of an opportunity to increase his wealth and his power by preparing a feast for a traveler that he liked.

Therefore, to increase your power and effectiveness—the shaman's proverbial goal—you must develop the capacity to receive with grace and humility. Never refuse a freely given gift, no matter how lowly or how opulent. When you receive another's gift, you honor them and you reinforce the harmony and balance between the spirit world and the ordinary world. Of course, you must be able to distinguish between a true gift and a bribe. Bribes are not gifts but an attempt to control you or buy you out. They have hidden or obvious strings attached and are conditional in nature. For example, an apparent gift of money or property can be a bribe for your "good behavior." Bribes need not be accepted because they are not given to you unconditionally.

To refuse a gift because you cannot pay the person back in kind is to miss the point. When the spirit world offers you a gift of talent or free advice on a matter, it does not expect repayment in kind. The spirit world expects you to use that talent or that advice for the benefit of yourself and others. That benefit spreads from person to person, creating more power, making the spirit world more powerful in the long run. In this manner, the spirit world keeps the ordinary world in balance. If someone offers you a free service or a gift of money and you refuse to accept it, you effectively stop this flow of power through you. You create disharmony.

The other important consideration about receiving is the style in which you receive. From a shamanic perspective, everything in your life is a gift—whether it is the food you eat, the clothes you wear, or the children you have been given to raise and care for. Taking gifts for granted or believing that you are totally responsible for their creation is a form of arrogance that ultimately reduces power. Minerals, plants, and animals deserve special thanks for their many gifts in the form of furniture, jewelry, building materials, foods, clothing and many of the articles we rely on for everyday living. Mealtimes are especially important times to remember the favors bestowed by the plants and animals for our benefit. Offering thanks ensures their continued support and enlists their help in times of need.

If you accept any gift with thanks and then simply store it without using it, you are reducing the flow of power. Love, money, and possessions have no power as long as they are dammed up or stored somewhere. It is their use that gives them power.

We know of a child who received the gift of a new red wagon for his birthday. He squirreled the box, fully wrapped, into a closet and refused to play with it, saying that it was too nice too open. He wanted to save it for later. All the other children were disappointed because they could not ride in the new wagon. That box stayed there for years. Eventually the boy became too old to play with the wagon and it was given away to someone else. The boy grew up to have problems with relationships and money. From a very young age he operated out of the belief that he couldn't have what was given to him.

This brings us full circle back to giving again. So you see that both giving and receiving are integral parts of a never-ending shamanic power circle that generates ever greater supplies of power for use in the ordinary world.

Now you have been exposed to the basic shamanic notion of the ever-balancing cycles of creation and destruction. When you know their basic principles, you are in a good position to:

- Clear your life of unwanted beliefs, goods, habits, and people.

- Know where you can find assistance when faced with obstacles that seem more powerful than you.

- Decrease arrogance, false humility, and guilt, and be able to have more of what you want in your life by defining it in clear specific terms.

- Increase your ability to have more real power and energy.

- Understand how to increase your own capacity for satisfaction in any area of your life by giving away or sharing the wealth in that area.

- Learn how to receive with grace and respect.

- Be in the position to make a much greater contribution in life.

CHAPTER 7

Shamans and Opportunity: Goals, Problem Solving, and Success

"What's he honking about?" Annoyed, Larry looked back at the driver behind him, honking and pointing wildly at the roof of Larry's car. "Oh my gosh! My tennis racket!" Larry pulled over to check the top of his Honda for what he already knew with a sinking feeling was no longer there. "How could I have been so stupid to leave my tennis racket on top of the car?" A tear welled up as he started to feel sorry for himself. Despite all the work he was doing on his goals and his ability to have, the Universe was just not on his side lately. Then Larry remembered a phrase from the goal-setting class he was taking—"Things aren't always what they seem." The big picture? he asked himself silently as he drove the rest of the way home. What *is* the big picture? The next day Larry went to the sports shop to buy the racket he had always wanted but never felt he could afford.

For many of us, life seems to be a series of situations we feel we must live through to get where we want to go. It is riddled with hardship and effort, and obstacles await us at every turn. A popular bumper sticker reads: "Life is hard and then you die." Unfortunately, this is the attitude that many of us have about life and its challenges. And yet those very same challenges are what make life interesting; it is the potential for success, for making it in the world, that keeps people writing New Year's resolutions and setting goals. The shamanic perspective on goal setting, problem solving, and personal change can bring a sense of balance and flow into these areas and make the outcome of your efforts more powerful.

Shamans regard goal setting differently from the average

130

person. They sense the difference between the goals desired by the physical self and those chosen by the spirit self. The goal of the physical self might be to buy a case of cheap wine, hide out, and consume it as quickly as possible. The goal of the spirit self on the other hand might be to refrain from such activity and develop skills in communication with others instead. Shamans have learned to distinguish between the two sets of goals. They know that when you align your sets of goals, you become balanced and conflict-free. In a word, you become powerful and nothing can stop you from reaching your goal. When the goals of your physical self and your spirit self are antagonistic, you experience stress, frustration, and you suffer from a lack of success in achieving your goals.

When we talk about setting and attaining goals in a shamanic sense, we also need to talk about problem solving, for you cannot accomplish one without first dealing with the other. If you always wake up at 7:00 A.M., for example, then waking up at 7:00 A.M. is not a goal to reach, but rather simply the status quo. But suppose you wanted to begin an exercise class that started at 6:30 A.M.? Waking up in time to get to your class would then become a goal, because it is something you want to accomplish that you are not doing now. To get to your goal of waking up at 6:00 A.M., you will have to change a well-worn habit of getting up at a later hour. Perhaps you even need to work on a belief system that dictates that such a change is impossible, e.g., "I am a late riser. I've never been able to get up early. I can't do it." So, you might say you have a problem that needs solving before you can reach your goal. Therefore, the moment you set a goal up for yourself, you identify the obstacles to reaching that goal. The next logical step is shamanic problem solving, an approach that in its broadest sense is a set of techniques used to change a situation from an undesired one to a desired one.

So far we have given you information about a variety of concepts that are prerequisites to setting goals and finding solutions to problems. We've talked about the spirit body and its uses; we've talked about presence and shamanic times; we've discussed the journey and spirit helpers or guides; we've explained the importance of surrender and how being too identified with your problem can be a block; we've told you about the abundance in nature, the concept of creating and destroying, and the principles of giving and receiving. And, last but not least, we've taught you the importance of shamanic visioning and given you techniques for enriching those visions. All of these concepts play an important role in successful goal setting and problem solving, as you will discover in this chapter.

The shamanic perspective on setting and achieving goals is based largely on the big picture. Shamans believe that unless a goal is in harmony with your true desires and what the spirit self believes is appropriate, then it probably will not manifest. You can endlessly visualize yourself getting that new position. And if you get it, it is in harmony with your inner self no matter how short or long a time it took to manifest. On the other hand, if the position is not in the interest of your spirit self, it probably will not manifest despite your efforts. From a shaman's point of view, no matter how hard your physical self tries to make something happen, it won't work unless it fits into the larger scheme of things.

This perspective is somewhat different from the one that teaches that any goal you happen to dream up should be attainable if you work hard enough and play your cards right. The "work hard and you'll get it" perspective is certainly an optimistic way of thinking, but it leads ultimately to feelings of failure about your inability to create what you want in life. In the shamanic outlook, failure of this type does not exist. For if you should fail to reach a goal that was never chosen by your spirit self, you are merely succeeding at staying on your truly desired course.

The shamanic method then deemphasizes undue effort, and focuses more on harmony and balance. If your goal is in harmony with your spirit self and with the rest of your environment, then it should come about easily with only the natural effort you would put into something you were truly excited about. We should caution you here that the "effort" it takes and the "time" it takes are separate issues; a goal may take a long time or a short time to manifest, depending on what is appropriate. This "timing" should not necessitate any more or less effort on your part.

Shamans also believe in getting their spirit helpers to help direct their goal setting through journeys and other visioning techniques. The goal is set the same way a good decision is made, after knowing all the facts. To return to our example, the goal of getting up at 6:00 A.M. to exercise is backed by inner information that this is indeed what the physical body wants and even needs; the enthusiasm is there, and the task becomes almost effortless.

For many of us, goal setting is a mundane and boring pastime, often conducted in relation to our business activities or personal agendas. Some of our goals might include such items as "I will clean the top of my desk off each night before I go home," or "I will eat only salad for lunch for two weeks in order to lose weight," or even "I will earn x dollars this year." Where is the fun, the excitement, the emotion?

Shamanically speaking, if your heart or your true desire is not involved in your goal, your success will be greatly diminished. For goals to be achievable, they must be realistic; and second, they must be something you really want to accomplish. For example, are you clearing your desk of papers every night so that the boss will pat you on the back (you know he or she hates messy desks) or because you feel a great sense of satisfaction and well-being when you see your desk clean at the beginning of a workday? If your cleaning attempt is to please your boss, your goal is ultimately doomed to failure. Perhaps you should focus on building a better relationship with your boss and how good that would feel. Maybe that goal would lead you to a different task altogether, like taking her or him to lunch at your favorite restaurant. That would be fun for you too. On the other hand, if cleaning your desk is for self-satisfaction, you are more likely to succeed only if you focus on the desired result. When you are setting that goal, you need to focus on how great you will feel the next day, not on the menial task itself.

It may be that your goal is actually a stepping-stone or a baby step toward a much larger wish. If so, the larger picture or wish is what you must keep in mind when you are setting that goal. For example, you want to increase your income for the purpose of buying a new house that will provide a better environment for you and thus support your well-being. It is the house and that feeling of well-being that should be envisioned in your process. Since money itself is just the means and not the actual motivator, it is the feelings themselves that fuel the desire and thus help produce the goal.

DETACHMENT

An aspect of goal setting important to its success is the concept of detachment or surrender. If you are emotionally too attached to your goal, it is likely that you will never achieve it. Have you ever noticed that the people who are really desperate for a relationship seldom find a satisfactory one? In our experience, it is always the people whose attention is elsewhere at the time who find the person they are looking for. Focusing your attention strongly and unceasingly toward your goal will, shamanically speaking, keep it earthbound or root-bound. Shamans know that birds cannot fly unless they are free to do so; likewise, the spirit must be free to journey in order to bring back needed information. And at the same time, the spirit world must be free to give or not to give as it sees fit. When you demand that the order of things be a particular and exact way to suit your goals, without allowing any flexibility, you are attached in such a way as to create an imbalance that leads to a loss of power. When you lose power you diminish your success.

What is required is a letting-go of expectations. To be successful you need to first set a goal and be as specific as you can describing it. Paradoxically, you then need to let go completely of your picture about both the specifics of your goal and how that goal is to be achieved. You need to state your goal, but then surrender to the higher forces of nature and your spirit self. This concept of surrender is also important in bringing possessions and experiences into your life.

Lena and I and our two children camped in the desert region of Southern California where the mountains are rich in minerals and mining is still very much alive. As the family walked up a steep canyon one late afternoon, Lena looked down and amidst the colorful desert rock she spotted a small piece of quartz, not a clear crystal, but quartz nevertheless. She gave this whitish iridescent rock to her son Carlos, five, who was standing next to her. Anna, the seven-year-old, very quickly decided that she also ought to have a piece of quartz and asked her mother to look for another one. "I'll certainly try but I can't guarantee anything," responded Lena to the somewhat demanding plea from her daughter. "You know, the one I found was probably just washed down from the canyon. And besides, it isn't a really clear piece," she added, trying to placate her. Anna, having been raised with the shamanic perspective since she was born, replied, "Well, I'm going to ask the mountain spirit to give me a gift; I would really like it to be a crystal and I don't really care how big it is or even if it's very nice. But I think the mountain spirit will hear me."

The family became silent for a few moments, noticing the deep rich colors of the rock mountain as the setting sun bathed it in its golden light. It was time now to turn back before dusk, so they headed down the ravine, back the way they had come up, being careful to avoid the thorny cacti growing between the rocks.

Suddenly Anna stopped and picked something up by her left foot. It was a beautiful piece of white rock with two perfect little crystals attached. "I forgot all about my crystal," Anna laughed with glee. "And look what I found; look what the mountain gave me." Jose, Lena, and Carlos moved quickly to where Anna was standing. "Do you think there might be more here?" she asked. They all started looking at the ground, stepping very slowly, until lo and behold, Jose looked up into a crevice on the side of the mountain and noticed a quartz vein that was full of crystals! The family spent the last minutes of daylight sifting through the earth and small rocks, laughing and finding crystals of various sizes and shapes. As they headed back, their pockets full of quartz, Anna reminded the others to thank the mountain spirit for its gifts.

This anecdote demonstrates that you need only ask with respect and a complete surrender to how it will be given, and you shall receive gifts from the abundance in nature. These gifts may come in a time frame that is different from what you wish or expect. As we have already mentioned, the balance in nature has its own time, shamanic time, and therefore you need to trust that your goals will be achieved at the appropriate time to maintain that balance. This requires an attitude of surrender and of trust.

KEEPING UP TO DATE

The other all-important principle related to timing is to be absolutely present with your goals. In discussing presence, we pointed out that being present is acting from the point of power. The same applies for goal setting. Not only should you be in the present when you set your goals but it is of utmost importance that you update your goals frequently to reflect your present orientation. Since the world is in a constant state of flux and change, it would stand to reason that your goals should change with your own growth.

As our situations change, so must our goals. The same principle applies with regard to being able to have as much as you can imagine yourself having. You may end up achieving a goal that is greatly outdated according to your present standards. If your goal was to be able to run a mile in eight minutes and now three years later you are still running a mile in eight minutes, then perhaps you have shortchanged yourself. Maybe by now you could be running three miles in twenty-two minutes. Perhaps you always wanted that boy or girl next door to notice you and now years later when he or she does, you have nothing in common because you've both changed so much.

We know a couple that planned to raise a family, a common goal. When they had one child, it was all they could do to keep their heads above water, so to speak, with baby, careers, and all. Their main goal was to finish the tasks each day that were required of them. Now, years later, not only are they raising three children, but juggling their original careers, volunteer work, and further education as well. Their capacity for having and doing has increased over time. If they had kept to their original goals, they would have outgrown them long ago.

How do you know if the goals you have set for yourself are the right ones? How do you know if they are attainable or in harmony with the balance of the universe? For these answers we recommend you ask for help from your guides or spirit helpers. Here is an exercise that incorporates the use of shamanic visioning, journey techniques, communication with your spirit body, and goal setting.

Exercise 1: Goal Setting

Sit down with a sheet of paper and a pen or pencil. Relax. Begin to write down the goals you have for yourself just as they come out of your mind. You can do this either for the years, the month, or the week. We also recommend that at some point you make a list of goals for five years, ten years and so on. This forces you to stretch your imagination about what you might see yourself doing in the future. Be careful though to update those goals frequently or they won't keep up with your growth.

Choose one of your goals. Close your eyes and ask yourself these questions: Is this a realistic goal for me? How do I feel about this goal? Is this goal something I wish with all my heart to accomplish, or is it something someone else wants for me? If so, who is this other person? Wait for the answers to come, either through visual images and symbols or by listening for the response within.

Create a vision of yourself achieving that goal, using all the visioning techniques you've been taught. Make sure to enrich your vision with colors and sensations from nature itself. Make sure that the "you" in the vision is the "you" in the present moment, not an old version of yourself.

Notice how you feel about achieving that goal in the vision. You may want to check in with your spirit body here and see what its reaction is to your image of achieving that goal. Notice any spots that are either energized or de-energized by the experience. Ask your spirit body if it's okay to proceed with your goal. For example, if you wish to lose weight and you have a goal of losing twenty pounds in two months, that may or may not be compatible with your spirit self; you need to find out.

With eyes closed, picture your cave or other opening into the Earth, meet your guide, and begin to journey. The focus of this journey is getting information regarding your goal. Since most goals include some physical time frame, create a symbol for time that you can use during your journey to give you information. For example, you may use a calendar, ruler, or time line as a symbol. If your goal is to meet a compatible lover within the next year, you may wish to ask your time symbol to show you what the time frame is that is appropriate for you to achieve that goal. During your journey you may also wish to ask whether or not this is an appropriate goal for you, and if not, what is in its place. Remember that as long as we have allies and spirit helpers, we're not alone, even in a task such as setting goals.

Always remember to thank both your spirit helpers and the source of information—whether it be the helpers, your own spirit self, or something else. You will know after this exercise whether or not the goal you were working with is the right goal for you.

If the signals are all systems go, then close your eyes and again envision your goal as completely and richly as you can. Open your eyes and write it down in detail. This makes the goal physical and aids the process of manifestation.

The last and most important part is to take action. It doesn't have to be the type of action that necessarily will bring you the best results, but an action that brings you closer to your goal in an emotional way. For example, if your goal is to own a new car within six months, it would be better

---

Exercise #1: The Steps

1. Sit down with a paper and pen.
2. Write out your list of goals.
3. Choose one goal to work with.
4. Vividly imagine accomplishing the goal.
5. Check with your spirit body.
6. Journey for information.
7. Thank your spirit helpers.
8. Repeat #4 and write down what you saw.
9. Take action.

for you to go to the car dealer and test drive that new car than to go to the office and work overtime. Sit in it; feel how it feels to drive it; close your eyes and smell how it smells; etc. Once you have recruited your senses into achieving your goal, then the rest will follow. If it means working overtime a few days, you will then gladly be willing to do it. For as shamans would say, it is the heart that motivates above all else.

PROBLEM SOLVING

Suppose you set a goal for yourself that is truly what you wish for, but in order to attain it you recognize that you must first either change your habits or beliefs, or change a situation that limits your ability to reach that goal. This usually requires problem-solving skills, our next focus in this chapter.

He Who Runs Like the Wind was not born with his name; he was initiated into it. All his growing-up years he could remember wanting to be like the great hunters who ran with the herds for days on end. He was born the stronger of two, his brother dying with the first moon, his mother with the second. The spirits had exacted their price from him too; the boy was born with a twisted foot from being confined in utero in such a small space with his twin brother. When the tribe had moved on, he would have been left to fate on his mother's grave if She Who Knows the Sun had not taken him as her own.

She Who Knows the Sun was a medicine woman, wise in the ways of nature and the spirit world. Sometime in his seventh year, the boy revealed to her his dream of running free and swift like the wind. The wise one looked at his crooked foot, then at his shining hopeful eyes and said, "You must know the Wind. It is the most powerful of all: It can tame water, wear away rock, and move earth. It can give you the freedom you are searching for if you know it."

Upon hearing her advice, the boy set out every morning for seven moons to a place she had designated. There he spoke with the Wind, slowly, awkwardly at first, then laughingly and lovingly. He journeyed within to seek help from his totem, the fierce and swift Hawk, and together with the Wind, Hawk taught his feet to fly. Limping at first and then with dancelike strides, the boy ran across the plain again and again, the muscles in his feet growing

stronger, his gait growing swifter with the passing of each
moon. And each day he thanked his allies for their help.

One evening near the seventh moon of his practice,
when the boy and She Who Knows the Sun were nearing
sleep, she whispered to him, "You must speak to your
feet who fly like the Wind now. You must tell them that
soon there is to be a test, an initiation. Tell them you must
know they are in readiness." With that, the old woman
went to sleep, leaving the boy to ponder her words. He
did as she told him and held an image of his winged feet
in his vision as he drifted off to sleep.

The following sunrise found the boy in his usual place,
playing with the Wind and the spirit of Hawk. Suddenly
the peaceful silence was shattered by an enormous roar
as the mountain above him opened and the molten earth
below came up through its peak. A river of fire was beginning to form, making its way toward the village. Without thinking, the boy ran with winged feet toward the
village, feeling the Wind at his back. Hearing his warning,
the tribe moved quickly and only one lodge was lost.

He Who Runs Like the Wind now thanked his name
giver and knew that he had done his task well. She Who
Knows the Sun smiled.

Problem solving, like goal setting, uses many of the principles we have already discussed. The most important thing
to remember in shamanic problem solving is sensitivity: sensitivity to your spirit body and its needs, sensitivity to other
people's spirit bodies and their needs, and sensitivity to the
spirit world itself, the spirit of all things and the balance in
nature. Only in this way will you find the truly powerful solutions to the problems at hand.

Shamanic problem solving also includes listening: listening to the advice of your guides or allies; listening to your
own spirit self or perhaps the spirit self of another person. By
listening, shamans adopt a win–win attitude in their problem
solving.

For example, if you need to increase your income, it cannot be at the expense of reducing someone else's income.
Think of the abundance in nature and find a way to increase
incomes across the board. Likewise, if you are competing
against four others for the same position at work, your greatest success will come from wishing the other four goodwill,
even if it means that one of them will get the position instead
of you. If that happens, something better is in store for you
that you cannot foresee. Remember that, as in goal setting,

detachment from the problem at hand and surrendering to its eventual solution is critical to successful problem solving. Have you ever efficiently solved any problem while engulfed in its emotional trauma?

Shamans would say that each one of your problems points you one step further in your life's direction, the path your spirit self has chosen. Likewise, they would say that each solution brings you closer to the ultimate goal, greater personal power. Therefore shamanic problem solving is about realizing those goals that your spirit self has set, not just those of your physical self. Each time you go through the process of problem solving the shamanic way, you understand yourself and your place among all living things a little better. Shamanically speaking, looking at the greater picture, the ultimate goal of every person is to become self-sufficient, realize their greatest personal power, and understand their connection to all life. This is the natural outcome of striving for balance.

The process of problem solving in a way that will ultimately empower you requires sensitivity and listening skills. Take for example a relationship between two people where a problem exists. What relationship doesn't have challenges and obstacles to be overcome? Relationships are the instruments of growth and, being such, they generate problems as surely as they provide the opportunity for breakthrough. Relationships are the ground where you can learn the most about yourself as well as about others. But in order to get the most out of dealing with relationships and their problems, you must first understand shamanic body language or the nuances and signals of a person's spirit body.

Usually, problems arise in a relationship due to unrealized expectations that each person has an emotional attachment to. In many cases, the problem would be identified as one or both people not getting what they want or not getting what they think they should have. Resentment tends to build and suddenly there is a stalemate where each, identified with their position, refuses to give ground. Imagine if entities in nature that rely on an internal balance for survival were suddenly to begin acting this way. Flowers would refuse to bloom, thinking they were not appreciated as much as they should be; bees then would make no honey and the rain would refuse to fall, saying that the flowers don't deserve it for refusing to bloom. In short, there would be chaos due to the imbalance generated by each obstacle. Our world would indeed be short-lived.

Seeing the larger picture here is certainly something shamans strive for. If you can show respect for another's place in
the scheme of things, even in the midst of a difficult situation, you have made the first giant step toward effective
problem solving. Shamans look at this process as the give-
and-take of power. They would say that if you delegate
power or empower someone else by respecting their position, you become empowered in the process. This is not the
same thing as giving your power away—letting another take
advantage of you.

Here is an exercise that uses the spirit body as a tool for
communication and problem solving in relationships. It is effective with lovers, friends, family members, business
partners, peers, acquaintances, and anyone else you happen
to come in contact with.

The goal here is to set the ordinary-reality personality
aside and deal directly on the spirit level, where true power
lies.

Exercise #2:Problem Solving with the Spirit Body

Identify the problem you wish to resolve. Start with one
that includes only one other person besides yourself. For example, you may have a problem with someone at work or
perhaps your spouse or other family member. Make sure you
mentally ask the person's permission to include them in this
exercise.

Close your eyes, relax, and, using your shamanic visioning techniques, re-create a vision or symbol of the problem
as it currently exists. Notice how you feel.

Let go of that vision and focus your attention on your
spirit body. Get a sense of it. Notice the area or areas that
are affected by the problem. This may show up as spots of
color in various locations, the absence of energy, or another
symbol. You will need to interpret this for yourself. An example would be seeing or sensing a turbulent fiery red streak
around your gut area that you would recognize perhaps as
anger. If you don't understand something, ask your power
animal or your own spirit body to tell you what it means.

Ask your spirit body to pretend that your situation is resolved and to show you what it would look like. Sense what it
would feel like if this problem truly did not exist anymore.

Now envision the other person standing or sitting in front
of you, as if you were going to have a chat. Get a sense of
their spirit body. Ask it to show itself to you as it appears
when it is affected by the problem. An example would be

perhaps seeing the other person's spirit body as having a dense or dark color around their heart area or seeing a noose around their neck.

Ask the other person's spirit body to show or tell you how and where it is affected by the problem. If you don't understand something, ask for it to be explained. Here you may obtain much information about the source of the problem. Sometimes power animals or guides can be thorough and long-winded.

Now ask the person's spirit body to pretend that the problem has been resolved and to show itself to you with the changes that would be visible. Ask the other person what they would like as a gift from you that would symbolize in some way a solution to the problem. Imagine yourself giving that gift to them. Examples might be a bouquet of flowers, a beautiful ring, tickets to a ball game, etc. Ask your own spirit body what it would like as a symbolic gift from the other person. Then ask for it. Imagine that other person giving you exactly what you asked for.

Bow down with your spirit body and imagine the other person's spirit body doing the same in a gesture of mutual respect. Remember again that to shamans, thoughts and feelings are actual forms. They go to the other person and affect them.

Exercise #2: The Steps

1. Select a problem involving another person.
2. See it as a symbol.
3. Sense how you feel.
4. Check with your spirit body.
5. Have it show you what the problem looks and feels like resolved.
6. Check into the spirit body of the other person.
7. Check how it is affected.
8. How would it look to them resolved?
9. Give gift.
10. Receive gift.
11. Bow in respect.

This exercise is effective not only in beginning the process of problem solving, but in opening up channels of nonverbal communication between your spirit self and that of another or others. A counselor we know who includes shamanic techniques in his practice recounted the story of a couple who had come to him on the verge of divorce. He taught them about the balance in nature, the need to give up control and their own agenda in favor of the bigger picture. He taught them how to be sensitive to their spirit bodies and how to read energy. This perspective proved to be invaluable to their process of reconciliation and the development of their communication skills. They ended their counseling closer than ever and with a newfound respect for each other as well as for all living things.

Seeing the big picture has its value in more ways than one. A problem you are working on may be only one piece of a much larger puzzle. The successful solution to your problem could depend on the successful outcome of all the rest of the pieces. Look at it in terms of the pieces of a picture puzzle; if one little piece is missing, the whole picture is incomplete.

Therefore, it is shortsighted and even arrogant to assume that your current difficulty is isolated from the rest of life. And if you treat the problem as if it were isolated and on its own, you will find a satisfactory solution more difficult to find. If, on the other hand, you work with the whole puzzle, you automatically adopt a win–win attitude, as the success of your solution depends largely on the success of others. In this way you also become empowered because you are in effect giving goodwill away. And when you give goodwill away, at the very same time others are wishing you goodwill that you receive graciously, and so the circle of abundance and empowerment goes.

Bess was a successful real estate agent. She had been working in the field for over six years now and considered herself one of the top salespeople in her office. But she recently encountered a tough problem. Her clients, Mr. and Mrs. Adams, had a house to sell and Bess had been trying to sell it for eight months. She was having difficulty doing so, regardless of what she tried, and Bess had tried everything. Instead, she experimented with her newfound shamanic perspective.

She sat down, closed her eyes, and began a series of shamanic exercises to see what she could learn about the situation. The process was revealing, to say the least. She saw that Mrs. Adams was quite attached to the house and was secretly unwilling to let anyone else move into the home where she had been raised, her children had been raised, and her parents had both passed away.

Furthermore, her biggest problem was not knowing where she was going, where they were moving to, and what her life in general would be like after 1624 Elm Street. Bess's guardian spirit represented this by showing her a picture of a blindfolded Mrs. Adams clutching a mini version of her house to her chest. To complicate matters, Mr. Adams had not yet decided which position he was going to accept out of two job offers that would determine what neighborhood the Adams would move to. Bess saw a picture of Mr. Adams running back and forth between two bosses and two little model towns. Bess likewise learned from her ally that there were in fact three families that had seen the house and that were possible buyers. But they had stayed clear of any negotiations because of the hidden message being given out by Mrs. Adams that the house was unavailable. This was illustrated by three families looking at a little house but being unable to reach it because Mrs. Adams barred the way.

Bess began to work on clearing the way for the Adamses to take their next step, using the shamanic journey and other problem-solving techniques. She communicated with both their physical and spirit bodies and helped them to "see" their way, make important decisions and clear the spirit of the house, making it ready for a new family to move in. Much of this was done without the Adams' conscious knowledge, although Bess had made sure to ask permission of their spirit to work with them in this way.

The results were amazing. Not only did the house sell within ten days of Bess's beginning the process, but the Adamses seemed happier and more relaxed than she had seen them in a long time. Bess felt a connection with them and their environment that she had never felt with any of her other clients. Not once had she thought only of her own goal and pocket book; she truly had their best interests in mind. Needless to say, every one benefited, Bess's bank account as well. Now, three years later, the Adamses still send Bess a card at Christmas time and she remembers her first empowering business experience with fondness.

When you work with the larger picture, problem solving often involves other people. Using the shamanic way and a win–win attitude will leave you with a greater sense of personal power and accomplishment. Here is an exercise that uses the journey method for solving problems. You can journey for yourself and you can journey for others. When journeying for others, the information received can then be communicated to them directly or via a spirit body communication exercise as you see fit.

Exercise #3: A Journey for Problem Solving

State your problem, then state the condition that you want. For example: "My relationship with my parents is tense and I wish to get along with them better."

Form the problem you wish to solve into a question. For example: "What are the obstacles I am encountering and what are the steps I need to take to dissolve them?"

Relax, close your eyes, and begin to journey. The idea here is to gather information about what the next step or steps to solving your problem might be. During your journey you may meet people related to the issue you are working on who are in need of help. Ask your power animal or guide to offer them assistance. Use your shamanic visioning techniques and "see" them overcoming their own obstacles and reaching their own goals on their own terms. Never force an agenda on someone.

If during your journey you were told to communicate something to another person involved in your problem, envision that person and their spirit body in front of you and communicate what is necessary to them via any shamanic visioning technique that works for you. If you are able, communicate to them directly as well.

Exercise #3: The Steps

1. State the problem and state the desired condition.
2. Reframe the problem into a question.
3. Relax, close your eyes, and begin to journey.
4. Have your power animal offer assistance to others related to your issue.
5. Communicate to others what is necessary.

Depending on how complicated the problem is and on the information you receive during your journey, you may need to repeat this exercise more than once for the same problem. Problem solving is a process; it seldom happens overnight and usually requires change. For example, if your problem is that you don't have enough money, you've never been able to get the jobs you really want, and you've always felt unsuccessful, then solving this problem will most likely take some time and many journeys. There also may be other people involved, as well as your upbringing and various other components. To solve this problem will surely require a great deal of change in your beliefs and personal patterns.

CHANGE

For the purposes of our discussion, we will define change as a process wherein a situation is transformed from an unwanted one to a wanted one. In order for this change to occur, the situation you no longer want must be clearly identified and the steps to transforming it mapped out. Thus the change wanted becomes the goal, and the obstacles that need to be overcome to reach that goal become the problems to be solved.

There are four main ingredients for successful change—commitment, agreement, surrender, and action.

COMMITMENT

Without commitment, there can be no lasting change. Many people go through life with "if onlys" and visions of "someday maybe things will change." Their goals are lukewarm in the sense that they don't really believe change will happen because it never has before. So when they do think about change, often the thoughts are "It's too much work," "I wouldn't know where to begin," or "Things could be worse so I'll just leave them the way they are."

Shamans would say that to want change without a commitment is like walking down a road in winter with only one shoe on when you said you wanted warmer feet. Let's say that you made a goal to have warmer feet, and you acquired a pair of shoes for that purpose. Only, let's say you have one shoe stolen at night by a wandering coyote. Since your action steps included walking on the road with your shoes on, you went ahead with your plan even though you had only one shoe left. The shamans would say that it was the part of you that was uncommitted that drew to itself the new obstacle to realizing your goal. Therefore your first step is to ask yourself: Do I truly want this situation to change? Am I willing to do everything it takes to change?

Once you make the commitment to change your situation, two things happen: your energetic or spirity body shifts, allowing for changes to begin; and unexpected help comes your way, seemingly out of nowhere. Because the help is unexpected, it often comes and goes unrecognized and is not taken advantage of unless you are open and sensitive to it. You might walk right by your other shoe, dropped by the coyote, without even noticing it.

AGREEMENT

After making a commitment, you will need to enlist the agreement of all the parts of yourself for this change. The parts that are skeptical, cynical, overly cautious, perhaps comfortable in your present situation, or fearful, need to be communicated with and enrolled in the program. For this communication, we recommend an exercise described at the end of this chapter. The agreement should be that all the parts remain committed for as long as it takes for the change to occur, and that all parts are willing to do what it takes and stick with the plan.

It is also important to get agreements of support from the people close to you, whether you must do it through an internal exercise or directly. Likewise, on a spirit level you can begin to change the way others have viewed you up until now. For example, if the people around you have seen you day in and day out as a person who weighs 230 pounds and has trouble moving around in the physical world, they have a fixed idea about you from what they see. If you are committed to losing sixty of those pounds and becoming physically fit, it will help if they change their fixed idea about you to reflect your goal. You can help this process by communicating with their spirit selves and showing them your shamanic vision of what you are out to accomplish. They will then be more able to notice your own energetic shift that occurred because of your commitment.

SURRENDER

By surrender, we mean your willingness to let go of your own agenda and give up your control of the events to come. Surrender is, however, not an easy concept to grasp. Holding on to your own script is like walking with blinders on: you won't be able to recognize some of those opportunities or take advantage of the unexpected help that comes your way. Focus on what you already have, rather than what you don't. This changes the focus from the concept of the half-empty glass to the half-full one. In this way too, the process of change can begin from a place of having rather than a place of not having.

The concept of surrender also includes, in this case, a real willingness to do whatever it takes, whatever your shamanic instructions are to bring about the change. What you think you may have to do for the change and what you actually need to do could be very different. For example, you may think that you need to sue someone else to get justice, but your spirit self may tell you that you should seek arbitration instead. This depends on who or what else is involved in the process, for when you consider the bigger picture you need to remember that your change cannot occur at the expense of someone else. Therefore, if your original plan was not in harmony with those involved, your agenda may be slightly changed. Trust your spirit self, who always sees the bigger picture. It knows what is best.

Sometimes fear enters into the picture, usually in the form of fear of giving up control or fear of the unknown. Hopefully, by now you have learned not only that your higher or spirit self knows what's best for you, but also that the universe is based on harmony and balance and will never throw something in your path that you are unable to handle. The goal of the natural world is maintaining this balance and what you usually find at the other end of change are feelings of self-fulfillment and exhiliration.

ACTION

Unless you physically do something to catalyze the process and make it real, your goal remains a dream, in the potential of the spirit world only. This again is another area where you can get stuck. For many of us, the very action we mistakenly think we need to take keeps us from attaining our goal of change. Many of those action steps you set for yourself, the ones that you really don't wish to do, result from the very belief system you are trying to change.

For example, suppose your goal is to be more open, less shy and awkward in social situations. Perhaps this is connected to a bigger goal of finding a committed relationship. You happen to believe that in order to be the way you want to be you must appear extroverted, funny, and enjoy going to bars and parties because you have seen that your friends who are successful in that realm have those qualities. You have tired this before unsuccessfully but this time you are really going to be disciplined about it. You are sick of your life the way it is, so you will grit your teeth and get out there in the front lines.

Already you have created an impossible situation. You will never change successfully because the change is not from the heart. What you really want is to be more at ease and connect with people, rather than be the party animal. It won't surprise you then that the parts of you that dislike the bar scene will not cooperate in your endeavor and will surely sabotage your action step of forcing yourself to the bar. A better action step here is to take a pen and paper and to write down all the reasons why people should be drawn to you the way you are. For your true goal is to draw yourself out, not to try and be like someone else.

Think of action as anything that you can do on the physical plane that brings you even a fraction of a step closer to your change. The action and results are your only measures of whether or not you are successfully changing. Set some tasks for yourself that you know you can handle and if you are committed, you will do them and, little by little, begin to notice results.

What can help you through a change? Shamans would tell you to look in nature and the spirit of all living things. Since shamanism is based on the natural order and balance found in all of nature, it would stand to reason that you could turn here for help. There are many properties of nature that are in a constant state of change or flux. Take, for example the wind. It is always changing and making changes to other natural things such as sand. Water, another strong symbol, is in constant motion and flow, like an ever-changing pattern. Molten lava becomes rock then changes into sand or dust with the constant forces of nature.

Nature is not as resistant to change as we are and it therefore has much to teach if we will only listen. We have a friend who visits the seashore anytime she is in a state of change. She will sit for hours seeing, sensing, listening to the sea, the swelling and crashing of the waves, the surf washing over the sand. There is a sense of balance that you get from becoming one with nature that can greatly aid your process of change. And since change usually requires letting go of one pattern or situation to make room for another, there can be a sense of loss involved. This loss is likely to be overlooked and remain unexpressed unless you can relax enough into the rhythm of change to allow it expression. Our seashore friend often finds herself crying in a state of emotional release, helped by the balancing qualities of the sea. Thus, if you can include the qualities of change found in nature in your own process, they will indeed help you with your change.

Here is an exercise for change that includes many of the techniques we have taught. It is a combination of spirit body visioning, sensing the elements, enlisting support of your allies, and the shamanic journey. We encourage you here to formulate your own sequence of shamanic techniques or modify this one to fit your process. The more complex the issue you are dealing with, the more complex your exercise may turn out to be. Use your imagination and the information given to you by the spirit world to take action.

Exercise #4: Change

Identify the change you wish to make and state it as specifically as you can. Ask yourself, is this really what I want? Is this change for me or for someone else? Am I willing to do what it takes to make this change? Get a commitment from yourself in whatever symbolic way you wish to. Some people write this down, some imagine it.

Envision your own spirit self and begin a conversation with it. Ask every part for thier agreement and commitment to this change. Be sure to listen if there are doubts or if there is resistance. Your spirit body may have a different agenda with your well-being in mind. Be sure to find out what it is. If your spirit self is not in agreement with the change you wish for yourself, find out why. Perhaps you need to reformulate your goal. If you have agreement, move on to the next step.

Do the same step but with your physical body, part by part. If you come across resistance here, it is probably based on fear of letting something very familiar go in exchange for something unknown. Spend some time communicating with each part, reassure it, and ask your physical body what you can do to help it feel safe and balanced during the process. This is an important step and should never be glossed over. People tend not to change when they feel too uncomfortable, so making the physical body as comfortable as possible is necessary.

Once you have commitment and agreement from your physical and spirit selves, ask for help from a power animal or an ally or even perhaps a natural element during your process.

Think of a natural element or phenomena that symbolizes change for you. Get to know the qualities of this element and how it feels through the sensing exercise we taught you at the beginning of the book.

Now you are ready to do a shamanic journey for the purpose of asking what your obstacles are to this change and finding out what your next steps are. This is similar to the journey for problem solving. Remember that surrender is an important ingredient to successful change, so take what comes in your journey even if it's not what you wish to hear. Take the information as it comes and without judgment. If you don't understand something, ask for a better explanation.

This step depends on the information you received during your journey. Here you will make a plan of action that you should try and stick with as much as possible. Your plan should include any further journeys or exercises that have been recommended. If during your journey you receive information that is vague and undefined, then try again and specifically ask for action steps.

Exercise #4: The Steps

1. Identify the change you want to make.
2. Get agreement from your spirit body to proceed.
3. Get agreement from your physical body to proceed.
4. Ask for help from your power animal or ally.
5. Create an image of change.
6. Take a shamanic journey focused on change.
7. Make a plan of action.

Change does not happen overnight and is usually accomplished through determination and a series of baby steps. During this process we recommend that you frequently check in with your physical and spirit bodies to see how they are faring. Rapid change is hard for the physical body to integrate and it may take time for it to adapt. The body tends to record all change, even positive change, as stressful. Baby steps allow your body to adapt gracefully to the changes you are making.

The exercise in Chapter 5 on symbolic dismemberment and reconstruction of your body is especially useful during times of intense change. This is particularly so if the change is directly associated with the body, such as losing weight or even moving to a different climate. When you picture your body being remolded, you will often see that it goes together somewhat differently from the way it looked before. You may notice that your body looks slimmer or in some cases more solid, depending on the changes you are making.

You can also benefit during this time from envisioning the qualities of the natural element that you chose in the exercise. This is especially helpful during those times when you are feeling overwhelmed and off balance. Use your resources, your guides, your power animals, and the technique of journeying as much as you need to. And don't forget the action steps. Your motivation to continue will be in seeing your successes, even if they are the accomplishments of baby steps.

The greater your capacity for having change, the greater your change can be. Remember the story of the two villagers and the herd of burros? The same concept applies to change. Your spirit self and your journeys will let you know if you have bitten off more than you can chew at one time. A change can always be broken down into smaller components. So take one step at a time. You did not go from twelfth grade directly into an executive position with a high income; nor did you all of a sudden find yourself fluently speaking a foreign language. One step at a time, and as the shaman would say, make sure each step is in the right direction.

CHAPTER 8

Finding Your Place in the Shaman's World: Maps and Trails

For shamans, knowing their place in the order of the world is of utmost importance. When you know your place, you can make order out of chaos and thus be in a position to exercise your power. When you have a map of the territory, you can then know in what direction to proceed. Without a map you are lost, proceeding aimlessly and without a known destination. In shamanism, those who have no organizing principle to their world are inherently powerless and as a result unsuccessful.

Shamans have several organizing principles that tell them exactly where they are at any moment. These organizing motifs, nature-based and perhaps quite simple at first sight, are actually rather sophisticated upon more reflection. Natural maps tell shamans where they are in relation to the center of the universe and help shamans orient themselves as they travel from place to place in their constant search for knowledge and power.

The first of these organizing themes, the "Tree of Life," is the supreme organizing principle of the cosmos. Massive in size, this tree has its roots in the core of the earth: the underworld or world of the dead. This is the land that shamans journey to when they want to retrieve lost knowledge or communicate with dead ancestors. It is also the place where shamans find much survival information and knowledge relating to the cure of diseases and infirmities. This land of the underworld is known as the storehouse of all instincts and knowledge related to survival in a physical body. Travel to the land of the dead without a guardian or an ally, however, is not a good idea because of the dangers that lurk there.

The trunk of the Tree of Life is located in the Middle World or the land that is magically equivalent to ordinary reality. In this land lie the answers to ordinary everyday problems. The trunk of the Tree of Life is often depicted as square, each side relating to one of the four directions. The four directions relate to the four seasons: east for spring and all new beginnings; south for summer, sun, growth, moving outward, and productivity; west for autumn, completions, death, and transformation; north for winter, gestation, contemplation, and rebirth.

The branches of the Tree of Life are located in the Upper World, land of inspiration and visions of the future. This is the realm of creativity, flight, and unlimited freedom.

Shamans regard no one world as better than another. The Upper World is not preferable to either of the other two. Each has its place in the cosmos and to neglect one for another is regarded as foolish. Each land has its own rules, its own characteristics, and its own offerings. Shamans must have their feet dancing in all three worlds as well as the ordinary world, so they can readily know where to go for the right information at the right time. Curiously, shamans from all parts of the world have similar maps to the different lands.

A shaman from Siberia can understand the journey of a shaman from the South Pacific by relating to its relative position on the Tree of Life. Although small local maps of specific spirit world destinations are common, surprisingly, there is no main written text or physically drawn central map that details this common experience. All shamans come to this knowledge through their own experience or through oral tradition.

The other main structure or map that shamans use to create order in the universe and to locate themselves is the mandala, circle, or medicine wheel. The medicine wheel is similar to the Tree of Life in that it is divided into four quadrants (or subdivided into eight) that relate to the four directions. The circumference and physical shape of the medicine wheel corresponds roughly to the Middle World. The sky above the medicine wheel relates to the Upper World and the earth below the medicine wheel relates to the Lower World. The center of the circle is the center of the universe; and all points on the circle, as well as those above it and below it, are moving, gradually spiraling toward the center. In the shamanic perspective, each person occupies a spot on the medicine wheel or mandala. That spot reflects where the physical person is at any given moment in relation to their own spirit center. No spot, however, is better than any other spot, just different. Therefore, from the shamanic point of view, all people are equal and all eventually discover their spirit center. When you consciously reach this center, you have access to all points on the mandala at once. You could say that each person simultaneously and paradoxically knows two places on the wheel: their physical-self position somewhere in the circle and their spirit self position at the center of the circle.

The greater the awareness that you have of the center, the greater the power available to you. Therefore, much of the shaman's work is related to achieving balance and becoming "centered." For this, the medicine wheel or mandala proves a helpful symbol.

Exercise #1: Finding Your Place in the Medicine Wheel

Close your eyes and relax.

Imagine a large wheel like a giant compass or dart board with concentric circles and two lines intersecting to form four equal quadrants. Label the tips of these lines with initials for the four directions: north, south, east, and west.

Make the dot at the center the same color as the rim and if you wish you can make each quadrant or concentric circle a different color, depending on your powers of imagination.

Allow each quadrant to be represented by a different power animal. Do not think about this much—just let them appear.

Now ask your own power animal or guide to show you exactly where you are on the medicine wheel right now. They may indicate it with a point of light or some other means. Note the quadrant and the proximity to the center. Also note the power animal that represents that quadrant.

You may wish to interview that power animal and ask what that position means for you right now.

Thank your helpers, orient yourself back to the room you

Exercise #1: The Steps

1. Close your eyes. Relax.
2. Envision a large medicine wheel.
3. Divide it into quadrants and color it.
4. Let power animals represent each quadrant.
5. Ask your own power animal to reveal your present position.
6. Interview power animals.
7. Thank them and reorient yourself.
8. Write down, draw, or paint what you experienced.

are in, and open your eyes. Write down what you experienced for your later reference. If you are artistically inclined, you can sketch, draw, or paint the mandala and your positon on it. Periodic check-ins with the medicine wheel will let you know where you are and how you are doing in reference to your center.

Shamans have noticed that most natural living forms are rounded and reflect the larger motif of the medicine wheel or circle of power. Tree trunks, plant stems, arms and legs, heads, the spinal column, bodily organs, shells, the sun, the moon, the stars, tornados, whirlwinds, pine cones, and a long list of natural forms, are miniature medicine wheels, reminders of that greater circle of life. Shamans have also noticed that when they close their eyes, the patterns usually reflected there are circular in form. It is not by chance that the tunnels they use to travel to and from the spirit world are round and the drums they use to help them on their way are round as well.

In fact, the entire matrix that holds the spirit world and the ordinary world in a state of balance consists of round tunnels that connect specific locations with one another. Shamans use any circular opening in their environment as a passageway into some location in the spirit world. In many cultures shamans create their own openings into the spirit world by digging a special hole in the floor of their dwelling or in the ground at their ritual spot. For example, the Hopis and Navajos dig a small hole called a Sippapu in the floor of the Kiva (circular ceremonial underground room) and leave an opening in the roof for similar reasons. Artistic shamans the world over create new openings by making circular drawings on cave walls, shelters, and rock faces. Tibetan Buddhist shamans create tankas, which are colorful circular paintings that depict the spirit world within us.

Interestingly, modern physicists have discovered the existence of black holes and postulated the existence of white holes in space, where massive amounts of energy seem to either disappear or appear. Whether these holes are related in any way to the shamans' holes remains to be seen. However, judging from recent comparisons of similarities between modern physics and mysticism, it is most likely.

In the following section we will decribe seven principal nonphysical holes or openings that have been alluded to by yogic shamans in India, Tibetan Buddhist Shamans, Native American shamans, and African shamans, to name a few. These openings to the spirit world are in addition to the commonly used cave entrances and other openings in the earth discussed so far.

TUNNELS TO THE SPIRIT WORLD

Tunnels or entrances to the spirit world exist throughout the environment. Caves, holes in trees, hot or cold springs, and orifices in the body are all gateways to enter into the world of spirit. This method of accessing power plays an essential role in the shamanic journey. Shamans travel through these tunnels into other worlds for the purpose of accessing and retrieving power, knowledge, and lost guardian spirits.

According to shamanic lore and many derivative mystical traditions such as Sufism, Tibetan Buddhism, and Hinduism, to name but a few, some of the most fundamental tunnels are to be found within the human spirit body itself. There is relative agreement cross-culturally about where these tunnels or energy vortices are located. And at the same time, there is some discrepancy as to how many there are. Some systems list three, some four, five, and some seven. For our purpose, we are going to follow the yogic system that describes seven openings. The Hindus and Buddhists call these openings "Chakra" or "Cakra," a sanskrit word meaning wheel or vortex. They are so named because to those who see them they appear to be rapidly moving whirls of colorful energy. Whatever their name, these round energetic openings are depicted both in religious and shamanic art throughout the world.

In a healthy person, the energy from each vortex extends within and outward in a complex of fine tendrils that form a colored, somewhat egg-shaped cloud around the body. Seven tunnels, each generating energy, form seven layers creating this egg-shaped spirit body. This, in fact, is the same spirit body you were introduced to and worked with in the first chapter. We are now going into greater detail with regard to its energetic makeup so you will begin to understand the intricacies of its inner workings, an understanding that will further help you in successful shamanic visioning.

Each layer that emanates from one of these energy vortexes is colored according to the frequency and the quality associated with that particular tunnel. In a healthy person, the colors tend to be pastel; in an unhealthy person they can appear to be dense, spotty, or dark.

The wheels themselves are like rapidly spinning tunnels or tubes that appear to go all the way through the spirit body from front to back. Located along the spinal column, there are seven main tunnels ranging from the base of the spine to the top of the head. Numerous other smaller tunnels exist in each joint of the body as well as along the energetic nerve paths or meridians described by Chinese acupuncturists. They may grow larger or smaller, depending on their level of activity. When they are highly energized and active, they tend to be more expansive, like the size of a small plate. When they are underused or shut down, they can appear dark or as small as a penny. For most people, when in balance, they are the size of a silver dollar.

All the tunnels are connected to each other via passageways that move up and down the spine. These channels allow the various openings to work in harmony and to remain in communication with one another. Occasionally these channels become closed or are shut down due to trauma, threat, despondency, or accident. A shamanic explanation might be that the person has become dispirited due to interference by alien spirits or loss of the guardian spirit who assists with that area.

Mahtee dodged the wet fronds as he made his way through the dense tangle of vines that clogged the ancient path. At last he broke out into the light of the clearing where Nata's village stood. Nata rushed out to meet him.

"At last you are here!" she cried, clearly distressed. "My sister Tia is not better. Can you see her after you have eaten?"

"Take me to her now," Mahtee advised.

Tia lay on a mat, stony and unresponsive. Mahtee sat silently for a moment, relaxing his body as he asked for guidance from his spirit allies. He pulled out his small traveling drum and began a rapid beat. Using his shamanic sight, he looked at her spirit body and saw that her power animal was missing. He also saw density and a blockage of dark color around her chest. Looking more closely, he noticed that from the opening to the spirit world in the top of her head there was oozing a black slime that appeared to be alive. He asked his guardian spirit, the python, what that might be and the snake immediately began to weep bitter tears. Then the snake asked Tia's spirit body if she wanted the slime removed. When she responded with a vigorous "Yes," the spirit pulled out the black slime and patted it into the shape of a young man who immediately ran away.

Tia let out a scream and then fell forward, sobbing uncontrollably. Mahtee quickly journeyed to find Tia's power animal with the help of his python. When he had spotted it four times, he managed to talk it, a small bird, into coming back. Then he quickly knelt over Tia's head and, blowing with all his might, delivered Tia's power animal through the spirit opening.

Mahtee said quietly to Nata, "She will be okay soon. Let her cry all she wants. She had a secret love with a young man from the next village. He left her when he found her without any power. She has neglected her power animal and it abandoned her, just as he did. Perhaps she has learned her lesson.

"Now I am hungry. Please bring me some food."

Each tunnel or vortex has its own quality and frequency of energy that governs specific parts of the body and energizes particular functions of consciousness. For example, the third tunnel governs survival issues (adrenals), while the fifth one relates to self-expression (vocal cords). Therefore, if you have a particular physical or energetic problem, knowing which tunnel to focus on could be quite useful and save you a lot of time figuring out what to do.

Tunnel 7: crown-pineal gland-spiritual wisdom.

Tunnel 6: brow-eyes-pituitary gland-perception.

Tunnel 5: throat-vocal cords-thyroid-communication and creativity.

Tunnel 4: chest-heart-thymus-affinity and self esteem.

Tunnel 3: solar plexus-adrenals-power and emotions.

Tunnel 2: abdomen-uterus-spleen-pancreas-sexuality-reproduction.

Tunnel 1: base of spine-bowels-gonads-survival.

While attending a workshop, a singer in his early thirties reported that his ability to write songs had dried up. During a simple shamanic exercise, he discovered that the spirit opening in his throat was totally blocked. With some guidance and inner work, he dragged out of his throat a toothy alligator that promptly spit out his father's lifeless body. At that moment he realized that he had written his last song before visiting his father in Boston six months ago. They had fought terribly and broken off communication.

Later he reported that he had called his father and they had made amends. He began to write songs again.

Exercise #2: Identifying the Seven Tunnels

Relax, close your eyes and use your shamanic vision to get a sense of your spirit body. Focus on the physical locations of each tunnel as we described, one at a time, beginning with the first one at the base of your spine. This is where the first tunnel should appear to you, red in color, and about the size of a quarter or a silver dollar. You may see a circular vortexlike pattern of energy larger than the size of the coin. This would be the filaments of energy generated by that tunnel and make up one of the layers of your spirit body.

Move up to the area just below your navel in the abdominal area and locate your second tunnel, often pink or orange in color.

Move up to the area above your navel in your solar plexus and locate your third opening, often yellow in color.

Move up to your chest in the vicinity of your heart and locate the fourth tunnel, often green or golden in color.

Move up to the cleft in your throat and locate the fifth tunnel, often blue in color.

Move up to the place between your eyes in the center of your forehead and locate the sixth tunnel, usually the color indigo.

Exercise #2: The Steps

1. Close your eyes and relax.
2. Using shamanic vision look consecutively at each tunnel.
3. First tunnel—base of spine; one inch in front of anus; red.
3. Second tunnel; abdomen; two inches below navel; orange.
4. Third tunnel; solar plexus; yellow.
5. Fourth tunnel; chest; green.
6. Fifth tunnel; throat; blue.
7. Sixth tunnel; brow; indigo.
8. Seventh tunnel; top of head; crown; violet.
9. Notice alignment and passageways between them.
10. Reorient yourself and open your eyes.

Move up to the top of your head at the crown and locate your seventh tunnel, most likely violet in color.

Notice with your shamanic vision whether or not your tunnels are aligned vertically and notice whatever connections and passageways exist between them. These passageways usually look like thin straws connecting one tunnel to another.

The tunnels also serve as storehouses of information preserved in the form of memories, fears, or blockages. When shamans journey through a particular tunnel, what they often literally meet are guardians of the information accumulated in that tunnel. We will give you examples of these in the following section. Let us now describe the functions of the seven major tunnels, beginning with the first at the base of the spine and proceeding through each one to the seventh at the crown.

THE FIRST TUNNEL OF POWER

Located at the sacrum or base of the spine, the functions of this opening are many and are vastly important for shamanic work. Here lies access to the storehouse of all instinctual and genetic information about survival. Here are the ancestral and archetypal (includes past-life) memories that lie latent until tapped by shamanic processes.

This first tunnel is also known as a storehouse for a powerful energy that, if released, rises up the spine, activating all the tunnels before rushing out the top of the head. In the Hindu tradition this latent energy is known as the Kundalini or serpent power. This serpent power can be activated by certain meditations, concentrations, or through the assistance of a yogi. According to Kung shamans in the Kalahari Desert, Num, a fiery energy stored in the base of the spine, can be released with pelvic movements in a special dance. The Num energy travels up the spinal column to the skull, where a transformation called Kia occurs. During this state of Kia, tremendous healing can take place not only in the dancer, but in others watching.

When shamans use this opening to journey into the spirit world, they are likely to meet initially with many of their fears. These fears often take the form of demons, evil spirits, or vicious insects, fish, and animals. After either avoiding these creatures, or successfully doing battle with them, shamans can then break into realms of unlimited resources.

The first tunnel creates the first layer in the somewhat egg-shaped spirit body, and is associated with the vibrant color red. The quality and vitality of this layer is the strong-est indication of the basic health of the body.

Looking into this opening can tell you where your level of survival happens to be. Incidents that are life-threatening or that bring up other fears of survival (finances) often blow the first tunnel wide open and can make you feel fearful, para-lyzed, and uncertain. When you experience a rapid opening of this tunnel in these situations, you get the energetic coun-terpart to the adrenaline rush. The process of change, which may threaten your basic survival beliefs, can also activate this first tunnel.

Memories stored in this center include childhood traumas, physical accidents, and even ancestral incidents that once threatened survival. People's grounding—the connec-tion with the Earth that helps make them feel safe—is also secured through this tunnel.

The Second Tunnel of Power

The second tunnel of power is to be found just below the navel in the abdominal area. The functions associated with this center are raw emotion, reproduction, fertility, sexual attraction, and sexual energy in general. Likewise, any blockages or problems in these functions can be identified and worked with through this tunnel. When shamans journey through this opening, they may initially confront memories of sexual traumas in childhood, adolescence, or past lives. Fertility symbols are often represented as well as demons or unsavory creatures that are common figures in traditional shamanism.

The color associated with this tunnel is usually pink or orange and the energetic field generated forms the second layer of the spirit body. Changes to or problems with this particular opening can manifest in a physical symptom in the abdominal area.

A woman attending one of our lectures told us that every time she dated a certain man, she would end the evening with the most fearful gastric pains in her abdomen. She attri-buted this condition to her excitement about being near him. But further scrutiny unveiled that her feelings for him did not support a level of excitement that would produce such a physical state. Needless to say, after tuning in and exploring the situation via a spirit vision, she found her companion setting up house in her second tunnel. That is she found his intrusive energy trying to influence her sexual response toward him. She cleared him out energetically and made the necessary adjustments to the opening to achieve a state of balance. She envisioned the opening to this tunnel reducing in size to the circumference of a silver dollar. The gastric pains disappeared, as did her date. She ended up dating another man who was less intrusive.

Working with the second tunnel is a valuable way of keeping your sexual and creative energy vitalized, a great help in initiating and gestating new projects and clearing out untenable ones.

THE THIRD TUNNEL OF POWER

The solar plexus, just above the navel, is the location of the third main tunnel. Yellow in color, it generates energy that forms the third layer of the spirit body. This tunnel is associated with action, assertion, visceral power, and the use of energy by the body. A few people use this center to enter and exit the physical body in out-of-body experiences such as astral travel. In this state many people describe "seeing" their spirit bodies connected to their physical bodies by a silver cord. Travel through this tunnel often reveals to the shaman personal patterns, ideas or misconceptions about power, and obstacles to the use of that power. Beyond the scary guardians of this information lie sources of real power that, if tapped, can truly be a key to success.

The powers available in the third tunnel can be used to command audiences, assist in leadership skills, or generally to become more noticeable. Think of some well-known opera singers or symphony conductors you have seen. They know how to access the power available through this tunnel successfully and they achieve their results whether they are conscious of it or not.

The Buddha is often depicted as having a very large belly, a symbol of great power and balance of energy in the Far East. Historically there is no evidence that the man who became the Buddha after his enlightenment, Siddartha Gautama, was actually a fat man.

Another and more subtle function of the third tunnel is to act as a generator of sorts and to monitor the energy distribution of the whole body. We are speaking here of the energy that makes up your spirit self. Although it cannot be measured physically, when it is not functioning properly you tend to feel listless, tired, and withdrawn. Checking with the third vortex is especially important before and after situations where you have to be assertive; need to use tremendous physical exertion, such as in a foot race; or when you notice yourself feeling powerless or withdrawn.

Tom, a young stock broker, described a situation that taught him about his third tunnel. He began to notice that every time he visited his high-powered and successful older brother, Josh, he found himself crossing his arms over his stomach area. All through their growing up years, he had been dominated by Josh. And now Tom was suspicious of how his solar plexis area felt whenever they were together.

Intellectually, he had come to no conclusion, so he decided to peek into the third tunnel with the help of his power animal. What he saw confirmed that there indeed was something going on. Just inside the entrance to that tunnel, he found his brother Josh blocking his way. Josh demanded a large sum of money from Tom to get past him. It was as if Josh owned Tom's power and charged him a fee for its use. Nothing had changed since those younger days.

Tom instructed his power animal to clear Josh out and keep him out. Next he printed his own name in large letters all over the walls of the tunnel indicating his own ownership. The next time he visited Josh, his solar plexus felt fine. Interestingly, after a short time, Josh excused himself, saying that he had forgotten another appointment.

THE FOURTH TUNNEL OF POWER

The fourth tunnel is found in the vicinity of the heart and chest areas. This opening is associated with emotion, affection, intimacy, self-esteem, and affinity for the environment. The fourth tunnel forms a bridge between the upper three spirit tunnels and the lower three and acts as a translator between the two sets. The color associated with this center is green and it forms the middle layer of your spirit self.

The shaman who attempts to journey through this tunnel often finds signs and symbols of grief states that tend to block this opening. Beyond these obstacles usually lie inspir(it)-ation and feelings of harmony and expansion.

Ever since Marjorie fought with her mother she noticed that she simply could not connect with anyone. Although she still felt that she was right, her self-esteem had fallen and all of her love feelings were noticeably absent. A quick scan of her seven tunnels revealed to her that the tunnel in her chest was tightly closed down. She asked her power animal to help her open it a little and as it relaxed she was overcome with grief. After the tears flowed, Marjorie felt that she could breathe again. She had remembered a time when her mother gave her kitten away as punishment for arguing with her. With the release of that sad memory, Marjorie could now feel loving again. She also went out and got herself a kitten.

This opening is probably the most noticed and worked with tunnel of all because of the inherent need we all have for love and acceptance and because of the importance of self-esteem. People in general are sensitive to the reactions of this vortex and the physical sensations they produce. Take, for example, someone you feel has charisma or whom you feel is kind and generous. Notice them with your shamanic vision. You will probably find yourself being drawn to their heart area as the source of those qualities. Likewise, at the other end of the scale, grief or loss causes us to feel "heartache" and sadness, usually concentrated physically in that area. Sobbing, for instance, is a physical reaction related to a release of emotion from the fourth opening. Because of the emotional nature of the fourth opening, working effectively with it can be a true key to success. Emotional interaction tends to be stronger than intellectual interaction. Thus, using the fourth tunnel can give you an edge when it comes to connecting with people and creating a bond of affinity with them. It can especially help you in problem solving when others are involved.

Storage in the fourth tunnel might include childhood memories associated with self-esteem, abandonment, and old griefs. This opening tends to be more vulnerable than others and protection is often necessary.

THE FIFTH TUNNEL OF POWER

Located at the cleft of the throat just above the chest area is the fifth tunnel, often a light blue color, forming the fifth layer of your spirit body. It is associated with creative expression and channeling ability. Also included in its scope of influence are the inner ears and the base of the skull. Using the fifth tunnel opens your abilities to communicate telepathically with others and to hear and recognize your own inner messages. Comedians, orators, teachers, and others with developed communication skills have learned to use their fifth center effectively, whether consciously or not. Psychic channels and other intuitives have also relied upon this passageway, particularly since it is connected with the inner ears.

Blockage in this tunnel includes childhood memories of invalidation of self-expression and communication. Thus, using this tunnel to journey often brings one face-to-face with these blocks represented by demons, dragons, insects, and animals with sharp teeth.

Unexpressed emotion, such as anger, causes constriction of this tunnel and is likely to be felt physically as a sore throat or a hoarse voice. The fear of expressing oneself, perhaps based on past invalidation, could also cause this sensation. It is a good idea to check in with your fifth opening after situations in which you were unable to express your emotions, as well as before situations in which you need sharpened communication skills.

The Sixth Tunnel of Power

The sixth tunnel is located at the brow, between your eyes and above your nose. This is the opening often known as the third eye or place of "shamanic seeing." Through the use of this passageway, you can see at a great distance or see things close-at-hand greatly magnified. The Egyptians depicted this opening symbolically as a serpent suspended over the forehead attached to a head band. The snake represented the ability to see into things microscopically.

People who develop the ability to use this tunnel at will do not need a microscope to see into tissue, bone, or any substance for that mater. This sixth opening allows one to discern disease and maladies and determine what is required for healing. On the other hand, one can use the same opening to journey and see what is far away. When people travel through this tunnel, they will often meet with obstacles to seeing: fog, darkness, dimness. Childhood memories may arise depicting events that shut down one's ability to see. Beyond these lie great visual vistas.

Judith loved to observe people. She loved crowds, loved to study many different kinds of people, trying to figure out what they were like. But at the end of the day she often wound up with a headache and pressure in her forehead without knowing why. When she learned about the tunnels, Judith discovered the reason for her problem. Through her curiosity about people, she attempted to absorb as much information as possible. Judith's tendency was to open her sixth tunnel up too wide and for too long a time, eventually giving her the physical reactions. She learned to monitor the opening, relieving her of her headaches.

Opening the sixth tunnel too wide in an attempt to see and clarify a confusing situation can cause sensation in the brow area resembling a headache. Headaches and eye tension are common malfunctions of the sixth tunnel and can be remedied by shamanic visioning.

The color associated with the sixth tunnel is indigo and the energy from it forms one of the outer layers of the spirit body.

THE SEVENTH TUNNEL OF POWER

The seventh tunnel of power is located at the top of the head and some shamans consider this to be the opening through which the spirit enters the physical body at birth and leaves it at death. The Hopis call this opening kopavi, meaning "the open door." For many shamans, this seventh opening is the passage through which their own spirit body (as well as their power animals) continually passes in and out of the physical body as they gather power and knowledge. When shamans return to their bodies down through this open door, they bring knowledge, wisdom, and all the energy that is then available for dispersal throughout all the tunnels.

As we mentioned in Chapter 2, both religious art and shamanic art depict the seventh opening as a halo or aureole from which rays of light stream out. The cross-cultural custom of bowing had its origins in the shamanic technique of blowing knowledge, energy, power, healing, or lost guardian spirits through this hole.

Every two years Andrew traveled to Northern India to visit his guru. Each time he said farewell to Guru Mataji, the guru called to him and held their heads together crown-to-crown. And each time Andrew was speechless for several hours afterward. In the days following the farewell, Andrew would discover that he knew more than he ever thought possible. He saw the world through the eyes of his guru, Mataji, and he was ecstatic. At the same time, however, he felt ungrounded for a long period of time. Eventually Andrew learned to close down his wide open crown tunnel after bidding farewell to the guru. That way he could return to the Western world with new knowledge and a sense of stability as well.

Although the seventh tunnel may be used as an opening through which to exit the physical body and travel to the spirit world, because this tunnel is such a powerful connector to the spirit world and because the knowledge that is accessed is usually of a higher spiritual nature, most people are not as physically aware of its function. At best, you may occasionally feel a tingling or crawling of the skin at the top of your head when your seventh opening is expanding or contracting. You can learn to become more aware of this activity by turning your awareness to the crown of your head when you feel a slight sensation there.

The color associated with the seventh opening is violet and it forms the outermost layer of the spirit body.

The best way to learn about your own tunnels of power is by experiencing them first hand. Here is an exercise to guide you through the exploration of each one.

Exercise #3: Exploring Each Tunnel

Always use the journey method to do any work or exploration within the seven tunnels. Do not go inside the tunnels without the protection of a guardian spirit or ally. They are high-powered openings to the spirit world and you will need the services of a guide. If you meet with obstruction in any of the tunnels, let your ally clear it up for you. If the obstruction looks very disagreeable—like a vicious beast, insect, or slime—do not attempt to deal with it all by yourself.

Recall that to do effective journeying of this kind you should be feeling relatively healthy and strong. If you have the flu, are depressed, or are under the weather, it is best to ask a friend to journey for you. They can simply lie down next to you, touching you at the shoulder, hip, and ankle, and follow the instructions below. Whatever they discover will be about you and your difficulty. They can ask their own power animal to assist you in whatever way is needed. Simply remain silent during the process. Afterward you can confer.

It is preferable to lie down on your back for this exercise. You can also sit comfortably in a chair with your spine straight as an alternative. Relax and close your eyes. Use a drumming tape or have someone drum for you.

Request the help and guidance of your guardian spirit,

ally, or power animal. Meet your guardian at the entrance to a tunnel. This tunnel will be the entrance to the opening in the top of your head. Tell your ally that you wish to explore a particular tunnel, or state the problem and then ask which tunnel you should explore.

Accompanied or led by your ally, travel down the tunnel until you reach the main branch tunnel at your forehead, also called the sixth tunnel. If this is where you want to explore, then follow your ally through that tunnel. Have your ally remove or clear any blockages that you come across.

If you wish to proceed to one of the other tunnels, then continue past this branch until you reach the branch you want to explore, corresponding to your throat, heart, solar plexus, abdomen, or base of your spine. You can then proceed down that tunnel and let it take you where it will. You can count on the fact that you will encounter experiences and information that relate to the issues you have stored in that area of your body.

As always, return rapidly via the same route that you took to arrive wherever you went. Always thank your ally for the valuable services rendered.

Exercise #3: The Steps

1. Lie down or sit comfortably. Relax and close your eyes.
2. Request the help of your guardian or power animal.
3. Meet your guardian at the entrance to the seventh tunnel (top of your head).
4. State the problem. Identify the tunnel to be explored or ask for assistance.
5. Travel down to the appropriate tunnel.
6. Explore the tunnel.
7. Return by the same route.
8. Thank your guardian.

GUARDING AND MONITORING THE TUNNELS

Very few people are aware of the seven main spirit tunnels on a conscious level. However, if you watch people's body language, you will notice that they often cover these vulnerable openings with their hands, crossed arms, and legs. How often do you see someone cross their arms over their chest or solar plexus when they feel uncomfortable? Perhaps you nave noticed people fingering their throat areas when doubtful about what to say or tapping their foreheads when they are inwardly pondering something. Why do people bow or bare their heads when they are praying or in the presence of a higher authority? Why do people fold their hands over their hearts when feeling devoted or focused on prayer? Have you noticed that some people cross their legs tightly and stick their hands in their laps when they are decidedly nervous or anxious about something? These are all signs of the unconscious spirit-tunnel monitoring that people do on a daily basis. However, these unconscious physical methods of covering up, warding off, or checking out are not nearly as effective as consciously manipulating and guarding the tunnels with the help of your power animals.

In the shamanic perspective, information transfers from one person to another person through the intensity of thoughts and emotions. These thoughts and emotions are generated by the activity in the various tunnels. To the shamanic way of thinking, the brain is just the physical organ that organizes the communications.

The tunnels within a person's spirit body constantly exchange information among themselves via their connective channels. At the same time, in the constant interchange of communication from person to person, the tunnels act as radio transmitters and receivers between people. Typically, this exchange of communication is normal and nonthreatening, but occasionally a transmission is too intense or powerful for the other person's comfort. When this happens there is an automatic physical response of discomfort or protection. You can see this response in a room where a highly dominant individual, like a preacher, is berating a group of people many of whom have their arms crossed over their solar plexus.

This intense type of communication is not always obvious to the naked eye. For example, you may end up with a severe headache after you spend time with someone who is quietly but intensely curious about what you know. They are literally climbing through your sixth tunnel to see what you see. This is unacceptably intrusive and should be guarded against for your own health and balance. On the other hand, you may wonder how someone that later turned out to be such a heel so easily seduced you. These people know how to open up your fourth tunnel and own it for themselves. Remember the story about the woman who got gastric pains after dating a particular man? Perhaps you have awakened in the middle of the night, unable to get someone you met off your mind. These are other signs of penetrating spirit intrusion that you need not put up with.

There is a difference between genuine love between two people and intrusive attention that may be mistaken temporarily for romantic feelings. Genuine love includes respect for the other person's personal space. There is no need to manipulate them or merge with them because the relationship is based on trust and mutual empowerment. They intrude upon you only when there is an emergency and they need to get your attention rapidly.

If you use your power animals to guard and protect your tunnels, you will not fall prey to the melee and discomfort that can occur if you do not. You can tell them when you wish privacy and when you are open to communication with others. Here is one way to set up guardian protection and monitoring for your power tunnels.

Exercise #4: Protecting the Tunnels

Relax, close your eyes, and open up your shamanic vision. Check into each of the seven principal tunnels as we showed you in the first exercise.

Ask your guardian animal or ally to assign a separate power animal to each tunnel. Ask yours to select ones who will represent each tunnel well and are in affinity with your spirit body. Discuss your needs with each guardian and ask them to report to you whenever you are imbalanced or are having some difficulty regarding a tunnel.

As problems occur, ask them to protect you and help you restore your power in that area. For example, if you are experiencing a headache, ask the guardians of both your sixth and seventh tunnels to let you know who is thinking about you and why. Ask them to extract that person gently and seal off their focus or point of attention on you.

Always remember to thank these guardians. If you want

Exercise #4: The Steps

1. Relax and close your eyes.
2. Check each of the seven tunnels, using shamanic vision.
3. Ask for a power animal for each tunnel.
4. Discuss needs with each one.
5. Ask for protection and help in problem areas.
6. Thank your guardians for their help.

them to stick around, remember to ask them for help regularly.

You may not always need to add protection to your tunnels to fend off unwanted intrusion. In fact, you may find that one or more of your tunnels have become overly protected and that you are no longer able to receive desirable communications from other people. It is not unusual in western culture for this to occur for the fourth or heart tunnel. The results can be depression, alienation, isolation, or feelings of loneliness. If you are feeling overly shut down in a particular area, ask your power animals to help you open that tunnel up using the methods described in exercise 2.

There are times when you may want to establish specific communications with other people by sending messages to one of their spirit tunnels. Perhaps you want to communicate support or love to them when they are at school taking an exam, at work in a tough business meeting, or unavailable for immediate telephone contact. Here is a simple exercise that will allow you to communicate with another person at a distance, without intruding unnecessarily in their spirit body.

Exercise #5: Communicating with Others

Relax, close your eyes, and tune into your own shamanic vision. Focusing on your own sixth tunnel (at your brow) can greatly assist you in developing your shamanic sight.

Using your shamanic vision, focus on the other person's tunnel that you wish to support or communicate with. For example, if they are nervous about giving a speech and you want to support them, focus your attention on their throat tunnel and send them a communication.

Talk to them silently there, just as if you were supporting them in person. You can say something like, "Relax, you are a good speaker and you have all the knowledge and information you need to give an excellent talk. Tell them X, Y, and Z, etc."

Notice: Do not intrude inside the tunnel! All you need to

Exercise #5: The Steps

1. Relax and close your eyes.
2. Focus your shamanic vision on the other person's tunnel.
3. Talk to them silently. Do not intrude.
4. Sign off; end the communication.

do is speak to it and the other person or their guardian spirit will hear it and take the necessary measures.

Remember to sign off; let them know your communication has ended. Keep it short, as you do not want to distract them for very long while they are busy. They may or may not be consciously aware of your communication. Nevertheless, their spirit self will respond, with or without their knowing it.

HEALING OTHERS USING THE TUNNELS

Occasionally someone will indirectly ask you for help regarding one of their tunnels. For example, someone may ask you to help them use their intuition more skillfully or help them visualize more clearly. Using your own shamanic visioning, you can picture their sixth tunnel and see how it looks. Tell them who or what you see there obstructing their vision. Then you can ask their power animal to clear that tunnel out and help them see better. If their power animal is not apparent, ask your own power animal to do the job.

Under no circumstances should you use your own energy to help them, nor should you try to send your own energy to them, because they will be unable to use it. They can only use their own energy frequency to make repairs or find balance. When people are imbalanced, confused, or ill, they simply need some information or communication. They do not need foreign substances. Your energy is a foreign substance. Use it only for communication. They can easily disperse whatever little energy you send in delivering the communication.

When you try to heal another by sending them copious amounts of your own energy, you will not only feel drained and dispirited, but you will compound the other person's problem; it becomes varnished with a layer of energy that they cannot digest or process. It may stay there for years until they finally get rid of it. This is why many so-called helpers and healers, despite the best intentions, do more harm than good.

Master shamans know that ultimately, all healing is self-healing. They are good at naming the problem, targeting the problem area (blocked tunnel), contacting power animals or guardians, communicating silently, and staying out of the way. They do not deplete themselves nor do they falsely believe that they alone are able to heal. They are the go-betweens or midwives between the power of the spirit world and the physical landscape.

CHAPTER 9

The Sacred Marriage: Discovering Balance

HEAD, HEART, AND GUT PEOPLE

Once upon a time there were three sisters. The first sister was smart, articulate, and knowledgeable about a great many subjects. She was an avid reader and could carry on intellectual discussions about philosophy, politics, and economics with true acumen.

The second sister was an actress, given to intense drama both on stage and in her own life. She could produce tears at the drop of a hat or just as quickly burst out laughing at nothing at all. A touch psychic, she somehow always knew what was going to happen next.

The third sister was a real whirlwind of activity, given to adventure and the rough-and-tumble of life. It was said that she never sat still.

Now, it so happened that all three sisters fell in love with the same man, a mysterious man whose past was a well-kept secret. He gave each of them equal attention and took turns dating them. This caused the sisters to fight and quarrel bitterly among themselves.

One day the mystery man disappeared, leaving the three without any warning. The intellectual sister buried herself in books. The emotional sister boo-hooed and carried on in a frightening fashion. The adventurous sister lost herself in endless activity. The sisters quarreled again, each saying that her way of dealing with the loss was best.

Finally the three sisters went to see a wise old woman they had heard about with the hope that she could tell them where the mystery man had gone. The wise old woman listened to each of them separately and then gathered them together and asked them one by one, "If there were a fire in your house, what would you do first?" The first sister said, "I would figure out where the fire was coming from and then I would call the fire department."

174

The second sister said, "I would know that a fire was coming and I would scream so the others would be warned." The third sister said, "I would grab some sheets, tie them together, and get myself and the others down the rope to safety." "So who is right?" asked the old woman gently. Each sister again argued that her way was best.

The old woman smiled. "Each of your approaches is needed and each is incomplete without the others. Together you make an effective team." The sisters then asked, "But what of our mystery man?" The old woman spoke again. "He was a part of yourselves looking for one whole woman, not three quarreling parts. But he did get you to reflect on your different styles and approaches. You are each very talented. But you have not worked together. He will return when you can work as one. Now go." The old woman smiled knowingly to herself.

We live in a world of indescribable diversity and infinite creativity. Both the ordinary world and the spirit world contain myriad forms and types even within the same species. Shamans know that each being, whether the spirit of a mountain range or the spirit of a lady bug, has specific purposes and jobs to do. Each species has specialists who contribute their part to maintain that dynamic tension between the ordinary world and the nonordinary reality. Within the world of rocks there are hard metals and soft metals, light lava rocks and heavy granites, sharp crystals and stratified marbles. Plants too demonstrate their diversity through not only size and shape, but color, texture, and function. Insects, reptiles, birds, and mammals each occupy their niches in the natural environment, making their particular contribution to the whole.

Shamans have discovered that this tremendous diversity exists not only in the ordinary world, but in all realms of the spirit world as well. The Upper, Middle, and Lower World all reflect the vast creativity witnessed in ordinary reality. Physically speaking, each rock may have a different shape, size, and color, but in the spirit world each has a unique imprint and energetic pattern. While it is true that at the foundations of the web of power all spirit is one and the same, at the surface levels each part has its distinct expression and character.

At all levels of reality, there are categories that classify groups of similar types within a species or general class of beings. For example, in a beehive there are classes of bees with different temperaments and jobs to do. Some are more aggressive and act as guards and warriors, protecting the queen and the hive. Others are service-oriented, geared toward caring for the larvae. Still others are dedicated to producing the wax and building the hive structures to house the honey and the larvae.

With so much diversity in all worlds, it is natural to find this same level of diversity among human beings. And as with all other kinds of beings, there are classes or subtypes of human beings that are specialists in function and type, each contributing to the survival of the whole. Knowing how to communicate with people of different specialties is a key to successful negotiations with them. Knowing your own specialty and learning how to use it is equally important. Although you have your own specialty, you have elements of all people's specialties and styles within you. Your challenge is to contribute your distinct talents while developing those parts of yourself that are weaker and less familiar to you. In this way, you move toward the balance that shamans are continually seeking.

Let us now look at one of the ways that people specialize. The types that we are going to describe here do not exclusively belong to the world of shamanism, but they are alluded to and referred to among a great many mystic traditions. Let's take the Navajo approach to illustrate the different styles.

Think of the human body as a large country with the national boundaries being the skin outlining the body. Think of the major organs of the body as cities and the glands and smaller organs as the townships and villages. The major arteries and veins are the freeways and roads linking the cities and towns, and the nerves are the communication lines between them. These cities, roads and communication links are configured similarly in each human being, but their relative size and strength are what makes up the differences in people. In some people the brain is the capital city, in others the heart is the capital, and in still others the gut is the center of commerce and government. Roughly speaking, these are then three major classes of people: head people, heart people, and gut people. From a shamanic point of view, knowing exactly how each operates can be a key to power and knowledge.

These different orientations determine how a person responds initially to any situation. A head person reacts to any stimulus with thoughts, a heart person with emotions, and a gut person with actions. Here is a more complete description of each class of people, accompanied by ways that you can better communicate with each type. Keep in mind that one of these types is your own and by coming to understanding yourself, you can become more balanced.

TYPE	RULE	STRENGTH	LIMITATION
HEAD	thought	analysis; language; logic; philosophy; insightful	slow-acting; cold; remote; alienated;
HEART	feeling	perceptive; quick; expressive; inspirational	irrational; subjective; sentimental
GUT	action	coordinated; athletic; active; instinctual	impulsive; frenetic; mechanical

HEAD PEOPLE

Head people are those who have developed the brain and vocal cords as their principal tools. Theirs is a government where thoughts and words are the chief tender. Head people are known for their excellent vocabularies and their ability to express themselves well. They rely on the relatively slow but precise use of words to process their experience and communicate it. They are the talkers and writers who are good at analysis, philosophy, and rational thought. A tendency to chop up experiences into bite-sized words makes them proficient at taking apart a problem to get to its source. In this way, they are able to conceptualize situations and get to the reasons why they occurred. This makes them good scientists, researchers, and business people.

Head people like to give reasons why they do things and they expect you to do the same. They think in terms of a linear time frame and want ideas to be presented logically. Their favorite question is "Why?" They say, "I want answers." You cannot respond to a head person with a feeling or emotion and expect to satisfy them. In more extreme situations, they will tend to dismiss feelings as hysterical, irrelevant, or bothersome. To them, feelings are not to be trusted.

Head people are not prone to take swift action. They would rather ponder the situation and analyze it heavily before moving on it. It is much more interesting for a head person to think or talk about something than act on it. This makes them good planners but not good producers unless the product is an article, book, or speech.

Because of these tendencies, head people can cut themselves off from their hearts and guts. Their country's capital lies in the remote region of the head and the other important cities are ignored or given a back seat in important government affairs. They can become trapped in endless analysis in a heartless sort of way, without considering the human element, and become cut off from taking action, the specialty of the gut region.

For head people, the heart is a satellite city relegated to serve the capital in the head. Feelings and emotions are experienced only in relation to the thoughts they are thinking. That is, they tend to use their hearts to worry about their thoughts. Likewise, the gut is a satellite of the head and all actions coming from it are a direct result of their thoughts.

HOW TO COMMUNICATE WITH A HEAD PERSON

Here are some of the things you can do to get along with a head person.

- First of all, you must always let a head person do some talking first, it makes them feel better. This is especially true after some journey work. Do not, however, let them talk endlessly. Listen up to a point and then come to a decision or conclusion.

- Try to help move the person away from pure theory to actual experience.

- Be patient and try not to act or move too quickly. The head person tends to process things slowly. They think in words and that takes time.

- When head people have a real problem, the last place they look for resolution is in their feelings or actions. If they have lost a loved one through death, they will try to think about what all the ramifications will be instead of giving in to their grief. They need gentle help and permission to admit those frightening feelings. Then they will need some assistance in taking appropriate action.

- Head people are proud of their ideas, sharp insight, and ability to analyze. Remember to compliment them on these special talents. Give them instructions and structure. They like it.

- Head people are great at recalling the details of a vision or journey. They may need assistance however in recalling the feelings of nuances of the journey elements that could make all the differences in its meaning. They do have these feelings, they just tend to deemphasize them out of habit.

- Head people become more balanced by doing physical exercise, taking action (gut), listening to music, and singing (heart). On the other hand, they are unhappy if they are deprived of reading, writing, or engaging in philosophical discussions.

HEART PEOPLE

Heart people have emphasized the heart and lung region of their bodies. For them, these are the centers of trade and commerce, the head and lower body being relegated to the backwaters. For them, feelings, emotions, and inspiration are the legal tender and primary focus of attention.

Heart people are incredibly perceptive and tend to be rapid in their assessment of a situation or problem. They do not process verbally, but through direct perception. They can walk into a room and immediately know that something is wrong or misaligned. They know immediately whom they can trust and whom they should avoid. However, they are hard pressed to tell you why they feel that way. Their way of knowing is broad-brushed and less incisive and specific than the head person's style.

Heart people do not process linearly but more in a matrix style that defies analysis or definition. They move rapidly into the future, past, or present, interweaving all of them to come to their final conclusions. They tend to drive head people crazy with their "harebrained" methods and their uncanny ability to be accurate much of the time.

Note that heart people are quite accurate in assessing a situation when they are not overly identified with it or attached to its outcome. Emotional perception is not the same thing as being attached. A head person can be attached to their ideas, an action person may be attached to their activities, and a heart person can be attached to their feelings.

Heart people tend to use the head city as a backwater, referred to only when an analysis of a feeling is needed. Therefore, heart people tend to think and talk about their feelings even when they are not actually experiencing them. For heart people, the gut city serves only to act out feelings as in dramatics, dancing, or compulsive buying.

Heart people can get into trouble with their sentimentality and the subjectivity of their feelings. Sometimes they mistake sentiment for genuine perception and as a result are totally inaccurate in their conclusions. They may have blocked off the roads to the head and, as a result, find themselves unable to understand their situation. In addition, they can cut off avenues to the gut, where action arises, so that they get stuck wallowing in emotion without moving on to something new.

How to Deal with Heart People

- First, allow the heart person time to express feelings first, whether or not they make any sense to you. Then gradually move them toward more objectivity by asking pertinent questions and creating a verbal structure.

- Help the person focus on the power and strength of their lower bodies, especially their legs. This helps to ground them into that part of their body that supports concrete action and limits chaotic emotional reactivity.

- Give up trying to get a heart person to follow a well-thought-out set of instructions or organized plan. They either won't, out of rebellion, or they simply can't do it, and you will bring on an unpleasant incident if you force the issue. Do, however, get them to give you a deadline for work completed. Get everything in writing.

- Trust heart people when they get an immediate hunch or sense. They are probably right even if it seems crazy to you.

- Heart people are great artists and poets. Always use metaphors when you are explaining something to a heart person or trying to get them to follow an activity. Better yet, use visuals and skip a lot of the words. Heart people respond to color, size, shape, and designs.

- Heart people are usually very good at journeying, but they can overdramatize their experience and at times distort it. Help them tell you exactly what happened. Help them to show you in specific movements what actually happened.

- Heart people are wonderfully empathetic and sensitive but can become overly identified with their own or other people's problems. Help them see that problems are challenges and are in fact opportunities for growth.

- Heart people become balanced when they do more physical exercise (gut) and when they read or apply themselves in mathematics (head). However, they will throw a fit if they are deprived of emotional expression.

GUT PEOPLE

Gut people are focused on the action-oriented qualities of the solar plexus and the lower body. For them, action and production is the legal tender for their government. All thoughts and emotions are screened through an action-oriented sieve. All ideas and feelings are in the service of action.

Gut people have natural coordination and athletic ability. They know how to use their bodies instinctively, without the interference of thoughts and feelings. They also know all about production and the exact movements needed for machinery, tools, and bureaucracy to work efficiently and effectively. They make great pilots, athletes, engineers, tool makers, designers, and percussionists.

Gut people are the doers and movers of the world. They have difficulty sitting still and are not happy unless they are traveling somewhere, even if it is confined to their thoughts or feelings. When they are unable to move physically, they often imagine themselves doing things and going places. Even their emotions tend to impel them to move or act something out.

Gut people use their hearts to give emotional expression to their movements, as in dance and gesture. They tend to harness their heads to think about and analyze their movements, as in choreography or engineering. If they get an idea, they immediately want to put it into action. Philosophizing is not their interest. They want "results and productivity."

However, when gut people cut off the roads to head and heart completely, they can become robotic and machinelike, even dangerous, as people who do not think or feel before acting. In this negative vein, they can be trapped in aimless doing, producing endlessly without any rational motive or perception of the greater need. Unfortunately, gut people can also have trouble with addictive behavior because of their impulsive tendencies. An uncomfortable feeling or thought can lead to drinking or drug taking quite easily. This is one reason why professional athletes have trouble with drugs.

DEALING WITH GUT PEOPLE

- Gut people need space to move in. They hate to be confined or trapped. Therefore never pen them in. Give them tasks that allow them to walk, drive, fly, and generally move about.

- Give gut people an opportunity to use their bodies. If you are trying to teach them something, get them to go through the movements first. They learn kinesthetically, by doing, not by a set of verbal instructions or by color codes. They do respond to three-dimensional models that can be manipulated to demonstrate how to do something.

- Compliment and acknowledge gut people for their incredible coordination. Give them credit for being capable in this physically oriented way. After all, who would you want flying the plane in an emergency?

- Gut people recall sensations and movements. In journeying, get them to identify these actions first, then help them identify the feelings and meanings that accompanied them. They have these but simply deemphasize them.

- Gut people may be impulsive, spontaneous, and on occasion belligerent. Learn from their spontaneity and compliment them on it. Help them to get in touch with their deeper feelings and emotions before they act self-destructively. Help them think through an action on a major issue before embarking on it, even if briefly. Help them to be dynamic rather than pushy.

- Gut people are balanced by listening to music, dancing (heart), or reading (head). They will be most unhappy if they are not allowed to move or at least move with their thoughts and feelings.

SUBTYPES

Each person specializes in one of the three styles, head, heart, and gut. In addition you may find that you have a subspecialty as well. If you are a heart person you might also be fairly good at head matters and poorest at gut activity. If you are a head person you might be fair at gut reactions but poor in the heart category. This gives you a more exact description of the actual way you operate in the world. Here are the six subtypes.

SUBTYPE	DOES LEAST	STRENGTH	LIMITATION
Emotional head person	act	empathetic	worries
Active head person	feel	prolific	obsessive
Thinking heart person	act	poet	introvert
Active heart person	think	expressive	dramatic
Thinking gut person	feel	productive	ruthless
Emotional gut person	think	dynamic	impulsive

BALANCING THE BODY

Your specialty and subtype gives the world diversity and ensures that there are experts in all spheres of life.

However, the head, the heart, and the gut were never meant to operate completely separately or in isolation from one another. Shamanically speaking, the body is meant to act in harmony, each part balancing and contributing to the activities of the others. When these three major regions act in harmony with one another, they are then capable of interacting effectively with the source of power, the spirit world. This leads to success in all spheres of life.

Shamans are dedicated to finding balance within themselves. They purposefully exercise all three aspects of themselves in order to become more effective human beings. Among their many skills, they have a reputation for being intellectual giants in their communities as well as being poets and artists. They are additionally known for being active, healthy, spontaneous people who travel both physically and spiritually.

Exercise #1: Balancing

This is a journey for balance. First ask your current guardian spirit or power animal for assistance in becoming more balanced. In your case you are unsure of your main style, ask your ally to tell you. You can even ask your guardian spirit to tell you what your subtype is; that is, a thinking or an acting heart person, an emotional or a thinking gut person, or an active or feeling head person. Then request help on a journey where you will go in search of information or knowledge that can help you strengthen the two weaker aspects of yourself.

Exercise #1: The Steps

1. Relax and close your eyes.
2. Ask your guardian or power animal for help in balance.
3. Ask for assistance in knowing what type you are.
4. Journey for information.
5. Thank your guardian.

Exercise #2: Balance for Head People

When caught in endless analysis, do something, not about the problem, but about something else. Get your body moving. Listen to emotional music, sing, draw, or paint.

Head people tend to be most comfortable with the fifth and sixth main tunnels of the spirit body. However, the second, third, and fourth tunnels are often blocked. This is where you need to explore and clear the most with the help of your power animal.

Exercise #3: Balance for Heart People

When caught in sentimentality, subjectivity, or a quagmire of emotion, move the body. Dance, shake, crawl on your belly like a reptile. Pick a subject or object and figure out how it was made or how it got that way. Let your energy drop down a notch to your belly or raise up a notch to your head. Do some talking.

Heart people are most comfortable with the second, third, and fourth main tunnels of power and less familiar with the sixth and fifth tunnels. If you are seeking balance, these are where you could benefit the most in your journeys.

Exercise #4: Balance for Gut People

When caught in action without rationale or feeling, listen to music, pay attention to what is happening in your chest area. Breathe deeply. Stop and think. Talk to someone about what you intend to do. Express your sexuality with heart.

Gut people are most comfortable with the first, second, and third main tunnels and least acquainted with the fourth, fifth, and sixth tunnels. Exploring these less familiar tunnels helps to balance gut people.

MAGNETIC AND DYNAMIC: FEMININE AND MASCULINE PRINCIPLES

Another way that people specialize is through their sexual role. Being male or female is a specialty that brings unique talents and abilities to life experience. On the other hand, from a shamanic perspective, each is a polarization of the other, half of the whole, and by definition an imbalanced state of being. This does not refer solely to the sex of the body type, but to the sexual orientation and identity of the person occupying that body. Because a person is a woman does not mean that she has a magnetic way of thinking and because a person is a male does not mean he has a dynamic way of thinking. There are males that are more magnetic than some females, and females that are more dynamic than some men. The important thing from the shamanic point of view is the state of relative balance a person has or is able to achieve in reference to both.

For shamans, this state of balance between the feminine and masculine, magnetic and dynamic, yin and yang aspects of themselves is of supreme importance. Many shamans have believed that to be a truly excellent shaman, one must bring together these polarities into harmony and balance. Historically, there are many accounts of shamans cross-dressing and living as members of the opposite sex either for a time or permanently. There are accounts of this ritualized merging into the opposite sex among Native American shamans from the Arapaho, Cheyenne, and Ute tribes as well as South American, Northeastern Asian, and Indonesian shamans. This is not caused by a cross-cultural sexual disorder, but is done purposefully as a practice to attain balance. Shamans are looking for that supreme internal unity that brings together the male and female aspects within themselves into a sacred marriage. They are so incredibly dedicated that they are willing to take extremely challenging measures to reach their goal of balance. Here is an example of that process in a traditional context.

Mantuk was a powerful man, large by Eskimo standards, and an excellent hunter and fisher. Just last year, he had won the intervillage competition for fish-laden–sled-pulling and spearfishing. That was before he fell ill with smallpox and lay in a coma for many days, awash in deep visions and dreams. He was watched over by Pestak, the village shaman, who gradually nursed him back to health. Although Mantuk recovered fully from his bout with disease and regained his old strength, he somehow knew his life was changed forever. He tried to hunt and fish as he had done in the past, but his heart wasn't really in it anymore. He knew it was because of the visions he had seen during his long coma.

In one vision, Mantuk met a beautiful woman who told him that he would recover, but that afterward he must follow the healing way, the way of the shaman. But to do so, he would have to undergo the most severe test he had ever been through, even tougher than his present illness. She told him that he must become like her. He did not understand and asked her what she meant, but she only repeated the same message each time Mantuk saw her.

When he recovered, Mantuk had tried to resume his old competitive way of life without success. Finally he told Pestak everything that he had seen and heard in his vision. Pestak sat still and mulled it over for a long time. Then Pestak told him, "You have received your path but you avoid it. You know that you will fail if you fight her. She is stronger than you and you fear her. The only solution is to do as she bids and become like her. That means giving up the hunter's life and finding another way. You must learn to heal and nurture. You must become receptive and feeling. Then you will find power and strength and she will not defeat you."

Mantuk was horrified, but he knew that Pestak was right. For the next year Mantuk gave up the life of the hunter and instead lived in Pestak's house, dressed as a woman. He learned the healing ways. This was indeed the most severe challenge he had ever undertaken, harder even than sled-pulling or spearfishing, or illness. Mantuk became a great shaman.

You need not practice such drastic measures to find your own state of internal balance. However, if you want to be a powerful and successful person, you must come to terms with these polarities within you. You need to get to know the side of you that has been repressed or ignored in favor of your specialty.

We are not suggesting here that, if you are a man, for example, you become a woman. Rather, we would suggest that you sense your level or ratio of dynamic and magnetic energy. Those amounts can then tell you where to concentrate in order to bring yourself into greater balance. For example, if you are a woman but you determine yourself to have 75 percent dynamic orientation and only a 25 percent magnetic orientation, then you need to focus on raising that 25 percent magnetic aspect of yourself. Likewise, if you are a highly feminine woman you need to bring your masculine side out more. Similar focusing for men with much higher percentages on one side or the other of balance is also true.

Exercise #5: Discovering Your Dynamic and Magnetic Balance

Close your eyes and relax. Shamanically envision a large mandala or medicine wheel about three feet in front of you. Imagine that there is a line down the middle of it. Label one side dynamic and the other side magnetic as you see fit. Imagine that each side is shaded with a different color. This represents the absolute balance of 50 percent yang and 50 percent yin energy. Now ask your power animal to shift that line over one way or another to reflect your actual balance of the two. See one side grow as the other side shrinks. Which side is larger, the magnetic or the dynamic? Assign percentages to this new ratio. This tells you which side needs more focus and attention.

Exercise #5: The Steps

1. Close your eyes and relax.
2. Invision a mandala or medicine wheel.
3. Divide it in the middle.
4. Label the two sides dynamic and magnetic, each with a different color.
5. Ask your power animal to shift the line to reflect actual ratio.
6. Assign percentages to your sides.

Most likely, if you are a man in western culture, you have been taught to suppress your magnetic side and become more "macho." This is unhealthy in shamanic terms because it causes you to suppress some of the most powerful shamanic tools you have: creativity; imagination; intuition; emotion; and flexibility. In order to develop these tools, you will need to drop the overly dynamic posturing and open up that feminine side. This does not mean that you become like a spineless jellyfish, which is probably your greatest fear.

Remember the goal is balance, not a parody of the opposite extreme. The power is always in the middle position, never in extreme polarity.

If you are like many traditional Western females, you have suppressed the more assertive and dynamic aspect of yourself in favor of a compliant, submissive, or manipulative posture. You may have found that this persona offers you unique advantages in terms of being protected and supported by the stereotyped males of our culture, but you have traded away some of your most important resources in the process. You have given up your power and your ability to go out and get exactly what you want in life. Lost is the ring of authority and the feel of independence that goes with that dynamic side. Shamanically, what is needed is a move toward the center, a gradual shift toward that male side that has been under wraps for so long.

Exercise #6: Balancing the Dynamic and Magnetic Sides

Here is a list of things you can do to begin to integrate your suppressed side. The first list applies to overly masculine people, the second list applies to overly feminine people. Remember that this refers to energy and not actual gender. We are sure you can add your own personal touches to the lists.

If you are the overly dynamic woman or man:

- Bring yourself into the company of people who you feel display a good balance of both sides. Being with other overly masculine types will only compound your problem. Usually you will find that older people have accomplished this better than younger people. They have had more time to transcend the social stereotypes and discover their own balance.

- Make a practice of listening to music or going to films that open up your feelings. You may find that your strongest suppressed emotion is grief, and sobbing is what you need more than anything else. There may be a sadness felt about all the effort you put out to keep yourself so strong all the time. You may also find that the emotion that comes most easily to you is anger. It is necessary to exercise some discipline to allow the sadness underneath to emerge.

- Lock up the drugs, beer and liquor supply. It's usually just a narcotic to suppress your anger and grief or cover up your fear.

- Take walks in nature and make a point of noticing the details. Realize that everything you are looking at is alive, even the rocks, and they have something to say to you.

- Avoid any tendencies to be fascinated with violence on television, movies, books, etc. This is just an old program that keeps the status quo. Avoid contact sports for a while.

- Find an older person, a child, or an animal whom you can nurture and care for. Listen to them.

- Sing.

- Prepare food and make a point of sharing it. Bring your own dish to a party or gathering.

- Get out the art supplies and paint or draw your impressions of the world around you.

- Get out the old photographs of yourself and your family as you grew up. Get in touch with how you felt then. Talk mentally to your father, mother, brothers, sisters, and all the significant characters represented there. Tell them everything you always wanted to say to them but didn't. Get out the hanky.

- Make a point of telling someone how you feel every day. Silence may be macho, but it kills you off early and ruins shamanic practice.

- You are probably used to hiding your fearful feelings even from yourself. Begin to admit to your fears and tell someone else about them. It's okay when you are afraid.

- Learn to be able to accept help from others. You are not an island. You cannot exist without support.

- Spend more time being, less time doing.

If you are the overly magnetic woman or man:

- Make a practice of being direct. If you want something, go to the person who can do something about it, not the one who will agree with you and pat you on the head. Avoid gossip.

- Cut the chatter and take action.

- Do aerobic exercise daily to build up physical strength and inner power.

- Make a list of everything you feel helpless about. Do whatever is needed to begin to handle these things for yourself. This may require you to study or take a class in auto repair, for example. Change a tire, repair a light switch, get those hands dirty. If you didn't get dirt under those nails, you didn't do enough.

- Go to at least a few films that make you uncomfortable in terms of aggression. Go to an erotic film. Identify with the more assertive party.

- Do something productive with friends. Build something together. Start and carry out a program to take food to the elderly or homeless. Take action.

- Get dirty. Real dirty, and don't wash it off for a while.

- Try as many new things as possible. Go to places you have never been before. Have an outdoor adventure.

- You are more comfortable with depression than any other emotion when you feel bad. You are more likely to stuff anger or ignore it because you fear it. Give a voice to your anger. Make sure it is directed at the object of your anger. Avoid passive aggressive acts like agreeing to meet someone and then not showing up because you are angry with them.

- Do things for the sake of doing them and the pleasure it gives you, not just for the effect your actions have on other people.

- Make a list of all the people you feel dependent on and list what you depend on them for. See how many of those things you can do for yourself. Next time you get in a bind, get yourself out of it using your own power.

- Spend more time doing, less time being.

Exercise #7: A Journey for Integration

Begin to journey using the techniques you have learned. Explain to your guardian spirit that you want to balance your dynamic and magnetic sides and that you want help with this. If it is appropriate, ask them to take you to a place where you can meet up with and confront your opposite.

If you are highly magnetic, your dynamic side may at first appear to be frightening and primitively aggressive. You may have to approach it many times before you can merge with it. Use your own discretion here. If you are highly dynamic, your opposite will often appear to be witchlike, malevolent, or cunningly dangerous. Again you may have to approach it many times before you can befriend it.

Feel free to rely on your guardian spirit to assist you or provide you with relevant advice. You will, however, basically have to carry out the confrontation on your own.

Return and apply any suggestions to your practice.

Exercise #7: The Steps

1. Relax and close your eyes.
2. Begin to journey.
3. Ask your guardian or power animal for help in balance.
4. Ask them to take you to meet your opposite or weaker side.
5. Approach and merge with that side.
6. Ask advice of your guardian.
7. Return.
8. Thank your guardian. Apply suggestions to your practice.

Exercise #8: Imagining Opposites

Using your imagination, envision yourself as you would be if you were the opposite sex. What would you look like if you were male? Female? How would you act? What would be your preferences? What kind of person would you be attracted to? How would it make a difference in your life? Would you be able to accomplish the same things? Would your goals be the same? If you have the courage to do so, imagine yourself as the opposite sex. What is he/she like? How does he/she move? This is not unlike letting your power animal come through you. Although it may be uncomfortable for you, it will not in any way harm you. It can give you powerful insights into your orientation and how you suppress that other half of yourself. To understand another, walk a mile in their moccasins. This is a variation on the old Native American proverb, "Don't judge me until you've walked a mile in my moccasins."

We have described two ways that you can become overly specialized in your life's focus, and we have given you a number of exercises to help find the balance needed for shamanic work. This requires the ability to handle major change in your life. So, if in doing the exercises in this chapter, you

have opened yourself up to a major change, go back to
Chapter 7 and review the section on change. Use some of the
suggestions to help you here. A shaman's life is not a static
one by any means, and this path requires cultivating a high
degree of flexibility and expansiveness.

CHAPTER 10

Transformation Through Ritual and Ceremony: Practices

The meeting had been heated and intense and when it was over the room had that thick, cut-it-with-a-knife feel to it. Marian's living room was spacious enough to hold the fifteen or so people who came together each month to debate community projects; and she had not minded the meetings. What she had minded was the way the room had felt afterward. Marian found that she could barely stand going into her living room for several days after one of these meetings. It seemed that all the debate and tension from the heated discussions remained in the room long after the meeting itself was over. But things had changed.

This time, after all the people left, Marian opened the windows wide and carried in a clay bowl that she filled with smoldering dried leaves and stems from the sage bush. She had picked the sage herself on her vacation to the high desert in Utah. Memories flooded in: how she had sat with the sage bushes for a time and had asked their permission to pick a few branches. The bushes had been generous and enthusiastic in their response. Not only did they offer their branches to her, but they also gave Marian information about the specific qualities of sage and instructions on how to use it for cleansing the atmosphere in her house.

Marian stood in the center of the room and raised the bowl of sage up to her eye level with her arms outstretched. Then, slowly turning around, she described an imaginary medicine wheel with the bowl. Marian stopped for a moment to invoke each of the four directions. She raised the bowl up above her head and then lowered it to the floor to invoke the Sky and then the Earth. Marian let the smoke drift over her body, using her hands to guide it to her chest, and from there over her head and then around the rest of herself. Next she carried the bowl around the room, letting the sage smoke drift to all areas, especially the eight corners of the room where the air tended to get particularly stale.

Despite the thickness and smell of the smoke, Marian suddenly felt that she could breathe again. Breathing the sage-scented air deeply, she felt her body relax. Thank you Sage for your cleansing powers, she thought. Her living room was now livable again.

Rituals and ceremonies are ancient shamanic forms practiced cross-culturally to access power and honor the spirit world. For shamans, rituals are a way of bridging the spirit world with the world of ordinary reality. They make use of ordinary elements of nature: sage and herbs, fire, crystals, the six directions, circles and other natural phenomena. All the senses are employed in rituals or ceremonies to enrich the experience and to raise its power to shift, transform, and create change.

When shamans want to manifest power, they do so ritualistically and ceremonially. Through ritual, they are reminded of the important source of power in the spirit world and the shamanic perspective they need to remember to keep. The ritual helps them remember to ask for what they want. It acts as a kind of focus where they can articulate their goal, ask for assistance with it, sense connection with the web of power, and surrender old agendas for new results.

Let us look for a moment at the common ingredients found in rituals and ceremonies throughout the world of shamanism. Most of these elements can be found in modern-day ceremonies actually based on ancient shamanic practices. Consider the opening ceremonies of sports events or the pomp and circumstance of graduations, political events, and international summits. Observe the rituals of any religious service or holiday festivity. Although, ceremonially speaking, they are often watered down, these events still have most of the ingredients listed below.

Both rituals and ceremonies are characterized by:

• Invoking the power of sound such as music, drumming, rattling, singing, and chanting.

• Invoking the power of motion such as gestures, postures, hand movements, and dancing.

- Invoking the power of smell by burning incense, sage, salt crystals and the like.

- Invoking the power of location by being performed in traditionally sacred spots or actively giving a location power through its performance there.

- Invoking the power of the guardians, allies, and power animals by inviting their presence, participation, and assistance.

- Invoking the power of all those physically present by requesting their prayers and joint focus of attention.

In addition, both rituals and ceremonies are:

- Performed on significant dates and times such as the equinox, solstice, new moon, full moon, day of the dead, midsummer, or arrival of monsoons and the like.

- Performed at significant rites of passage such as birth, puberty, marriage, death, or initiation into lodges or positions of authority.

- Performed to open or close important meetings. They signal the sacred time of focus, as when a council meets to form new agreements or laws.

- Performed to signal a transfer to a different state of consciousness, such as the beginning of a journey, or a trance state.

- Performed to celebrate or commemorate important events such as peace treaties and agreements, the birth or death of a great leader, the liberation from oppression, or a successful hunt.

- Performed in connection with a profound event such as the healing of a disease or an emotional or physical wounding.

In Marian's tale, you see how sage can be burned ritually to clean a room or space and the people in it before or after an important event. Often in rituals such as these, several ingredients are brought together or used in conjunction with one another. Invoking the four (or six) directions and the Sky and Earth, for example, is a common way of starting a journey or beginning a meeting of any kind. Invoking the six directions grounds an event and gives it a central location of importance in the cosmos. The six directions are also used in conjunction with the invocation of the medicine wheel, the sacred circle that honors the spirit world and gives power to the event.

In many of the rituals we describe here, we suggest that you use the rattle, an ancient shamanic tool. A rattle seems like a strange device for adults to use because in modern-day Western culture, we usually associate them with babies and their teething toys. Yet rattles have an ancient history and have been used by shamans on every continent of the world. They must therefore have a powerful significance in the world of shamanism.

Rattles are usually made of dried gourds with beans or pebbles placed inside for sound. These may have been collected at a sacred site or passed on from a powerful shaman. The gourds themselves are attached to a stick and decorated in every way imaginable. Often they are made to resemble animals or creatures from the spirit world, because shamans believe that the sound of the rattle aids in opening the doorway to the spirit world. Rattles are used to call forth the aid of allies and guardians. So, whereas the drum is used to carry the shaman himself to and through the spirit world, the rattle brings the spirit world and its inhabitants closer to ordinary reality.

Rattles are also used as a kind of directing device, much like the magician's magic wand. Energy can be mentally sent through them and out into the environment. The rattle can describe a sacred circle or distribute healing energy within a sick person's body.

The sound of the rattle creates a high-pitched frequency that helps invoke an altered state. In our experience, it is hard not to respond to the sound of rapid rattling. It creates an atmosphere of imminence, that something out of the ordinary is about to happen. We recommend the use of rattles in ceremonies because they have proven effective tools for setting the stage and opening the doorways to power and creativity.

SIMPLE OPENING RITUAL

Smolder some sage and use it much like the cleansing ritual described in Marian's story. If you are in a group, you can simply pass it around, allowing each person to clear themselves with the smoke, using their hands to do so. (A feather is nice to use also.)

OPENING RITUAL FOR JOURNEYING OR OTHER SHAMANIC PROCESS

Using a rattle, stand in the center of the room facing east. Pivoting around clockwise, describe a circle with the rattle while shaking it. If you are in a large group, you can walk clockwise all the way around the group, shaking the rattle over each person's head.

Stand in the center of the room and, again facing east, invoke the power and spirit of the east. Shake your rattle above the head for the upper world. Then, at position level with the chest for the middle world; then below the chest around the waist for the lower world. You can say something very simple like, "Spirit of the East, season of spring and place of sunrise, please bring your inspiration and creativity to our gathering. Thank you for your illumination."

Moving clockwise, face south, rattle, and say something like, "Spirit of the South, season of summer and place of productivity, growth, and harvest, please bring your energy and productivity to our gathering. Thank you for your warmth."

Moving clockwise, face west, rattle, and say something like, "Spirit of the West, season of fall, and place of preparation, please bring your powers of introspection to our gathering. Thank you for your insight."

Moving clockwise, face north, rattle, and say something like, "Spirit of the North, season of winter, and place of purification, please bring your powers of renewal to our gathering. Thank you for your patience."

If you wish, you can include the Sky above and the Earth below as the fifth and sixth directions.

If you are in a group, it is often effective to ask for volunteers to stand in the position of each direction. The volunteers should choose the direction that means the most to them at this time. For example, someone may be feeling inspired, a feeling related to the east; a person might feel sunny and productive which is related to the south; another person may feel introspective and this would correspond with the west; yet another person may feel they are in a place of renewal, a state related to the north. Each stands facing into the middle of the circle from the direction that they have selected. They each can speak a few words from the heart about that direction.

Opening Ritual: The Steps

1. Using a rattle, stand in the center of the room. Face east.
2. Pivot clockwise, describing a circle with the shaking rattle.
3. Face east. Invoke its power and spirit.
4. Shake rattle for the upper, middle and lower worlds.
5. Move clockwise, face south, west and north.
6. Rattle for Sky and Earth as fifth and sixth directions.

POWER SONGS

While there are a great many traditional songs and chants that accompany shamanic ceremonies, shamans usually have their own spirit or power songs. These songs come to them spontaneously and may or may not become a permanent part of their shamanic toolbox. Typically, a song is given to shamans by their guardian spirits as a gift of protection or a method of calling up power. The power song may be long and elaborate, but more commonly it is a simple verse or series of sounds set to a rhythm or tune. It may be accompanied by simple drumming or sung unaccompanied. Here are two examples of simple power songs.

1

Oh waters, you are my friend,
Oh waters, you are my friend,
You carry me in your bosom,
You fill me with strength,
You surround me, you guide me,
Oh waters, waters, oh waters

2

Hah hey, hah hey, hey hey hey
Hah hey, hah hey, heh hey hey
Fly me, bear, fly me, bear
To where you fill the sky,
Fly me, bear, fly me, bear
Your name I always hear,
Fly me, bear, fly me, bear

> Fill me with your power,
> Fly me, bear, fly me, bear
> Surround me with your fur,
> Hah hey, hah hey, hey hey hey
> Hah hey, hah hey, hey hey hey.

These power songs remind shamans that they are protected from harm by their guardian spirit. In singing them, they honor their allies and call forth their powers to protect and help them. The songs are also a constant reminder that they are connected with the spirit world, not lost in the "dream" of ordinary reality. Singing a power song fills them with power and a sense of certainty.

Power songs are usually sung at ceremonial times, during rites of passage, or in situations where assistance is wanted. For example, a power song might be sung just prior to a healing ritual or a journey for specific information to solve a thorny problem. You can sing a power song prior to a challenging interview, meeting, or test situation, where more power would be of value. Singing a power song just before a surgical procedure or medical intervention would be excellent.

Here are some hints at discovering your own power songs.

- Take a journey using the methods we have outlined specifically to find a power song. Tell your ally that this is what you are looking for. Allow your ally to take you somewhere where you can find one or be given one. Upon returning, practice it until you get the words, sounds, beat, and tune clear.

- Using a drum, begin a methodical beat, and allow yourself to relax with the idea in mind that a power song is looking for you. The power song will find you via the beat of the drum if you are open to it. As you begin to get fragments of words or sounds, gradually alter your beat to accommodate the new song. Don't worry if it feels like you are making it up at first, because that is the way most shamanic work intuitively feels. Take a risk and continue to plug away, letting something come through. Be persistent but playful and proceed without effort. If it feels like work, quit and try it another time. There is no limit to the number of power songs you can have, but generally you will probably rely on one or two favorites.

Power songs are valuable because they introduce a new element to your approach. Singing bypasses the usual mind chatter that tends to reduce your power, and also allows you to shift into a different mind-set before taking on a difficult task or challenge. Power songs remind you of your hidden resources and great guidance and support system. They let you know that you are not alone.

SHAMANIC DANCING

Dancing is an integral part of many shamanic ceremonies and rituals, for good reason. It is an excellent method of creating balance and harmony between the web of power and the ordinary physical world. Movement through shamanic dance is both an expression and liberation of emotion, and a vehicle for transformation. It allows the dancer to shift from one state of consciousness to another extremely rapidly and promotes the kind of trance states so valuable for shamanic work.

Shamanic dance has a number of important functions. First of all, it communicates a story or a set of feelings to those watching. The dance transforms the atmosphere so that everyone observing becomes the participant of a vision, a hunt, or an adventure. Everyone present, including those watching the dance, are transformed in the process and thus prepared for the communion with the spirit.

Additionally, the patterned movements of the dance—the postures and gestures—create openings through which the spirit world becomes accessible. Shamanic dance prepares the dancer for deeper internal experiences. Through the shifting movements of the dance, shamans unleash powerful energies within their own bodies. The vigorous flow of gestures releases the energy dams at all the joints. This is important because at the vertebrae are located the seven main spirit tunnels and at the other joints between bones are located many smaller ones. Dancing creates harmony and balance within the body, aligns and helps to unblock the tunnels, and sets up a proper foundation for extensive journey work.

After or during a journey, dancing helps people put their experience into form, helping them remember what happened. Dancing the experience not only communicates it to others, but increases the likelihood that the dancer's vision will manifest into reality. Dancing a successful hunt seen in a vision, for example, increases the possibility that the next hunt will indeed be bountiful.

The many forms of shamanic dance range from group-oriented methodical movements to wild spontaneous gyrations spun from deeply personal ecstatic experiences. Often the more spontaneous movements emerge after a series of formal or traditional dance steps have set the atmosphere for a shamanic trance state.

We suggest that you start out learning to dance privately or solo. Then, if you wish, you can include other people. The dances recommended here have no set steps or routines. They are simple and require no expertise in dancing whatsoever. In shamanic dance it does not matter how you look, it's how you feel that counts. It helps to be physically fit however, or you will get winded quickly.

Dance Ritual #1: The Preparation Dance

Set up a private environment where you will not be interrupted. Clear out an area where you can move without bumping into things. It helps if the room is semi-dark. You may wish to cleanse it with sage first or invoke the six directions.

To the sound of your own small hand-held drum or rattle (or tape recording), begin to make simple movements up and down as you may have seen in some African dances. You do not have to go anywhere. This is something like jogging in place. It helps if you can drum or rattle loudly.

With your eyes half-closed, concentrate on the sound of the drum or rattle. While keeping a small amount of attention on maintaining your position without bumping into anything, mentally travel to a natural place where you have always felt powerful. This could be a seashore, a forest, a meadow, a mountain ridge, a desert, a cave, or anywhere you have felt your spirit free and empowered.

Continue to move this way for as long as you like, but not for less than five minutes. Shamans do this for hours at a time, but they are physically fit and capable of incredible endurance. You need not follow their example, although in time you certainly should increase your own endurance to dance for fifteen minutes or so.

Signal the end of your drumming with three strong beats and rest for five minutes or so. Then, if you wish, embark on a shamanic journey, focusing on anything you want. You will be surprised how helpful the dancing is prior to your journey work.

The benefit of this dance is that it helps you develop the ability to keep one foot in the world of ordinary reality and the other in the spirit world at the same moment. The dance

---

Dance Ritual #1: The Steps

1. Set up the environment.
2. Begin to drum or rattle (or start tape). Begin to move.
3. Mentally travel to a place you feel powerful.
4. Continue moving for as long as you want (not less than 5 minutes).
5. End with three strong beats.
6. Journey if you wish.

---

helps you practice that ability and prepare for situations where you want to access the spirit world quickly for advice while remaining undetected in a social setting. In many situations you will not be able to dance but you will have developed the skill to be in both worlds at once. In this sense the dance is like a drill to prepare you for that.

Dance Ritual #2: The Journey Dance (Advanced)

Prepare the environment as you did in the first dance ritual. Use a rattle if you wish. It helps here to have someone else drum for you or use a drumming tape. You may discover some rhythmic music that works for you, but it should not be too oriented toward a specific emotion.

Stand in the center of the room with your eyes closed and call upon your power animal or guardian spirit. Tell them your problem; ask them your question and then follow their instructions.

As you experience the journey, dance it, using hand motions and gestures to illustrate what is happening. Use the

---

Dance Ritual #2: The Steps

1. Prepare the environment.
2. Begin to rattle or turn on drumming tape.
3. Communicate the focus of your journey to your guardian.
4. Follow their instructions.
5. Dance your journey experience.
6. End with three beats.
7. Thank your guardian.

---

rattle to describe events and activities in the vision. The challenge here is to lose absolutely all self-consciousness, so that you are completely at one with the experience.

Allow the journey to climax and come to a natural conclusion. Signal the end with three strong beats of the drum or shakes of the rattle.

USING QUARTZ CRYSTALS FOR PROTECTION AND EMPOWERMENT

Among all the rock spirits, crystals are the most universally used in shamanic practice. Shamans believe that crystals are more sentient than other rocks and have special properties that are useful for shamanic work. Most shamans carry crystals in their shamanic toolbox (medicine bundle). Principally, crystals are excellent for increasing visionary powers, producing clarity of insight, and are extraordinary energy-transfer devices. In addition, crystals have a reputation for amplifying energy as they channel it from one place to another according to the will of the shaman. Crystals can be useful in healing rituals, mentally transferring the guardian spirit's healing energy to a diseased part of the body. Or they can be held up to the forehead with the intention of shamanically seeing what is happening at a distant place, just like a fortune teller's crystal ball.

OBTAINING AND PREPARING A CRYSTAL

Traditionally, shamans have felt that the most powerful crystals were the ones they either found themselves or received as gifts from another shaman. Today however, with modern conditions, most crystals must be bought in rock shops or at outlets that carry them. A purchased crystal is perfectly fine, provided you cleanse it first before using it.

The clarity, shape, and size of the crystal affect its power and specific abilities. Shamans have special regard for pure, clear quartz crystal without chips or breaks within it. They like to have the point clear and sharp and the facets equal in size and shape. The fewer the chips and irregularities, the better the crystal can transmit.

Shamans prefer to keep their crystals private, rather than displaying them openly around their necks the way people do when they use them as jewelry. Quartz crystal acts as an amplifier, and they usually don't want all their experiences amplified. They like to keep their crystals cleansed and fresh for the next time they use them. Washing them in ocean water, burying them in salt, bathing them in sage smoke, or freezing them are all methods of cleansing crystals of accumulated energies. Freezing is especially effective because the lower temperature helps the crystal to release its store of used energy. This process is similar to the way you might erase a tape or a computer disk electronically.

TUNING YOUR QUARTZ CRYSTAL

You may wish to tune the crystal to your own spirit in the following way:

Freeze the crystal for several days in your freezer or in the snow in winter, if you live in a cold place. Hold the fresh crystal up to your forehead, point upward and say something like, "Hello, Crystal Spirit, I'm glad you have come to me. Thanks for your help. Do you have any special properties I should know about?" Listen for a mental response or visual image. Then continue. "I would like to tune you to my own spirit energy now. My name is . . ." Project your name three times into the crystal. Then intend to use the crystal for whatever you plan to use it for: to help you see better shamanically; to transfer your guardian spirit's power into your projects; to use as a healing device; or all of the above. Intend that you will use it only for the benefit of yourself and others.

Bring the crystal down to your chest over your heart, point upward, and flood it with a positive emotion you feel with regards to using the crystal.

Your crystal is now tuned to you. Keep in mind that you will have to do this each time you cleanse the crystal. Cleanse the crystal whenever you feel subjectively that it is time.

CREATING A CLEAR, SAFE, AND POWERFUL PLACE

You may have a personal work space or place of meditation that you like to keep clear and peaceful. In addition to occasionally burning sage there to cleanse the spot, you might want to create a higher frequency energy field in that space. You can accomplish this by positioning quartz crystals around that space in different configurations. The resulting amplification can help you to think more clearly and creatively and provide you with more inspiration as well. You will also find that you can do enhanced journey work there as well. Your journeys will be clearer, more lucid, and more powerful than you ever thought possible. Here is one of many crystal configurations:

You will need at least four crystals for this ritual. They can be any size, depending on the size of the field you want to create. The larger the field, the bigger the crystals needed. Four two-inch-long crystals are fine for a personal space of about one hundred square feet.

Cleanse the crystals, tune them, and tell them what you plan to do with them. Tell them that you want to use them together to create a safe powerful field where you can work or play. Ask their permission to go ahead.

Mark off a circular or rectangular area surrounding your work space (desk, office, art studio, dark room, meeting area, whatever).

Set one crystal pointing inward at each of the four directions. If you have six crystals, you can set two in the middle, one pointing upward and one downward (propped) for the upper and lower worlds.

You now have an amplified work space where your productivity can increase multifold. Avoid going into this space if you are feeling cynical or overly negative.

CREATING YOUR OWN POWER SPOT

Creating a power spot is similar to the ritual of using crystals to create a safe place. This spot is sometimes known as the medicine wheel. It's a place that you can use again and again for rituals, journeys, or gatherings, depending on how big you make it. Sitting in the middle of this mini personal power spot will energize you and empower you.

Select a site, preferably outdoors, that is flat, free of traffic, and feels good to you.

Collect rocks, pine cones, or other natural objects that appeal to you, that you can use to outline the circle.

Outline a circle approximately eight feet in diameter. (This is optimal for one person but you can make it any size.) Cleanse the entire area with burning sage. Each participant helping to construct the circle or wheel can cleanse (smudge) with sage as well.

Either dig a small fire pit in the center or place a large rock or power object in the center. Invoke the spirit of the Sky above and the Earth below.

Place one larger rock or object at each of the four directions and while doing so, invoke the power of that direction. You can place crystals at these locations for amplification if you wish. Place rocks also at the midpoints of the directions: northeast, southwest, and so on.

You may wish to add additional rocks or objects around the circle. Use the circle to journey in, or simply to be in for a lift in your power. You will notice that it will tend to attract birds and small animals, especially cats, who are very sensitive to energy fields.

VISION QUEST

The vision quest is a timeless symbolic pilgrimage to a personal power spot for inner guidance and clarity. Traditionally the vision quest tests and develops your personal strength as you exercise patience and perseverance in your wait for a vision. There are many forms of vision questing from every continent of the world. Some are year-long isolated walks in wild country that test survival skills as well as spiritual fortitude. Some are treks to power locations, where the questor remains for three days in hopes of a vision. Still others are inner journeys spent in the darkness of a sweat lodge or sealed room for days at a time. A vision quest can be as simple as an afternoon of solitude on a hillside or the beach.

Whatever the form of your vision quest, it can be life transforming if you plan it and carry it out with purpose and humility. In our experience, people from all walks of life, both young and old, have received tremendous benefit from this time-honored ritual. It helps to quiet yourself, focus, tune in to the web of power, and retrieve the answers to some of your most difficult problems. It can even help you map out your life's path or the major tasks you want to accomplish before you die.

There are some traditionally common ingredients to setting up and carrying out a vision quest, no matter how strenuously or simply you have designed it. Keep these in mind when you design one.

CHOOSING THE PLACE

Select an isolated spot, free of public traffic and preferably in the countryside. Choose a place that you have always loved. Always let someone know where you have gone and when you expect to return. Even better, go with someone who will do a vision quest in the same general area over the same time period.

CHOOSING THE TIME

Decide how long your journey will be. Longer is not necessarily better. There are no macho points in shamanism. If you are unclear how long you need, ask your power animal for advice. If you are going overnight or for several days, you may need to take more things with you than for an afternoon quest. Select a time when you will be free of most of your commitments. Birthdays and other important anniversaries are usually good dates for vision quests if you are not already heavily committed socially.

CHOOSING THE QUESTION

Reflect on what you are asking about. Are you looking for a general direction in your life or are you seeking the answer to a difficult problem? Ask your guardian spirit for advice on this matter. Reflect on your question for a few days before the quest.

PREPARING FOR THE QUEST

Fasting is a traditional practice both before and during a vision quest. It is seen as a personal sacrifice and a sign that you are seriously asking for help. There is no need to undergo severe fasting however, because in many cases it can be injurious to your health unless you are already an expert. Lowering your food intake for a couple of days before and abstaining from alcohol and drugs is recommended. On the quest itself, you may want to limit your food intake to a little juice or have water only. Your own state of health and any medical conditions will determine your special needs.

MATERIALS NEEDED

Your materials need be few. Water, drum, rattle, sage, matches, jacket, blanket, sunglasses, journal, pen, or tape recorder may be part of your paraphernalia. Sometimes people bring an inspirational book, poems, I Ching, Tarot deck or the like. In general, however, the fewer distractions you have, the better. Leave radios and munchies at home.

WHAT TO DO

When you have arrived at the general site of your quest, find the exact location for sitting by using your rattle. Shake the rattle in front of you and let it lead you to a spot where it does not want to leave. You can use one of the methods described earlier on finding power spots as well. This, of course, is all very subjective, but effective.

Invoke the six directions and create a power circle around you using twigs, small stones, or pine cones. When you do this, you transform the area into a natural doorway in which the spirit world can manifest itself.

Make yourself a comfortable place to sit and, closing your eyes, say hello to your surroundings: the local plants, trees, insects, and any elements present. Ask for their help in offering you guidance and assistance on your quest. It is a good idea to spend a lengthy period of time on this.

Feel freer to journey or use any of the methods in this book during the vision quest. Sing, dance, sit quietly, listen, look, and visit with nature.

Some people find the experience more meaningful if they stay awake throughout the night(s), while others prefer to sleep a few hours. Decide what is best for you.

WHAT TO LOOK FOR

Spend your time getting to know the immediate area that you are in. Small natural signs are gifts to you from the spirit world and can be powerful messages related to your question or issue: a feather, a visit from an animal or butterfly, a cloud passing overhead, the cry of a coyote. These ordinary things and events become significant in the nonordinary environment of the vision quest. Remember that the spirit world often uses natural signs to communicate with you in response to your requests. Don't expect the opening of the skies or earth-shattering visitations and the like. The spirit world is subtle, not overly dramatic. Learn to listen and hear with refinement. You do not have to be hit over the head to learn something.

OBSTACLES

Vision quests, while sometimes intense, are also filled with boredom and mental and physical restlessness. You may be distracted by memories, mental chatter, and worries about the details of a thousand things you need to do when you get home. You may get tired and wonder what you are doing out here in the middle of the night when you could be comfortable at home in bed. You might find that all you can do is think about food—lemonade, beer, or hot chocolate. You may even consider quitting and going into town for a bite to eat or going home early. It is best to ignore these typical distractions and simply say to yourself something like "And this too." This helps to remind you that what you are thinking or feeling is not to be resisted, simply acknowledged and let go. If you try to fight these distractions they will only get worse. In our groups, we have found that those who stuck with their original plan gained much more from the experience than those who bailed out. These obstacles are all part of the experience and are not a negative reflection on you. In fact, they can teach you a lot about yourself.

COMPLETING THE VISION QUEST

When you have come to the end of your allotted time, thank the spirits of that place and restore it back to its original natural state. Erase all evidence that you have been there. Clean up any trash left over by former visitors.

Do not worry if you have not received any clear answers or messages during your vision quest. Often the insights do not immediately penetrate into your physical body, but within several days you will begin to have insights and clarity that will surprise you. Occasionally these insights will be weeks, months, and even years in coming. Remember that shamanic time is different from the ordinary time you are used to.

SHARING

You can share your insights and experiences with a friend or group who are supportive. Ask them not to analyze or try to interpret your experience from their own point of view. This could distort your own benefits. However, you will find that just talking about your vision quest will make it real and help you understand and gain from it. Certainly writing about your experiences can be very helpful during the integration process.

Sometimes it is appropriate to keep the experience private and share it or parts of it with no one. Some shamanic traditions encourage sharing, while others recommend against it. We see advantages to each at different times under different circumstances. Use your own discretion with regard to this.

HARNESSING POWER THROUGH LIGHT

Shamans the world over have a special relationship with the sun and with its properties of heat and light. Although much of shamanic work is done in the darkness of night or with the eyes closed, storing light is an important part of a shaman's work. Traditionally shamans have enjoyed sitting in the sun for hours, collecting and storing sunlight for their more nocturnal activities. Many ancient shamans were sun worshipers who appeared to stare directly into the sun to receive its powers. Actually their purpose was to let as much sunlight as possible enter their eyes.

Under no circumstances should you stare directly into the sun or even indirectly, as you might damage your eyes irreparably. Nor, with the current destruction of the ozone layer, should you sit naked in the sun for any period of time. Nevertheless, being outdoors and absorbing much sunlight through the skin and eyes even indirectly under the shade of a tree is an excellent shamanic practice to absorb power.

You have now learned many rituals, ceremonies, and practices that shamans use in their quest for power and self-knowledge. Keep in mind that these rituals have countless forms and are subject to infinite personal interpretation. Remember also that shamanism is a deeply personal practice, without dogma or rigid guidelines. Making these practices work for you is the important thing.

CHAPTER 11

Playing the Shamanic Game of Life: The Big Picture

The ratty old volkswagon bounced over the ruts of the desert track, a road barely discernible in the dawn light of a cold December day. The steep climb out of the seldom-traveled north end of Death Valley slowed the ancient bug down to a crawl. Rain slanted down, finding its way through the old convertible roof, dripping onto the ponchos of the travelers.

"So it never rains in Death Valley," growled Lena as she worked the coat hanger to make the wipers work. She looked askance at Jose, who was silently maneuvering the old car up the incline. "My hand is freezing and is that what I think it is?" Lena pointed to the white stuff by the side of the road, the first signs of snow on the pass.

"Don't worry. I brought the chains," mumbled Jose, trying not to get breath on the inside of the windshield.

Sure enough, after not more than a mile, the snow had built up on the road to such a degree that it was time for the chains. Jose released the front trunk, stumbled out and fished around for the chains. "Aha, here they are," he yelled triumphantly.

A few minutes later Lena heard curses coming from under the car. "What's wrong?" she shouted irritably. The cold night in the damp tent had taken its toll.

Jose came to the window, a look of disbelief on his face. "The chains don't fit. I must have brought the ones for the Honda, they're way too small. Damn! And we have only enough gas to get to Lone Pine this way. So we can't turn back at this point."

Lena gave him an incredulous glare. "I thought you tried them on." With that she threw open the door, slammed it shut, and stomped back down the snow-covered roadway in utter frustration. "What a miserable situation," she complained angrily, kicking the snow with her boots. She felt extremely sorry for herself and she was fed up.

After a few minutes, shuffling along and looking at her feet, animal tracks in the snow caught her attention. "Hmmm, what are these?" she wondered. As she began to decipher the tracks, Lena looked about her at the natural landscape. Well, this isn't so bad she thought. "Animals make a home here and they live with the snow when it comes on rare occasions. They make the best of it." Her thoughts began to shift. Lena remembered her own power animal and was reminded of the potential untapped power in this landscape. "Nature always works," she said to herself and she began to chuckle at their seemingly hopeless predicament. The feelings of anger and frustration faded and were replaced by the familiar feeling of ease and certainty that she had come to know through her shamanic practice.

She heard the distant cry of a bird and once again she thought of her own power animal, the great horned owl, an ally she could call upon. She closed her eyes, called it forth, and asked it, "What would you do in our shoes?"

Owl sat on the thick branch of a pinyon pine and gazed at her. "You are right to sense power in these desert mountains. They are healing for you. What is your hurry? You wished for healing emotionally and now you are in a prime location to absorb it from the minerals here. Let them give you balance. When you have had enough there will come a way out."

Lena laughed, "You mean this is actually a healing experience?"

Owl cocked its head sideways and nodded. "It could be."

Lena thought a moment and said, "OK, I think I get it. Time to let go and receive."

Meanwhile, back at the car, Jose had exhausted his attempts to makeshift the chains. After the obligatory curses and frantic casting about for solutions, he gave up and went for a walk up the road. His mind was filled with the warnings he had read and dark thoughts about desert passes in winter. No maintenance, no services, and no traffic. And he was feeling bad that he had dragged Lena into this. It took him some moments to simmer down and regroup.

Oh, well, he thought, I've been in these situations before. We'll get out. I might as well enjoy this. Let's see what I can discover. He stood quietly for a moment, consulting his deer guide.

Deer spoke: "You should be glad because you have shown power. After all, you are realizing an old dream. Did you forget? You've always wanted to see it rain or snow in Death Valley. Now you have it. Can you enjoy it? You can build more power by having your dream. That will pave the way for the next step."

I guess I confused those chains for a reason, thought Jose. My spirit self made sure I'd stick around enough to enjoy it. I need to change my attitude. We have food and supplies. I guess we'll just have to wait.

Two hours later, walking in the snow to the crest of the rise, Lena and Jose looked out over the slick road as snowflakes continued to fall silently and gently in the desert. Suddenly a movement caught their eyes. Rounding a bend and coming slowly down the road was the impossible. An old snowplow was working its way down from the pass on this isolated rut of a road in the middle of nowhere—not a county machine, but a miner's snowplow.

The ride through the rugged snow-covered desert mountains could not have been more beautiful. The old convertible bumped and sloshed behind the snowplow for miles, slow enough to deeply appreciate the experience. Jose and Lena laughed at their own foolishness and marveled at their exhilaration. The big picture always felt this way.

Let's review the principles of the shamanic approach so that you can quickly recall the key points of this powerful practice. Remember for starters that shamanism is an ancient, cross-cultural personal strategy for accessing power and gaining self-knowledge. Requiring only discipline and practice, it can be used by anyone, anytime, and anyplace without detection, if so desired. There is no hierarchy and no dogma. There are, however, certain broad themes and common discoveries, the so-called rules of the game listed below. When you know these rules, life becomes easier and more fun. As illustrated in our story above, you feel more in charge of your destiny, and your enthusiasm for living takes a leap. For shamans, the rules of the game are as follows:

• There is an ordinary world that works according to the everyday laws of physics ad chemistry.

• There is a nonordinary world, or spirit world, that works

according to an entirely different and more flexible set of rules.

- There are three main levels to the spirit world; the Lower World, place of challenge, mystery, and confrontation with fear; the Upper World, place of inspiration and cosmic knowledge; the Middle World, place of balance and integration.

- There are universal maps to the spirit world that let all shamans know where they are in relation to it. The medicine wheel or mandala and the tree of life are instantly accessible maps to all levels of the spirit world.

- The ordinary world is dependent on the spirit world for its existence. All forms in the physical world have their source in the spirit world. Elements, rocks, plants, animals, and humans are alive and have spirit bodies that function according to its rules.

- The flow of power moves from the spirit world or web of power to the conventional world.

- For shamans, it is worth knowing how to directly access and maneuver their own spirit bodies in the spirit world because that is their key to power and success.

- Doorways or tunnels to the spirit world can be opened using special shamanic techniques. When you open these doorways, the rules of the spirit world prevail over ordinary rules. Thus you can manipulate time and space and you can mold reality directly.

- Imagination, concentration, and will are the vehicles that open these tunnels or passageways to the spirit world.

- Rituals, ceremonies, drumming, and rattling enhance your ability to open the doors to the spirit world.

- If you are to travel to the spirit world to access knowledge or information, a guardian spirit, ally, or power animal is essential as a guide and advisor. Developing a good relationship with them is an integral part of effective journeying.

- Using the power you gain to help yourself and others at the same time is a wonderful way to become even more powerful.

- Knowing how to use power spots and power objects is a key to enhancing your personal effectiveness.

- Creation and destruction are two sides of a single coin. A knowledge of their principles is a necessity for success. To create you must learn to destroy appropriately, for death is required for rebirth. You must transform old beliefs into new ones to see change in your life.

- You must dissolve limitations to create the possibility for expansion. Since the universe is expansive and expanding, going with that flow is fruitful.

- Expanding and growing means coping with change. There is only so much change your physical form can accommodate at one time. You must go step by step on your patient climb toward meeting your goals. When you try to go too quickly, you may lose your power and lose your advantage.

- Forming clear attainable goals, then taking action is essential to actualizing them.

- Success involves understanding people's specialties in life and knowing how to communicate with them. Discovering how to balance your magnetic vs. dynamic sides as well as your head, your heart, and your gut is a key to developing power.

- Knowing how to dance, sing, play, and laugh allows the power to flow in ever increasing amounts.

HOW TO KNOW THAT YOU ARE BEING SUCCESSFUL AT SHAMANIC PRACTICE

Once you establish a good connection with the spirit world and are filled with power, there are important signs letting you know that you are on the right track. First of all, you experience a series of remarkable coincidences that might appear to you as extraordinary good luck. Things work for you or go your way. Obstacles are removed from your path one after another, while other people around you may continue to struggle.

It is not uncommon to have synchronistic meetings with people in remarkable places. During his travels in Asia, Jose was exercising shamanic techniques regularly. When he was traveling in Nepal, he stopped into a hotel lobby in Katmandu for directions and ran headlong into his former acupuncturist from Berkeley, California. She was heading for an isolated monastery to visit her teacher, a high Tibetan Buddhist lama. It just so happened that this was of great interest to Jose, who had been hoping for just this sort of thing, an inside chance to study with a good teacher in Nepal. She invited him to come along and there began an extraordinary adventure that was to transform the next few weeks.

These apparently coincidental events happen to everyone, but when you have been practicing from a shamanic perspective, the magical quality of events begins to pick up in speed and regularity. To shamans, this is regarded as most auspicious.

Next you may notice a heightening of your intuition and your awareness. You find that you can sense obstacles before they grow too big and you know the most fruitful path to follow for satisfaction and enjoyment. You often anticipate what people are thinking and feeling and you establish rapport with them much more quickly. You know what is happening around you and you spend less time in confusion.

Another sign of successful shamanic practice is an increase in your creative abilities. You notice that you are able to quickly come up with excellent solutions to problems that once stumped you. You are able to see how obstacles are really opportunities that challenge you to grow stronger and more powerful. Artistic urges happen more often and you look for ways to express the bountiful and rich life developing within you.

Your compassion increases toward others and you can no longer run roughshod over fellow creatures on the planet whether they be animals, plants, minerals, or other people. Your capacity for love and affinity grows to the point where you want to see everyone win in as many situations as possible. You want to alleviate suffering whenever possible. You find yourself growing in respect for others and their experiences each day. You can no longer negatively judge people because you understand them and realize that they, like you, are valuable living parts of the web of power.

Likewise, you notice that your own self-esteem and capacity for loving yourself expands exponetially. You treat your body with greater care and respect by exercising it and giving it the kind of food it needs for vitality and energy. Your health noticeably improves and you become more capable of using the power you have learned to channel from your shamanic practice.

When you have been successful in your shamanic practice you find that you see the world in a much broader context. You experience awe for the source of the incredible internal gifts that you receive along the way. You develop a humble perspective, knowing that you yourself are not the source of power and light, but just one of many vehicles for it. You lend your hand to allow the universe to work through you. The more power you are able to channel, the less you take credit for.

HOW TO GO FURTHER

Now that you have been exposed to time-tested shamanic techniques that can enhance your living skills and increase your personal power, you may wish to pursue shamanism more seriously. For this, it will be helpful for you to find teachers or guides with whom you can study or with whom you can apprentice. We cannot tell you whom to approach because this is a matter of personal discretion. However, you have learned how to use your shamanic power to call the appropriate teachers or guides to yourself, whether they be the internal kind or the physical kind. Perhaps you will find that your best teachers are the animal, plant, or spirit guides whom you meet during your inner journeys. On the other hand, you may find that you want to study with a physical human being who can show you the ropes and help you in your path as a healer.

Remember that there are all kinds of people out there who may call themselves experts in shamanism and will gladly tell you what to do. Many of the best shamans these days, however, do not call themselves such and do not look like traditional shamans. On the other hand, the guide that suits you best might be a very traditional-looking shaman. Therefore, you must look more than skin-deep to find the right guide for you.

You may wish to travel to another country to study shamanism in an exotic and stimulating environment. Sometimes removing yourself from your everyday surroundings can open the inner doors to your own powers quite rapidly. You may, however, find it difficult to translate what you have learned in a foreign context back to your own cultural setting. The true test of your abilities comes when you are back in your own environment with the typical stresses of your everyday life.

Nor should you think that you can learn all about shamanism on a quickie two-week tour. Real learning takes discipline and practice over a long period of time. For example, for the Lakota Sioux the formal training takes sixteen years.

Today, there are strong feelings from different camps about who can and who cannot be a shaman. Some feel that middle-class whites interested in shamanism have no right to practice its ways because they have no tradition of it behind them. Others feel that shamanism is for everyone, regardless of race or cultural background, and that no one has the exclusive right to this powerful body of knowledge. Although we suggest you make up your own mind regarding these matters, we believe that all people are entitled to learn and know more.

Here are some pointers on how to assess and select the best teachers for yourself.

We suggest you look for a teacher who:

- Has a good sense of humor.
- Helps you laugh at your bumbling self.
- Is able to play.
- Has a powerful presence.
- Shows respect for all living things.
- Demonstrates respect for the environment.
- Models self-respect.
- Shows kindness or compassion.
- Is able to tell the truth and be direct.
- Is able to teach by setting the example.
- Has a global point of view.
- Has a "We're-all-in-this-together" point of view.
- Is inclusive rather than exclusive.
- Has a good reputation.
- Allows mistakes.
- Isn't perfect.
- Is flexible.
- Isn't afraid of emotions.

We suggest you avoid a "teacher" who:

- Has a superior attitude.
- Excludes members of any race or cultural group.
- Expresses an us-vs.-them point of view: "They're out to get us" or "We're better."

- Is bigoted.

- Is shortsighted.

- Is attacking or violent.

- Is insensitive.

- Is overly serious.

- Has a "Do what I say, not what I do" point of view.

- Drinks heavily or consumes lots of drugs.

- Is ingratiating.

- Is controlling.

- Makes you wrong or an outcast for questioning.

- Teaches by belittling or making you an example in front of everyone.

- Wants lots of money up front.

- Has assistants, cohorts, or senior students who act inappropriately in your view and whom you are expected to obey.

- Believes the form of ritual is more important than the results.

- Pretends to be perfect.

- Is overly idealistic, not practical.

No matter what teacher you are drawn to, or whom you study with, you will ultimately learn everything you want to know. In a sense, you cannot go wrong, no matter what you do because you are simply occupying a temporary position on the medicine wheel, a position that is endlessly shifting and rotating you toward the center. Even if you decide that shamanism is not for you, you will be making the right decision. Shamans know that this is so; they make a point of being where they are, present and in the moment, not resisting the place they occupy on the power circle. Yet they do have goals that help them proceed toward positions on the medicine wheel that give them greater satisfaction and knowledge.

We hope that you have benefited from what we and our helpers have written in this book. We hope that you will turn to those magnificent inner resources that are available within you and become strong and powerful. We hope that you will always use those resources for the benefit of yourself and others.

Although throughout this book we have spoken of spirits, allies, helpers, and so on, we want to emphasize that despite the many forms the spirit world takes, we believe there is one all-encompassing spirit that is the true source of all power. We believe that we are all co-creators with that Great Spirit of which we are part. May you walk the path of truth, the path of beauty, the path of love, and the path of power.

APPENDIX

Shaman's Resource Guide

Drums, Rattles, and Other Resources: There is a great variety of drums, rattles, crystals, tapes, and other useful paraphernalia helpful in shamanic work. You do not have to have anything fancy or historical in order to carry out the techniques.

Drums: In a pinch, almost any drum will do. For excellent sonic sound, rawhide drums approximately 16″ in diameter by 8″ high work well. They are manageable and mobile. Drums 16″ high provide a deeper and louder sound for larger group work. Water drums provide a rich, deep resonance but require care and specific knowledge for preparation. Cassette recordings of drumming are completely adequate for journey usage provided you have good speakers or reproduction equipment. We have used them with good results.

When you buy a drum, test out a number of them for sound. Select the one that has a good deep sound. This is a personal ritual that you will enjoy. When a drum is cold it tends to go flat. Bringing it into a heated room or heating the skin over a fire will tighten it again.

Rattles: Native American rattles and other ethnic rattles are usually made from dried gourds with pebbles or seeds within, to make the sound. Suppliers of Native American crafts usually carry them. Our favorites are the brightly colored Hopi rattles that are often decorated like animals. Huichol rattles also provide a good high-pitched sound for shamanic work. You can use maracas for rattling as well. According to Michael Harner, the Professional Maraca (LP 281) available at music stores produces an excellent sound. Warning: Rattles tend to be fragile and they crack with any kind of rough handing.

Crystals and Other Minerals: Most good rock shops carry crystals and other specimens that you can use for personal energy work. See Chapter 9 on rituals for information about selecting crystals. You do not have to spend a lot to purchase many good healing rocks and minerals. In fact, some of the best ones are not particularly attractive for jewelry making and they can be obtained very reasonably. Flourite is a good example of an excellent cleansing mineral that is both inexpensive and easy to find.

Sage and Sweetgrass: These are easily available from the suppliers below or from local herbal stores in your community. They are both excellent for cleansing and renewing an area. A bit of charcoal will help the sage to smoulder. Use a clay pot or bowl for this purpose. Be fire safe.

Further Resources

Jose and Lena Stevens, Box 5314, Berkeley, CA 94705. Write for information about workshops and lectures on shamanism, prosperity, personal growth and other books by the authors (*Tao to Earth, The Michael Handbook,* and *The Personality Puzzle*).

The Center of Shamanic Studies, Box 673, Belden Station, Norwalk, CN 06852. Excellent two-sided drumming tapes and workshops with Michael Harner.

Shamans Drum: A Journal of Contemporary Shamanism, Box 2636, Berkeley, CA 94702. This is an excellent quarterly journal (by subscription) about the practical everyday pursuit of shamanism. It also carries an excellent list of shamanic-related resources.

The Bear Tribe, P.O. Box 9167, Spokane, WA 99209. Their catalogue has a large inventory of hard-to-find books and objects related to shamanism and they publish a quarterly newsletter called *Wildfire*.

Rock Shop, 468 Santa Clara Ave., Oakland, CA 94610. An excellent source of good healing rock specimens as well as ritual objects, drums, rattles, and books.

Pacific Western Traders, P.O. Box 95, 305 Wool Street, Folsom, CA 95630. They have an excellent selection of Native American ceremonial objects including drums, rattles, books, sage, crystals, craft supplies, recordings.

Taos Indian Drum Company, P.O. Box 1916 D, Taos, NM 87571. Write for price list and information on ceremonial drums.

Bibliography

BOOKS

Acterberg, J. *Imagery in Healing: Shamanism and Modern Medicine*. Boston: Shambhala, 1985.

Andrews, L. *Medicine Woman*. San Francisco: Harper & Row, 1981.

———. *Flight of the Seventh Moon: The Teachings of the Shield*. San Francisco: Harper & Row, 1984.

———. *Jaguar Woman and the Wisdom of the Butterfly*. San Francisco: Harper & Row, 1985.

———. *Star Woman: We Are Made from Stars and to the Stars We Return*. New York: Warner, 1986.

———. *Crystal Woman: The Sisters of the Dreamtime*. San Francisco: Warner, 1987.

Campbell, J. *Primitive Mythology*. New York: McGraw-Hill, 1978.

Castaneda, C. *The Teachings of Don Juan: A Yaqui Way of Knowledge*. New York: Ballantine, 1968.

———. *A Separate Reality: Further Conversations with Don Juan*. New York: Simon & Schuster, 1971.

———. *Journey to Ixtlan: The Lessons of Don Juan*. New York: Simon & Schuster, 1972.

———. *Tales of Power*. New York: Simon & Schuster, 1974.

———. *The Fire Within*. New York: Simon & Schuster, 1984.

———. *The Eagles Gift*. New York: Simon & Schuster, 1981.

———. *The Second Ring of Power*. New York: Simon & Schuster, 1985.

———. *The Power of Silence*. New York: Simon & Schuster, 1982.

Cirlot, J.E. *A Dictionary of Symbols*. New York: Philosophical Library, 1962.

Clark, K. *Animals and Men*. New York: William Morrow, 1977.

David, J. *Michael's Gemstone Dictionary* (2nd ed.). Orinda, CA: Touchstone Books, 1987.

Eaton, E. *I Send a Voice*. Wheaton, IL: Theosophical Publishing House, 1978.

———. *The Shaman and the Medicine Wheel*. Wheaton, IL:

Theosophical Publishing House, 1982.

Eliade, M. *Shamanism: Archaic Techniques of Ecstasy;* Solligen Series LXXVI. Princeton, NJ: Princeton University Press, 1964.

———. *From Primitives to Zen.* San Francisco: Harper & Row, 1977.

Epstein, G. The experience of the waking dreams in psychotherapy. In J. Fosshage and P. Olsen (Eds.) *Healing: Implications for Psychotherapy.* New York: Human Sciences Press, 1978.

Freud, S. *The Interpretation of Dreams* (2nd ed.). New York: Macmillan, 1915.

———. *Totem and Taboo.* New York: Random House, 1946.

Halifax, J. *Shamanic Voices.* New York: Dutton, 1979.

———. *Shaman: The Wounded Healer.* New York: Cross Road, 1982.

Harner, M. J. *The Way of the Shaman: A Guide to Power and Healing.* San Francisco: Harper & Row, 1980.

Heinz, R. (Ed.). *Proceedings of the Third International Conference on the Study of Shamanism and Alternate Modes of Healing.* Wisconsin: A-R Editions, Inc, 1987.

Jaffee, A. Symbolism in the visual arts. In C. G. Jung (Ed.) *Man and his Symbols.* New York: Doubleday, 1964.

Jung, C. G. *Man and his Symbols.* New York: Doubleday, 1964.

Kakar, S. *Shamans, Mystics and Doctors: A Psychological Inquiry into India and its Healing Traditions.* Boston: Beacon Press, 1982.

Kier, A. (Ed.) *Magic, Faith, and Healing.* New York: Macmillan, 1964.

Lamb, F. B. *Wizard of the Upper Amazon* (2nd ed.). Boston: Houghton Mifflin, 1975.

Larsen, S. *The Shaman's Doorway.* New York: Harper & Row, 1976.

Leadbeater, C. W. *The Chakras* (10th ed.). Wheaton, IL: Theosophical Publishing House, 1973.

Little, M. & Foster, S. *The Book of Vision Quest.* Covelo, CA: Island Press, 1980.

Lopez, B. H. *Of Wolves and Man.* New York: Charles Scribner's and Sons, 1978.

Motoyana, H. *Science and the Evolution of Consciousness.* Brookline, MA: Autumn Press, 1978.

Mukerjee, R. *The Symbolic Life of Man.* Bombay, India: Hind Kitabs, 1959.

Murphy, J. M. "Psychotherapeutic Aspects of Shamanism on St. Lawrence Island." In Ari Kiev (Ed.), *Magic, Faith, and Healing*. New York: Free Press, 1964.

Neihardt, J. *Black Elk Speaks*. New York: Pocket Books, 1972.

Neihardt, J. G. *When the Tree Flowered: an Authentic Tale of the Old Sioux World*. New York: Pocket Books, 1951.

Nicholson, S. (Ed.), *Shamanism: An Expanded View of Reality*. Wheaton, IL: Theosophical Publishing House, 1987.

Nowak, M. & Durrant, S. *The Tale of the Nivsan Shamaness: A Manchu Folk Epic*. Seattle: University of Washington Press, 1977.

Park, W. Z. *Shamanism in Western North America*. Chicago: Northwestern University, 1938.

Pearce, J. C. *Magical Child: Rediscovering Nature's Plan for Our Children*. New York: Dutton, 1977.

Pearce, J. C. *Magical Child Matures*. New York: Dutton, 1985.

Schwarz, J. *The Path of Action*. New York: Dutton. 1977.

———. *Voluntary Controls*. New York: Dutton, 1978.

———. *Human Energy Systems*. New York: Dutton, 1980.

Segal, J., Ed. *Imagery: Current Cognitive Approaches*. New York: Academic Press, 1971.

Sheehan, P. W., Ed. *The Function and Nature of Imagery*. New York: Academic Press, 1972.

Shephard, P. *Thinking Animals: Animals and the Development of Human Intelligence*. New York: Viking Press, 1978.

Shorr, J. E. (Ed.). *Imagery: Its Many Dimensions and Applications*. New York: Plenum Press, 1980.

Singer, J. *Imagery and Daydream Methods in Psychotherapy*. New York: Academic Press, 1974.

Stevens, J. *Power Animals, Animal Imagery, and Self Actualization*. Dissertation. California Institute of Integral Studies. San Francisco, CA, 1983.

———. *The Michael Handbook*. aka *Essence and Personality*. Orinda CA: Warwick Press, 1987.

———. *Tao to Earth: Michael's Guide to Relationships and Growth*. Berkeley, CA: Affinity Press, 1988.

Storm, H. *Seven Arrows*. New York: Ballantine, 1972.

———. *Song of Heyoehkah*. San Francisco: Harper & Row, 1981.

Underhill, R. M. *Singing for Power*. Berkeley: University of California Press, 1938.

Wabun, Sun Bear. *The Medicine Wheel: Earth Astrology.* Englewood Cliffs, NJ: Prentice Hall, 1980.

JOURNALS

Fabrega, J. R. & Fabrega, D. S. "Some Social and Psychological Properties of Zancanteco Shamans." *Behavioral Science* 15: 471–86, 1980.

Gowan, J. C. "Role of Imagination in the Development of the Creative Individual." *Humanitas* 14: 221–23, 1978.

Khatena, J. "Training College Adults to Think Creatively with Words." *Psychological Reports* 27: 279–81, 1970.

Krippner, S. "Alterations in Awareness ad Discovery of the Self." *Humanitas* 14: 2, 1978.

Peters, L. and Price-Williams. D. "Towards an Experimential Analysis of Shamanism." *American Ethnologist* 7: 397–418, 1980.

Silverman, J. "Shamans and Acute Schizophrenia." *American Anthropologist* 69: 21–31, 1967.

Stevens, J. *Dance of the Tonal.* "Shaman's Drum: A Journal of Experiential Shamanism." Fall, 1986.

BARRY LOPEZ

**DESERT NOTES: Reflections in the Eye of the Raven and
RIVER NOTES: The Dance of Herons**

71110-9/$7.95 US/$9.95 Can

"Barry Lopez is a landscape artist who paints images with sparse,
elegant strokes…His prose is as smooth as river rocks."

Oregon Journal

WINTER COUNT 58107-8/$3.95 US/$5.50 Can

Quiet, intoxicating tales of revelation and woe evoke beauty from
darkness, magic without manipulation, and memory without
remorse.

GIVING BIRTH TO THUNDER, 71111-7
SLEEPING WITH HIS DAUGHTER $7.95 US/$9.95 Can

In 68 tales from 42 American Indian tribes, Lopez recreates the
timeless adventures and rueful wisdom of Old Man Coyote, an
American Indian hero with a thousand faces—and a thousand
tricks.